That things are "status quo"
is the catastrophe.

—*Walter Benjamin*

# Black Box

A RECORD OF THE CATASTROPHE

VOLUME ONE

The Black Box Collective emerged after several years of symposia, reading groups, summer camps, wood-splitting, and barn-raising. The poets, journalists, academics, metaphysicians, artists, and strategists of the collective gather regularly at a retired dairy farm in the foothills of the Cascade Mountains north of Seattle to explore consciousness, community, and the circulation of communizing/commonizing currents. *Black Box: A Record of the Catastrophe* is our first attempt to assemble a critique that might awaken us from the dream world that is so efficiently reproduced by capitalist culture.

### EDITORS
Stuart Smithers, Brendan Kiley, Eirik Steinhoff,
Bethany Jean Clement, and Nadya Zimmerman

### DESIGN DIRECTOR
Corianton Hale

### FEATURED ILLUSTRATOR
Peter Wieben

### INVALUABLE SUPPORT FROM
Smoke Farm and its affiliates

www.blackboxcollective.org

Please send correspondence and submissions to theblackbox@riseup.net

ISBN: 9781629631233
Library of Congress Control Number: 2015930904

PM Press
P.O. Box 23912
Oakland, CA 94623
www.pmpress.org

10 9 8 7 6 5 4 3 2 1

Printed by the Employee Owners of
Thomson-Shore in Dexter, Michigan.
www.thomsonshore.com

# Contents

**ARTISTIC CONTRIBUTIONS:** Peter Wieben, John Criscitello, Carl Lehman-Haupt, Kathleen Cramer, John Beauparlant, Corianton Hale.

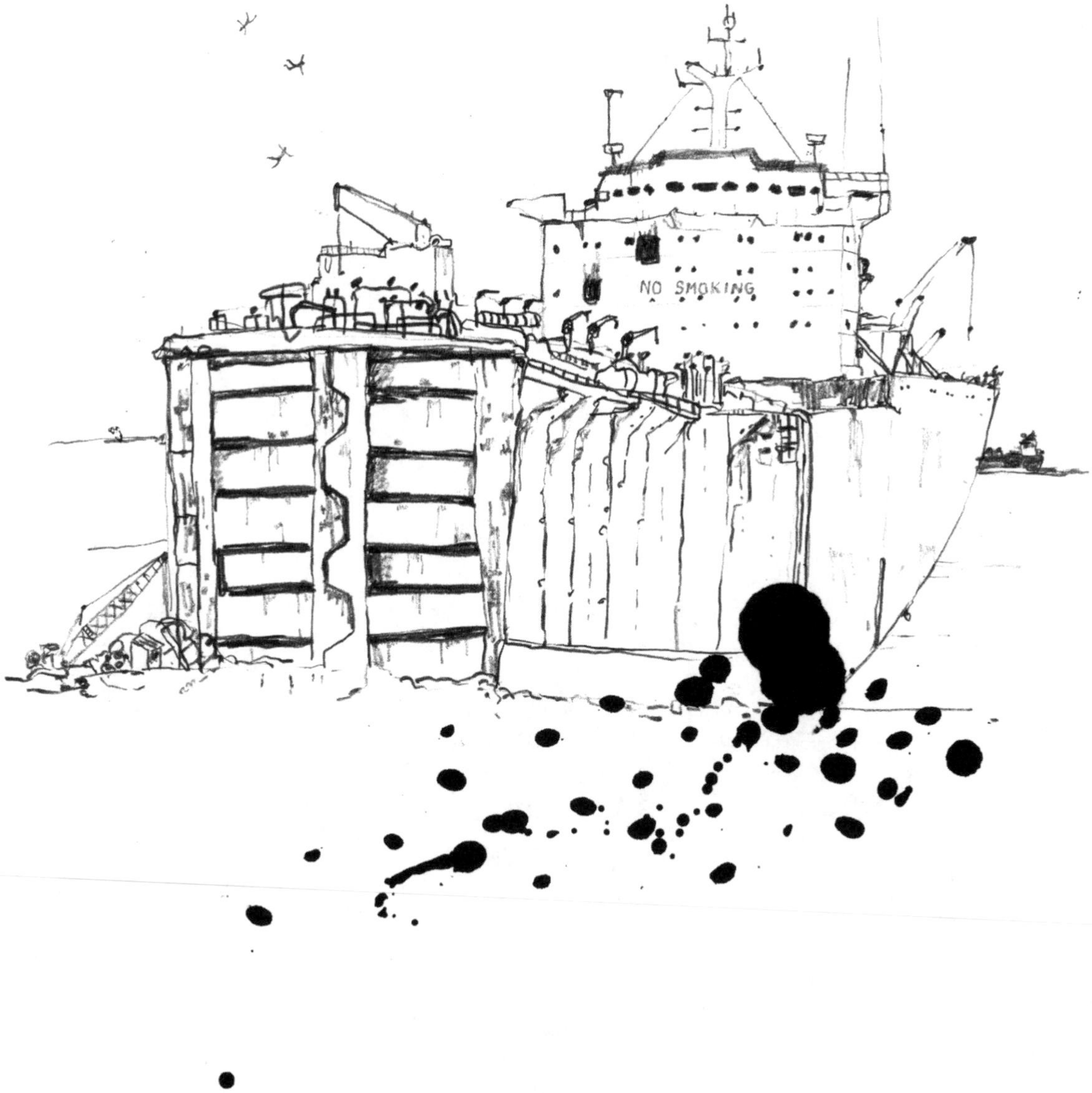
NO SMOKING

# The Weight of All Those Machines

## PETER WIEBEN

There are many men there, thousands of them. But they do not weigh as much as the machines. The men are crawling all over the ships. The ships have been pulled out of the water using big winches that are sunk into the sand on the beach. The winches alone outweigh the men. They pull the ships up onto shore, then the men are released to swarm them. They cut them to pieces with oxygen torches and acetylene torches. The pieces they cut fall off and are very large. Sometimes, the pieces are as big as buildings. The fat man, the owner of lot 161, told us that five men die in Alang each year. Will sensed that he was lying, and I did too.

Once the pieces are on shore, they are dragged up the beach by the men. Sometimes the machines help. The pieces are just slices of ship. Sometimes, the slices come from the front of the ship, like bread slices. Other times, the slices come from the sides, like turkey slices. Either way, they must be picked apart.

It is interesting to see what is inside a big ship like that. I got to look right inside. I could see the rooms. Sometimes the plumbing is visible, or stairs. Sometimes the insulation is. Will told me that one reason the number of deaths is higher than five is because there are no masks or filters in the ship-breaking yard. Whatever comes out of the ship, if it is not scrap metal or something usable (like a lifejacket), is set on fire.

Sometimes an oil tanker arrives. In these cases, the tanker is cut open on shore and the oil spills out. That is why the Alang coast is brown. I thought that anyway, and I told Will. Will told me that the coast is always brown in India, not just in Alang. I walked down to the mud and smelled it. It smelled like shit. Will told me that is because the workers do not have any plumbing in their homes.

Will is a factory worker from Tulsa, Oklahoma. For this reason, he was more adjusted to the environment of the Alang ship-breaking yard. For example, when we approached the ships, after we were frisked and interrogated a little, we walked over a piece of metal that was being cut by two men wearing no shoes. The cutting was happening with what was either an oxygen torch or an acetylene torch. The sparks were quite hot, but we walked right through them. There was very little air to breathe. The smoke, combined with the chemicals, the exhaust of the machines, and the stinking ocean made it so I hated my own breathing. Will said that was normal. I was unable to cover my mouth with my T-shirt because I was supposed to be a hardened factory worker like Will and not just some idiot with a notebook.

I saw a worker there and I told Will that he couldn't be older than 15. Will said that was bad. But then he told me that he started work in a foundry when he was 17. It wasn't good, he said, but he really couldn't judge.

Later, we stood underneath a crane that was handling a large piece of a ship. It was swinging over our heads. I was nervous to be beneath this piece of ship. The piece was bigger than a van. I was afraid the piece would fall and crush us, but again Will said this was fairly normal. The ship they were breaking was Japanese. It was constructed in 1999.

I asked Will if he thought human rights abuses were happening in the shipyard in Alang. I told him that I had read in many newspapers that these ship-breaking yards were the scene of human rights abuses. In fact, I believed that I had seen some with my own eyes. Will said he didn't really think so. He said the pay was better here than in many parts of India. Besides, he said, the conditions were not that much worse here than in the average factory. The reason the shipyards were big news was because Westerners felt guilty that their ships were being broken up here.

We sat with the owner of lot 161. His face was so round and so pudgy that his eyes were really squinty and gangster-looking. I do not know if he was actually evil, though. While we were with him, he received a delivery which he unwrapped and passed around for Will and me to look at. The delivery was a very ornate box. The box was made of very fine wood and had beautiful engravings all around it. Inside of the box was a book with what looked like original Persian miniatures on it. They depicted a king with his entourage. The king was on a horse. Inside the book was a wedding invitation. "Save the date, only," the fat man said.

The fat man was wearing a gold watch and had tea delivered to us. I did not take any. I told the fat man's assistant that I was sick to my stomach. The assistant became afraid of angering the fat man, who rarely hosted foreign dignitaries such as ourselves. After all, foreigners could not be trusted in a place like Alang. They tended to leave and say nasty things about the operation there. They tended to distort the truth and exaggerate things like

human rights abuses and environmental catastrophes. Foreigners were obsessed with Alang, the fat man said, because they did not understand it. We were seated on a veranda overlooking the struggling shipyard, which was teeming with workers. There was a noise like thunder from the next lot. A thick plume of smoke intermittently blew into my face. It was dark brown.

While we were sipping tea and examining this ornate box, two men were disassembling a cylinder that was composed of hundreds or thousands of greased-up pieces of wire. The wire was thick like rebar. Each piece was stuck through two circular metal plates. Heat exchanger, Will said. The men were removing each piece of wire by hand, but it was so greased up that their hands kept slipping. Each piece took them five minutes or so to remove. They were not even close to finishing. The cylinder was more than a meter in diameter. The men had to strain a lot to remove the wires. Behind them, a group of seven men lifted one giant piece of scrap after the other into the bed of a large Indian dump truck. They lifted as a team, like this: "Ho! Ho! Hup!"

We drove along the beach at Alang to see how big the place was. It went on and on. For 10 kilometers there was one giant ship after the other. I liked looking at these ships and seeing their insides, but it was very depressing to consider that each of these lots had a fat man, an ornate box, and men pulling wires out of cylinders. Each lot had a tall gate and a mean-looking man in front of it to keep out people such as ourselves. The gates were painted with motivational messages such as "Clean Alang, Green Alang" or "Safety Is Our Motto."

Will loved to look at the big engines. They were bigger than a house. They were covered in valves and exhaust pipes big enough to walk through. "What happens to them?" I asked Will.

"Scrap."

We were not supposed to be in there. We didn't have a permit or anything. We were told that we could go to jail if we were caught.

Nowadays, the value of a big ship like that is only determined by its weight. The human labor and knowledge and design and so on are negligible to the price. That is how cheap human labor has become. Nowadays, things like ships are measured by the kilo. This is something the fat man explained to me, as we were standing beneath that crane, beneath that piece of ship that was bigger than a van.

The homes for the workers at Alang are made of plastic sheets and scraps of wood and tarps and so on. When they need to use the bathroom, they wander out into the ocean.

The ships are bought as is. That means that when they are hauled up on to shore, everything is still inside of them. The beds, the maps, the lockers, the exercise equipment, ropes, lifeboats, blenders, spoons, and so on are all still there. Outside Alang, there are open lots or rudimentary warehouses holding all of these things for sale. I saw a whole warehouse full of tread-

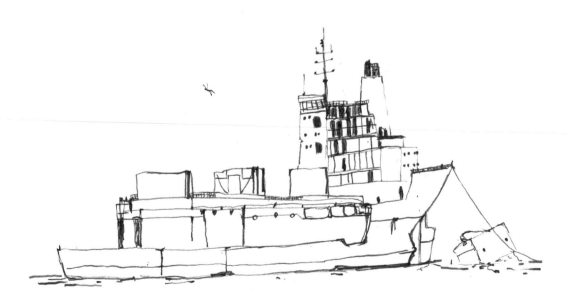

mills. Another was just couches. It was really amazing. All of these things were along one long road leading to the ships themselves and the brown beach. I measured the distance from one end of this road to the other, and the distance was six kilometers. On both sides of that road were continuous piles of ship stuff that reach higher than a house. I probably saw over one thousand blenders from all around the world.

Also with Will and me was the German intern. The German intern was interested in one day entering manufacturing or a related field. He, like Will, did not really seem to be disturbed by Alang. The two of them ate a lot of food at a restaurant right outside the road with all of the stuff on it. I could not eat though.

I told them that when I was a kid, I used to kill ants. I would squish their legs and then I would use a magnifying glass to cook them. The smaller my spot of sun, the better the ant would burn. It would pop and sizzle when it cooked and curl up as the ant got heated by the sun. "Yes," the German intern said. "That is universal."

---

Will is an engineer and he is pretty good at math and at figuring things out. I asked him after I returned from India whether he thought human beings weighed more or machines did. In other words, if you stacked up all humans on a scale, and then all machines, which one would be heavier?

"There are about 6 billion humans at about 60 kilos average," Will wrote to me. "That's 0.36 gigatons."

Will wrote that he read in a book by Vaclav Smil that humans use 1.5 gigatons of stuff each year just in order to "keep the 'human edifice' going. But that includes a lot of cement and sand and stuff."

He wrote that in his apartment, the machines he had weighed more than him. "Fridge, air conditioner, ghetto blaster, etc."

He wrote: "The total number of cars produced last year was 80 million. And the total number in existence is now more than a billion. The average car weighs more than 1.5t. This means that cars alone outweigh humans by four times: 1.5 gigatons of cars vs 0.36 gt of humans."

As we were leaving Alang, there was a truck that was painted in orange, with dots of every color on it. It had paintings of eyes on its front, and on the back it was written: "All is All." The truck was being loaded with scrap, which would be melted in a furnace somewhere and turned into auto parts, machine parts, gears, and so on. The ships' ballasts, giant redwood trunks made of forged steel, were taken away to be turned on lathes for weeks, making them into molds for the pipes that run beneath our cities. The lathes turn in a workshop in Ahmedabad. It is nice there. It is peaceful. The hum of the lathes never stops, these big redwoods turn and turn, spiral-shaped steel shavings pile up on the floor, and the men wade around through those, carefully checking the slow progress of the molds. Then the molds are brought to factories and filled with liquid steel. Then more cities are built. And ships are made to supply them with all the things they need.

In Ahmedabad, Will and I went up in a hot air balloon. It was tethered to the ground by a steel cable, and the cable was controlled by a winch, which was bolted to the ground. We could see for miles. The city was full of cars and motorcycles and dump trucks and construction equipment. The buildings were all falling down and rebuilt as they fell, so signs and laundry lines came out at odd angles. Police in khaki uniforms used long sticks to control the traffic, beating the cars like sheep. Women dressed in the brightest colors. People piled into any kind of motorized transportation. There was a ring of smoke around the city. Four industrial zones, all with hundreds of smoke stacks, released black lines that drifted the same way, out over the plain to the seaside. The industrial zones surrounded the city, so it always smelled like burning, even high up. "I hate to ask this," I told him, "but what do you think would happen if the cable broke? We would fly to space!"

Will laughed. "It wouldn't even make the news," he said.

I used to have this nightmare where I found myself standing inside of a giant mouth. The mouth was as big as the universe and was lined with sharp teeth pointing downwards. In the nightmare, I am holding onto a tooth and all around me, human bodies are falling down into the mouth. Millions of them, people from all over the world. I told Will about this. I said that was kind of the feeling I got when I was in Alang—that we were all falling down into some kind of abyss, and that it was completely out of our control to stop it. That it wasn't progress that was moving us, but gravity. I told him I needed a bit of time off from looking at machines.

———

A few days later, we were drinking whiskey and Will and the German intern were discussing Alang. They said that it was not a humanitarian problem or an environmental problem. They said that like all problems, it was an engineering problem. The solution to all of these machines, they kept insisting, was more machines.

I told them that I thought they were maniacs.

"Listen," Will said. "I'll draw it out."

He proceeded to redesign Alang with locks for raising the ships and for holding in spilled oil. There were big cranes to hold up the ships and the ship pieces so they wouldn't fall and crush the workers. He put robotic torches on robotic cars on these same cranes to do the heavy cutting. He insisted that it would be quiet and clean. He said that humans would only have to push the buttons. It could be a good operation, he said. Clean and efficient and humane. It would even be cheaper than it is now. More profitable.

I looked at his drawing and I had to admit that it seemed like a very good idea. Much better than the way it was now.

"So why don't they do it?" I asked.

"Folks are just too busy whipping their workers to think about the numbers," Will said. "Quite common." ⬡

# What Is a Life in Angola Prison?

## TANYA ERZEN

You Are Entering the Land of New Beginnings
—Sign on the entrance to Angola prison

Angola: Ain't No Place to Be
—Quote on T-shirts worn by members of the
Angola Lifers Association

John Floyd has been tending the peacocks since he arrived at his caretaker's shack at dawn. There are dozens of them roaming the expansive grounds, perched on trucks, reclining in tree branches, and pecking around the front porch of the ranch house. He's discovered a nest midway up the hill and he'll have to be canny in order to cajole the mother and her chicks down to the safety of the hutches and sheds he's built for them over the years. There are foxes, snakes, and whatever else could nab an unsuspecting peacock at night.

John knows each peacock, each guinea hen, each chicken, and each flower and plant because he's been here for 34 years. Now 64, a slight white man with a stoop and a squinty smile, he has spent half his life in a prison the size of Manhattan—decades without ever seeing the outside world. He is one of 6,000 men who live in this former slave plantation and convict leasing farm, nicknamed Angola because the plantation owner believed the hardiest slaves came from there.

Thanks to Louisiana's draconian criminal justice system, most of the over 4,000 men serving life sentences without the possibility of parole will die here. "We have more funerals than we have men going home," John explains. John is a lifer. He is one of the 1,000 or so "trustees," men who have inched their way to the

upper echelons of the prison hierarchy after dozens of years. They are cooks in the warden's home, automotive mechanics, newspaper editors, radio DJs, cattle wranglers, horse trainers, preachers, heavy-machinery repairmen, cowboys who compete in Angola's yearly prison rodeo, and coffin-makers.

John sleeps in a prison camp called the Dog Pen with other trustees who raise bloodhounds and breed wolf/German shepherd hybrids—the wolves alone were not deemed vicious enough. They train the bloodhounds to hunt prisoners who escape. There are no fences in Angola except around the individual prison housing camps, spread throughout the 18,000 acres. Wolf/German shepherds prowl between the double barbed-wire fences that surround the camps at night when men are locked into their cells or dormitories. Dense wooded hills teeming with snakes and the alligator-infested Mississippi River form a natural barrier to the prison.

If you did escape, where could you go? It is 20 miles to the nearest town, the road lined with ramshackle homes and the occasional decaying antebellum plantation. During the few occasions when the Mississippi has swelled and the levees that surround the prison burst, prison officials evacuated prisoners to higher ground. Angola is like a shallow bowl and the whole basin could flood.

How do you spend a life without the possibility of parole? For up to 15 hours a day, John passes time in the company of the chickens, peacocks, and guinea hens, mowing the lawn and tending the flowers. The animals belong to Warden Burl Cain, but this is John's tiny domain. "You can have a life here," a man who spent 28 years in Angola told me. But what is a life in Angola? The lifers and trustees are considered the "most rehabilitated" of prisoners. They have responsibilities, jobs, and a modicum of freedom to move around—to make their own days.

Burl Cain, the controversial warden of almost 20 years, who is tyrant, benevolent father, genial charmer, and king to the men inside, says the prison is here to keep the prisoners safe, not punish them further. "They want to have their lives make sense," he explains. "There is something for everybody." And it is true that in most other prisons it is hard to imagine all these men bustling from place to place. Warden Cain says: "You can move your way up all the way in the system until you almost feel like you're free."

So many men are serving life because Louisiana boasts the harshest sentencing laws in the nation. First- and second-degree murderers automatically get life without parole, but the majority of prisoners are incarcerated for nonviolent offenses, and the state mandatory minimums mean that a person can receive 20 years to life without parole for drug possession or shoplifting. Unlike most other places, which require a unanimous jury to secure a conviction, a person in Louisiana can be convicted on the votes of 10 out of 12 jurors.

According to the Prison Policy Initiative, Louisiana has the highest incarceration rate in the country, with 868 of every 100,000 citizens in prison. African Americans make up 32 percent of Louisiana's population but constitute 66 percent of incarcerated people in the state. White people in Louisiana make up 60 percent of the general population but represent 30 percent of the incarcerated population. Even the conservative Texas Public Policy Network and the Reason Foundation recently issued a joint report recommending that Louisiana drastically alter its sentencing guidelines to reduce its prison population. They argued it is out of step with even conservative states like Georgia and Texas.

Louisiana's numerous parish jails also house state prisoners, and it is a lucrative enterprise for rural sheriff's departments who vie for prisoners from New Orleans and Baton Rouge to fill their jails and coffers. They are a powerful and vociferous lobby against any alteration to the sentencing status quo. Just as the brutal convict lease system, what historian Robert Perkinson calls the "most corrupt and murderous penal regime in American history," replaced slavery and shored up the walls of white supremacy after the Civil War, today's prison system is big business for law enforcement and corporations. Our criminal justice system is an economic machine fueled by sending men like John to prison for life.

Despair is a prisoner's most potent enemy. Both the prison administration and the men inside seem to agree on this alone. For the staff, it means everyone works to stave off violence and chaos. The trustee system is meant to dole out incentives in the face of hopelessness. Angola had the dubious distinction of being known as the "bloodiest prison in America" until recently. Men slept with catalogues and phone books taped to their chests as shields against stabbing. Sexual exploitation was rampant, as Wilbert

Rideau—former editor of the *Angolite Magazine*, who spent 44 years in the prison—chronicled in his memoir *In the Place of Justice* and his co-authored book *Life Sentences: Rage and Survival Behind Bars*.

"You have to allow people to be creative or they will be creative in dark ways," says Cathy Fontenot, the assistant warden who retains a simultaneous vivacity and world-weariness after 18 years here. It's the first job she had out of college. To Fontenot, even being a field hand has value. Every day, all year round, hundreds of men are marched in a line, hoes balanced on their shoulders, to the immense Angola fields to pick beans, okra, squash, cotton, sugar cane, wheat, or corn. None of the 1,200 guards at Angola carry guns. The only exceptions are the field overseers, mounted on horses, with rifles beside them at all times.

Robert Mencie, a 31-year-old black man from California, expressed his incredulity upon being sent to the fields. "I didn't know people were still doing slave-type work. I didn't think they were doing that in America. Period. Until I come down here." And with black men making up 76 percent of the prisoners at Angola, the tableau of weary laborers could be a photo from the 1880s or 1920s. Robert might appreciate W.E.B. DuBois's classic quote about the failure of Reconstruction: "The slave went free; stood a brief moment in the sun; then moved back again toward slavery."

Cathy is adamant: "Here it isn't hopeless. They are safe, clean, and someone is paying attention." If she died at home, she frets about who would find her. She is between what she calls "wusbands," and her kids live with their father during the week. At least at Angola, where privacy is nonexistent, a dead body is noticed immediately.

Later, two emaciated hunger strikers stagger into the infirmary and Cathy mentions the yearly suicides. We visit hospice, a program initiated years ago by men in the prison. The workers there, most of them lifers, are devoted to caring for their brothers who are sick and dying, knowing they will one day take their place. They practice a selflessness rare in the free or unfree world. In the morning, they arrive to the stench of men no longer able to control their bodily functions. They bathe their withered bodies. They spoon-feed them. Their patients will never leave hospice, and their kindnesses and intimacies are perhaps the last these men will receive.

I wonder about despair when you are locked down 23 out of 24 hours a day in a cell with even meager possessions denied to you. No books. Nothing but the company of yourself, one metal bed, and a toilet. This is Camp J or "the Dungeon," where Angola exiles the "worst of the worst," men with repeated disciplinary problems. When I visit, the men are outside for their allotted 45 minutes of daily exercise, confined in 8x10 cages, dog pens built for human beings.

We pass in front of the men in cages and down the row of cells, the officer bellowing "women on the floor" as a warning. How is our well-being, those of us the prisoners call "free people," made possible by this dismal suffering? What is a livable life here? In his book *Inferno: An Anatomy of American Punishment*, Robert Ferguson writes that punishment diminishes the punisher and the recipient. There is no redemptive future for the humans in cages in Camp J. But what might happen if more people looked?

There are other lives in Angola, too. Close to 400 free people are born and raised inside the boundaries of the prison. A few miles from the main prison is B-Line, a town built for prison staff. There is a chapel, a pool, a recreation center, and the Prison View golf course. Although the prison began hiring African American correctional staff in 1975, B-Line is still a stronghold for white families who have worked here for generations. Their livelihoods depend on the men who spend their lives in Angola. John Floyd talks about small kids he observed growing up who are now prison lieutenants. Over half of the B-Line population is children under 18. To them, Angola represents home and security.

John is determined not to die here, and certainly not to spend eternity in Angola's grounds. After a brief tour and discussion about native Louisiana plants, he reenters his shack to retrieve a battered manila folder. Inside are photos of him with Emily Maw, director of the Innocence Project New Orleans, and her family. The Innocence Project has championed his case, which is marred by evidence suppression and police misconduct.

Thirty years earlier in the French Quarter of New Orleans, two gay men were discovered stabbed in the neck and chests within days of each other and a mile apart. Both had consensual sex with their assailant, who left a half-filled whiskey glass at each scene. The police discovered pubic hair belonging to an African American man at both crime scenes. John is white. No physical evidence, including blood type, ever linked John to either murder. Yet detectives relentlessly questioned him, plying him with numerous drinks at a gay bar he frequented.

John, who has an IQ of 59, lower than 99 percent of the population, and is highly susceptible to suggestion, confessed to both crimes. The judge acquitted him of one murder because the overwhelming physical evidence could not tie him to the crime scene, but convicted him of the other at the same trial. Since then, the Innocence Project has learned that the New Orleans district attorney's office failed to turn over significant evidence. Fingerprints on the glasses at both locations belong to the same person (not the victim) and are not John's. And so, after more than three decades, John continues to fight his case.

For John and the lifers, many of them old men, life outside Angola is a receding memory. What would it mean for John Floyd to walk out of Angola? The conundrum for so many of the lifers who have been in Angola for

# Prison "trustees" raise bloodhounds and breed wolf/German shepherd hybrids–the wolves alone were not deemed vicious enough. They train the bloodhounds to hunt prisoners who escape.

30 years is that though they might be the most well-adjusted—or "rehabilitated," in the prison's terms—they have adapted to the institution. Most of their families and friends abandoned them long ago. John, like many others, has never made peace with a life at Angola. You can build a life in Angola, and then there is life. Angola is always a qualification of a life. It is a constrained and diminished life. John's life can never be self-determined, and isn't that the definition of freedom?

John Floyd's story is his story, but it is also the story of thousands who will spend their lives in Angola and other prisons without the possibility of freedom. There are innocent and guilty men there. How long do we punish them? When is punishment enough? John's misery is daily, endless, and ordinary. His time is a form of suffering. His hope, like that of all the lifers I met, rests on the prospect of freedom. The question remains: Who is served by his life in Angola?

At dusk, I talk to Warden Cain outside his massive, immaculately clean, and shiny Silverado SUV. Soon, all I will hear are the night sounds of Angola: the beseeching screams of peacocks and distant yelps of dogs as the clusters of lights of prison camps blink in the darkness. John approaches us. "I know you're going to get out because you're innocent," Warden Cain says to him, almost nonchalantly. He turns to me and says: "He really is." John, stone-faced, doesn't respond. Instead he solemnly tells Warden Cain about the peacock eggs. They had been covered by a tarp, but it blew away in the wind. Now the eggs are broken and the chicks dead. The warden is distraught. "That's bad luck," he says. ⬢

Adorno *à la plage*

# The Logic of the Martyr

## STUART SMITHERS

...interior life (where the revolution always begins).
—Pasolini, *the last interview*

The sea is boiling, opening its belly. Revelation needs heat; brains that evaporate steaming thoughts. Then the mirage becomes reality. In agony, the light. In poverty, the future's birth. Then again the curse against the war machines uttered by the sun. But the sun is ever exploding death into life.
—Etel Adnan, *Seasons*

## Magic spell

We live today as if under a spell. The personality and ego formation that was somehow and at some time necessary as a mask became hardened and seemingly real, even to the point of becoming a form of life and having defense mechanisms. The ego represents nature's first attempt at and most sustained form of artificial intelligence. Adorno says that the process of dominance "keeps spewing undigested scraps of subjugated nature" while the spell produces a neatly dovetailed reality: "The reality principle, which the prudent heed in order to survive in it, *captures them as black magic*; they are unable and unwilling to cast off the burden, for magic hides it from them and makes them think it is life."[1]

---

[1] Theodor W. Adorno, *Negative Dialectics* (New York: Continuum, 1973), 347.

To break the magic spell of capital we need luck and cunning, fortitude and courage, but above all, it seems to me, we could do with a little magic of our own. We are always everywhere faced with the question of means: *how* to awaken from the spell of late capitalism. I am beginning to think of the Frankfurt School as a guild of magicians—Adorno, Horkheimer, Benjamin, and Marcuse—each with his own secrets and tool kit. Of course, the point of Frankfurt magic is simply to undo capitalism's magic: to engage critical means to awaken the dead, to make the scales fall from our eyes, as Horkheimer and Adorno say somewhere, to create the conditions for capital disenchantment. Susan Buck-Morss helped me with this thought, recognizing so much of Benjamin's particular genius when she wrote: "His legacy to readers who come after him is a nonauthoritarian system of inheritance," a system of investigation and exposition like the "utopian tradition of fairy tales which instruct without dominating," an approach that results in victories over forces of domination.[2]

Is this a hopeless task—to awaken humanity from the dream world and to liberate us from a mechanical, zombie-like existence? For both Adorno and Benjamin humanity has forgotten life and being behind the mask, just as individuals have forgotten themselves and their life possibilities. Adorno's magic elaborates thinking, a thinking that shines a floodlight on deception, lies, false promises, and mechanisms of fear. His magic exposes the architecture and engineering of the spell: finding the weak spots in capital's system of magic, recognizing and exploiting the spaces in between, the gaps and intervals in capitalism's logic.

Benjamin, on the other hand, enters the world of imagination, inhabiting the dream world of capital and the space of things, awakening the reader to the illusory surface of commodities and the transparency of things. His work often frees us from the hardness of reification and allows us to live in the dream world conscious of its dreaminess. He is a master of dream-yoga, a form of lucid dreaming in capital. Or perhaps we could think of his method as that of a hacker: finding the back door of the system, only to enter and exploit the system from within. Of course, the exploration of dream-yoga would be fetishistic if it weren't meant to demonstrate the nature of the dream world and the very real suffering that exists within in it.

## Virtues of Resistance

In Thesis IV of Benjamin's *On the Concept of History* (which he described in a letter to Gretel Adorno as more "a bouquet of whispering grasses, gath-

---

**2**  Susan Buck-Morss, *Dialectics of Seeing: Walter Benjamin and the Arcades Project* (Cambridge, MA: MIT Press, 1991), 336.

ered on reflective walks, than as a collection of theses"), we find an account of the virtues that arise from struggle for material existence:

> The class struggle, which is always present to a historian influenced by Marx, is a fight for the crude and material things without which no refined and spiritual things could exist. Nevertheless, it is not in the form of the spoils that fall to the victor that the latter make their presence felt in the class struggle. *They manifest themselves in this struggle as courage, humor, cunning, and fortitude.* They have a retroactive force and will constantly call in question every victory, past and present, of the rulers. As flowers turn toward the sun, by dint of a secret heliotropism the past strives to turn toward the sun which is rising in the sky of history. A historical materialist must be aware of this most inconspicuous of all transformations. [Emphasis added.]

In *The Coming Insurrection*, the anonymous authors of the Invisible Committee make the observation: "It's the privileged feature of radical circumstances that a rigorous application of logic leads to revolution. It's enough just to say what is before our eyes and not to shrink from the conclusions." But do we live in "radical circumstances"? Is the ongoing crisis radical, or should we agree that debilitating circumstances have become the norm and something radical is still missing? The Invisible Committee's statement might appear cold and cerebral, true but missing some element of passion that actually moves one from conclusions to action.

So if we wonder why there are so few revolutionaries today, we might ask: Is our logic off? Are we not rigorous enough? Are we avoiding conclusions? Are we lacking in virtue? Are we cowards?

Or: *What prepares the ground for the appearance of a revolutionary subject in a world where the fight for material existence seems to lack desperation?*

Certainly the struggle to feed oneself arises from a particular type of suffering, but in late capitalism we live in a system that both creates needs and largely fulfills those created needs. Do the "refined and spiritual things" in Benjamin's thesis—including the virtue of courage—arise only out of a desperate fight for material things? Living under the spell of late capitalism, turning a blind eye to suffering wherever possible, I would like to ask if there is some vital lesson to be learned from those who actually live in the most radical circumstances. If the tradition of the oppressed teaches us, what new lessons can we learn about the conditions for the appearance of a revolutionary subject who lives under the spell?

# Radical Circumstances

Grave digging, and washing and burying the bodies of the dead, is work for men in Islam. The women in Benghazi visit the graves of the new "martyrs" at night. For three days, Benghazi suffered the most brutal crackdown of any of the Arab uprisings with loyal troops even firing on crowds of mourners as they left the cemetery. Men carried the bodies of young men to their graves, bodies that had been ripped in half by assault rifles, as the funeral processions defiantly marched past Qaddafi's military garrison, the Katiba, with some 5,000 soldiers and officers inside, including his Special Forces.

Mahdi Ziu was an unlikely hero: a quiet, 49-year-old married man with two daughters, working as a middle manager at the state oil company. His family and friends say he had little interest in politics. But the brutal repression proved too much; he had buried too many boys and young men. Then something happened; he reached a tipping point in himself—*beyond a certain point*, as Marx wrote. This interior zone of rising up, the appearance of exceptional "fearless" courage and the determination to act, is the space where Benjamin's "refined and spiritual things" manifest in the struggle: These spiritual qualities appear during and through the act of resistance and rebellion, not afterward. The condition I imagine is one of both gradual and sudden transformation, the recognition of a transcendent solidarity—deep identity and relationship with the other, the young men of Benghazi both dead and living, with the families and friends of the dead and the living.

The residents of Benghazi resisted Qaddafi's desperate attempts to crush the revolt and saw their friends and brothers cut in half by anti-aircraft guns as they mounted their assault on the garrison with Molotov cocktails, stones, bulldozers, and fish bombs. Mahdi Ziu was "inconspicuously transformed"; his wife, his daughters, his friends knew nothing. He asked his neighbors to help him load four canisters of propane into his car and when they asked what he was doing, he told them the propane canisters had leaks and he was taking them to get fixed.

Mahdi Ziu drove his car in the next day's funeral procession and protest. When he was close enough to the gates of the Katiba, he swerved out of the crowd and floored his accelerator. Guards fired on him, but it was too late: The explosion blew a huge hole in the wall. The pile of concrete and twisted rebar is now called the "martyr's gate" in Mahdi's honor. Within hours, Qaddafi's forces had been defeated, many disappearing into the countryside, the feared Katiba abandoned. The tide had turned for the Libyan uprising.

The collective tipping point for the rebels had probably come earlier, but now the reality of their courage was clear. On the walls of the city, Arabic graffiti appeared: "We have broken the fear barrier. We won't retreat."

# Against Self-Preservation at All Costs

Two types of courage issue from a certain duality. One knows that one is afraid but determines not to be overcome by the fear that is all too evident to oneself. In this type of courage, one struggles not to be overwhelmed by fear. The other courage appears as a spontaneous event, whole, absolute, and complete—not as a struggle. This second kind of courage is no doubt preceded by struggle, but there is a sudden and definite shift. To call it courage may even be wrong, because what appears to be courageous action issues from a state of fearlessness. This is not an overcoming of fear in the sense that one is able to act despite fear, but an absence of fear. This second type of courage is naturally preceded by fear and other conditions, but appears unpredictably when an unknown tipping point is reached. As Marx says, this tipping point marks a distinct change in quality: "Merely quantitative differences, beyond a certain point, pass into qualitative changes." Both types of courage reflect different levels of freedom from the capture of self-preservation's urge. [3]

The courage during the Benghazi funeral processions was certainly honorable and remarkable, but media reports about the protesters did not reflect language that was particularly religious, only the most casual and formulaic statements about "God being with them" that day because their heads weren't blown off.

In the dream-world of late capitalism, the question of self-preservation must include questions of identity and ontology: *What* self is being preserved and *why*? And to what extent does a subconscious urge for self-preservation work against the spontaneous arising of a revolutionary subject?

Like the ego itself, the urge for self-preservation served some logical function in the distant evolutionary past when self-preservation of the species was precarious and difficult. Adorno identifies the ego drive as the instrument of self-preservation, and suggests that the power of the ego drive remains "all but irresistible even after technology has virtually made self-preservation easy..." [4]

## The Logic Is Not Logical Anymore

If I am reading this correctly, Adorno comes very close to Fanon's anti-identitarian objection when he declares his refusal to be a tool or be subject to

---

**3**  In *The Republic*, Socrates maintains that the guardian class should fear capture and enslavement more than death.

**4**  Adorno, *Negative Dialectics*, 349.

the power of a tool. This is to recognize the enemy within as the reified hardened ego, always seeking dominance and maintaining itself as the false master.[5] Adorno notes that the human species inherited something compulsive from animals with regard to self-preservation, but in the human it is qualitatively transformed because the reflective faculty of mind that might break the spell has instead entered into the service of the spell, become the instrument of the spell as reified consciousness:

> By such self-preservation it reinforces the spell and makes it radical evil, devoid of the innocence of mere being the way one is. In human experience the spell is the equivalent of the fetish character of merchandise. The self-made thing becomes a thing-in-itself, from which the self cannot escape anymore... In the spell, the reified consciousness has become total.[6]

The genealogy of the spell indicates that the reflected nature of the mind entered the service of capital's spell as reified consciousness—which, adding the ego's force, qualitatively changes the drive of self-preservation and creates a perpetual reinforcement for both reified ego-consciousness and the spell. In this form, risk-avoidance, conformity, and the secret mechanisms of fear become normative strategies of a spellbound consciousness that seeks to preserve itself.

## The Martyr Is Indeed Extreme

The martyr represents what we have denied ourselves. The martyr is a representation of pleasure—of all the pleasures we have foregone in fear of death, to stay alive, to preserve ourselves—and all pain. For most religious mentalities, heaven represents not so much the restitution of all-pleasure, but the survival of a status quo of compromised pleasure and the escape from the danger of hell, displeasure, and the fear of displeasure. Heaven is approached through fear (and desire). The martyr is

---

**5**  See especially the clarifying last chapters of Frantz Fanon's, *Black Skin, White Masks*, where he counters the hardening of bourgeois culture with an examination of incomprehensible (to the West, in any case) forms of courage: "For me, bourgeois society is a closed society where it's not good to be alive, where the air is rotten and ideas and people are putrefying. And I believe that a man who takes a stand against this living death is in a way a revolutionary" (New York: Grove Press, 2008), 199.

**6**  Adorno, *Negative Dialectics*, 345. The idea that the "self-made thing becomes a thing in itself, from which the self cannot escape anymore..." is not only a perfect description of the process of ego-enclosure, but of humanity's relationship to technology. In this further phase of ego-enclosure, the distinction between Frankenstein and human tends to become blurred.

a model of uncompromised fearlessness and pleasure.

Western politicians and pundits would like to brainwash us into believing that all "martyrs" are brainwashed. Stories about 72 virgins awaiting martyrs in paradise reflect the same pleasure-oriented dualism—desire for the happiness of heaven, fear of hell—that operates on some level in all religions. But the image of the "brainwashed" martyr is also an easy target for the media, where the rhetoric of modern martyrdom is presented in wholly irrational terms in order to rationalize our own fear and powerlessness in the face of extreme sacrifice. Someone like Mahdi Ziu—a comfortable, middle-class engineer with a family and career—is an unimaginable martyr. The idea and image of the martyr needs to be rehabilitated. Only when we finally begin to try to understand the unimaginable martyr will we begin to understand the fear and confusion behind the cartoon version of the logic of the martyr.

Why do politicians and the media insist that martyrs are "cowards" and extremists? It was striking in the immediate aftermath of the *Charlie Hebdo* massacre in Paris that the international media could only repeat worn-out ideological themes of cowardice and victory: *They* will win (if we don't). Anyone who watched the closed-circuit surveillance footage of the street encounter between the Paris police attempting to block the escape and the shooters couldn't possibly think these men were cowards. One could assign endless adjectives and wonder about their actions and motives, but "cowardly" would not apply. And doesn't the rhetoric of heroism, of a society determined to put its head down and march ahead— not determined to preserve life but preserve a *lifestyle*—really mean that we would prefer not to think? Some 80,000 French security forces were summoned to find the two "extremists." "Winning" only means to preserve an already suspicious life, but the meta-level of the contest suggests that extremists can't possibly lose.

The martyr is indeed extreme, but not all extremists are martyrs. The extreme dualism inherent in the difference between the Messianic and the profane (sketched out in Benjamin's "Theological-Political Fragment" written in 1921), runs counter to the preservation of a comfortable, compromised self. The dialectics of an extreme self has roots in Western metaphysics:

> I know thy works, that thou art neither cold nor hot: I would thou
> wert cold or hot. So then because thou art lukewarm, and neither
> cold nor hot, I will spue thee out of my mouth." (*Revelation* 3:15–16)

Bataille suggests that there is no society without an accursed share—that part of society that will destroy us, unless we destroy it—and the means to continue the life of the society is *sacrifice*. The contemporary contestation between the West and "extreme" forms of resistance could be viewed as a contest of *sacrifice*—a potlatch of sacrificial modes that the West is losing. Any rhetoric of sacrifice in the West is betrayed by an almost universal refusal to consider altering our *lifestyle*, while not hesitating to "sacrifice" the other in a vain attempt at self-preservation. The accursed share that is already turning on society is vast material accumulation and the attachment to comfort, pleasure, and self.[7] The two vastly different dimensions of sacrifice revealed by the martyr—refusing to sacrifice capital-driven lifestyle, versus the actually existing sacrifice of self—reflect two models of non-rational gestures, only one of which is grounded in a metaphysic of redemption. The martyr is traditionally the one who witnesses the world, and suffers for that vision and testimony. Socrates and Christ are the archetype of the Western martyr: witnesses who refused to renounce what they saw and described as the real world, and at the same time represented an unbearable presence and reminder for those who had no interest in, or feared, rocking the status quo.

The world system has even created a new type of secular martyr, the capitalist martyr. After the twelfth worker jumped to suicide at the Foxconn site in China that manufactures many of Apple's products, a worker-blog provided this posting:

> To die is the only way to testify that we ever lived. Perhaps for the Foxconn employees and employees like us—we who are called *nongmingong*, rural migrant workers, in China—the use of death is simply to testify that we were ever alive at all, and that while we lived, we had only despair.[8]

## Liquidating the Spell

Adorno continues his thought on the closed system of the spell, suggesting that it perpetuates a coldness in humans that could finally actualize our impending disintegration, horror, and catastrophe—a reality that might well explode the spell, causing the scales to fall from our eyes. But anyone who is not cold, "who does not chill himself," already suffers reality beyond the

7   See Daniel Hartley's essay in this volume: "Thoughts on Revolutionary Indifference; or, The Thermodynamics of Militancy."

8   Jenny Chan and Ngai Pun, "Suicide as Protest for the New Generation of Chinese Migrant Workers: Foxconn, Global Capital, and the State," accessed June 12, 2015, http://japanfocus.org/-Ngai-Pun/3408/article.html.

spell, and perhaps suffers that consuming fire of conscience as a demand or call for some kind of action. [9]

Does the process of domination likewise subsume conscience? As Horkheimer and Adorno observed, "conscience is being liquidated" by capitalist culture. Conscience remains a difficult concept. You might say that reified consciousness is reflected in the absence of conscience and the decay of the soul (defined by Horkheimer and Adorno as "the possibility of guilt aware of itself"). [10]

The process needs to be reversed so that the liquidation of conscience, the decay of the soul, and reification of consciousness is replaced by the liquidation of the reification of consciousness. In that process the nonaligned, liberated consciousness will consciously confront the fear barrier and discover the secret mechanisms of cowardice that allow the spell to continue. Finally, fear and forgetting should not be dominated, but self-liquidated in the light of a nonaligned consciousness.

The conscious movement toward risk reverses, so to say, the process of reification, de-crystallizing thingness. Internal struggle and conflict dissolve the totalizing reification of the ego as an illusion of unity that has been fed by the alignment of consciousness with enlightenment, power, and a bestial drive of self-preservation that attaches us to a bestial form of life that would condemn others to death and misery. The illusory unity of the ego-as-one is split into two with this inner struggle and confrontation: fear and courage, with the possibility of a third element as the reappearance of conscience, a feeling in between seeing and passivity, need and fear. Conscience always places us in front of the possibility of action, good or bad, liberating or enslaving.

But under the magic spell of late capitalism, the reality of a nonaligned consciousness—free from domination and free from the wish to dominate—is far from obvious. As Adorno and Horkheimer wrote with regard to the culture industry: "Amusement always means putting things out of mind, forgetting suffering, even when it is on display. At its root is powerlessness. It is indeed, but not, as it claims, escape from bad reality but from the *last thought of resisting that reality*." [11]

The magic spell offers cheap happiness and the sleepy forgetfulness of the suffering of others and one's own—a bad escape that spares us the inconvenience of thinking and revolution. Nevertheless, the limitless horizon of this infinitely bad escape does seem an unlikely possibility.

Jameson remarked: "The question of poetry after Auschwitz has

9   Adorno, *Negative Dialectics*, 346.

10   Theodore Adorno and Max Horkheimer, *Dialectic of Enlightenment* (Stanford: Stanford University Press, 2002), 164.

11   Ibid., 116 (emphasis added).

been replaced with that of whether you could bear to read Adorno and Horkheimer next to the pool." Both Adorno's original statement and Jameson's updated remarks already reveal that we are confronted with a possible moment of conscience. Whether the moment is unbearable and you hide Adorno and Horkheimer under someone's discarded magazines or, on the other hand, you decide that you might more righteously abandon the pool in order to read Adorno and Horkheimer in the sanctity of your study—in both cases, the crucial moment of conscience as conscious struggle has passed and the momentary suffering and disclosure of the ego's identity as totally representative of the self has ended with the return to the fully reified ego-consciousness, comfortable again with one's identity.

As I reflect on that question now, I imagine a tentative approach: We must read Adorno and Horkheimer to our friends and anyone within earshot, out loud, even next to the pool, perhaps especially next to the pool. In the current ongoing crisis, we might still be able to restore, in Jameson's words, "the sense of something grim and impending within the polluted sunshine of the shopping mall..." and find ways to evoke in ourselves and in others the sense of a forgotten conscience that might still be alive in our subconscious. At the same time, behind and before the reified consciousness, there is a free and nonaligned consciousness closely related to what Adorno often refers to as "thinking." The orientation and elaboration of a consciousness that is not just momentarily free initiates a process of the reversal of reification. Any revolution that lives the communizing current, no matter how weak or fleeting, will sooner or later be confronted by counter-revolutionary forces of domination; a new revolutionary subject is needed, one aware of the lived process of the reification of consciousness and the means of reversal.

To resist hypnotism and the magic spell, we need more than the normal program of instruction. There will always be more martyrs—but to fight the spell we also need more magicians. ⬢

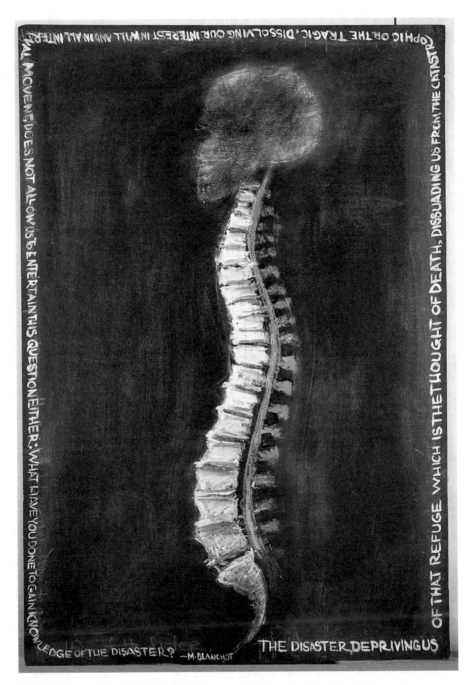

Carl Lehman-Haupt & Kathleen Cramer, *Writing the Disaster*, 2014

Now what we call "bourgeois," when regarded as an element always to be found in human life, is nothing else than the search for a balance. It is the striving after a mean between the countless extremes and opposites that arise in human conduct. If we take any one of these coupled opposites, such as piety and profligacy, the analogy is immediately comprehensible. It is open to a man to give himself up wholly to spiritual views, to seeking after God, to the ideal of saintliness. On the other hand, he can equally give himself up entirely to the life of instinct, to the lusts of the flesh, and so direct all his efforts to the attainment of momentary pleasures. The one path leads to the saint, to the martyrdom of the spirit and surrender to God. The other path leads to the profligate, to the martyrdom of the flesh, the surrender to corruption. Now it is between the two, in the middle of the road, that the bourgeois seeks to walk. He will never surrender himself either to lust or to asceticism. He will never be a martyr or agree to his own destruction. On the contrary, his ideal is not to give up but to maintain his own identity. He strives neither for the saintly nor its opposite. The absolute is his abhorrence. He may be ready to serve God, but not by giving up the fleshpots. He is ready to be virtuous, but likes to be easy and comfortable in this world as well. In short, his aim is to make a home for himself between two extremes in a temperate zone without violent storms and tempests; and in this he succeeds though it be at the cost of that intensity of life and feeling which an extreme life affords. A man cannot live intensely except at the cost of the self. Now the bourgeois treasures nothing more highly than the self (rudimentary as his may be). And so at the cost of intensity he achieves his own preservation and security. His harvest is a quiet mind which he prefers to being possessed by God, as he does comfort to pleasure, convenience to liberty, and a pleasant temperature to that deathly inner consuming fire. The bourgeois is consequently by nature a creature of weak impulses, anxious, fearful of giving himself away and easy to rule. Therefore, he has substituted majority for power, law for force, and the polling booth for responsibility.

— Hermann Hesse, *Steppenwolf*

# Catheter Enjambment

## CACONRAD

*for Chelsea Manning & Mattilda Bernstein Sycamore*

And our lips are not our lips.
But are the lips of heads of poets. And should shout revolution.
—Jack Spicer

Let's be honest about our culture and say that anyone who makes us remember we are naked animals under these clothes is dangerous. To remove the scandal of it would first require the total annihilation of every bureaucratic agency sending memos through our doors. It is 2012 and some of us have our boots holding back the Return to Modesty campaign. The American homosexual in 2012 unapologetically celebrates surrendering to the dominant culture's taste for marital equilibrium and WAR! A swift, unmitigated return to values acts like bookends many willingly throw themselves between. The opportunity to challenge these stifling, life-threatening institutions passes out of the conversation entirely in 2012.

Stupid faggots putting rainbow stickers on machine guns! I'm going to say it: GAY AND LESBIAN AMERICA HAS STOCKHOLM SYNDROME! The campaign to be included in the multibillion-dollar military-industrial complex comes at a time when three children die of war-related injuries EVERY SINGLE DAY in Afghanistan. And after 10 years of American occupation, Afghanistan has been deemed THE MOST DANGEROUS nation on our planet for women. No other place on Earth is worse for women than Afghanistan. How else can I repeat this so you hear it? America DESTROYS Afghan women and children! Did you hear it that time?

The genocide of thousands of gay men in Baghdad is a direct result of the American invasion and occupation of Iraq. The most famous homosexual apologist for fascism, Dan Choi, helped make this genocide possible while serving as an American soldier in Iraq. American gay rights are all that matter I guess? And the destruction of Iraqi gays is just another item on the list of collateral damage? WILL NOT SERVE! To be repeated, WILL NOT SERVE WILL NOT SERVE I WILL NOT SERVE! WILL NOT! Today I WILL LISTEN to only my voice for NOT serving this sanctioned, collective, and REAL evil. In the morning I performed Reiki on a long, thin piece of plastic tubing, Reiki with intentions to BE conscious throughout the day of being queer. Queer. Only queer. Today I will NOT ALLOW anyone to change the subject when I talk about what it means to be queer. Today I will NOT ALLOW the liars to step in front of me. Today I will talk about the frustration of watching war go unquestioned by the homosexual community of America. Reiki. I did Reiki for half an hour on this plastic tube, then lubricated every inch of it, then inserted it inside my penis. It was not for pleasure of pain, it was for a chronic reminder of HOW this culture inserts its will on my penis more and more each day. You may now be married under our rules. You may now engage in the murder of innocent lives by our rules. I had many strained, bizarre conversations this day, constantly FEELING the tube inside my penis while walking around Philadelphia, while walking around Occupy Philadelphia and talking about war, genocide, and oil. The following poem is the result of this exercise, which was more painful in spirit than was the tube inside me.

## IT'S TOO LATE FOR CAREFUL

melting glaciers
frighten me when
appearing on
my street as
downpours
a feeling I send
ahead of myself to one
day walk inside
people sleep while I
inspect their
flowers
not as
weird as

you think
I dreamt gays were
allowed in the military
isn't it great everyone
said
*what a nightmare* I
said
killing babies is less
threatening with a politically
correct militia
vices for the vice box
for
wards of the
forward state
who like different
things to kill alike
we CANNOT occupy Wall Street but
we CAN occupy Kabul
massage our
anger with a heart chakra green
blessings soaked into bed sheets
there's a way of
looking into
time for a poem
send it into the future
your footprint has
grown small what is
wrong with your footing?
what kind of American
are you? just buy it or
steal it but shut up
this poem is terrific for
the economy
the rich have
always tasted
like chicken
I'm not a
cannibal because
they're not
my kind
we CANNOT occupy Philadelphia but
we CAN occupy Baghdad

we're the kind of poets
Plato exiled from the city limits
FUCK Plato that
paranoid faggot
Don't Ask, Don't Tell?
HOW ABOUT
Don't Kill and say whatever you WANT
for instance
when I adopt a cat
I will name him Genet
"Genet!  GENET!" I practice
calling Genet
INTO my LIFE!
when you purchase
a car the factory's
pollution is
100% free
it's never easy
waking to this
bacteria and light
mucus and bone
a legacy of stardust
it is 98.6 degrees Fahrenheit inside all
humans
the freshly
murdered
their murderers
and the rest of
us between
my father lived to
see the fast-forward to
the cum shot
technology's
authentic
application
we CANNOT occupy Oakland but
the ghosts will occupy us
I will stay and
watch our
phoenix rise
I believe
in us

# Precarious Labor: A Feminist Viewpoint

## SILVIA FEDERICI

*This lecture took place on October 28, 2006, at*
*Bluestockings Radical Bookstore in New York City as part of the*
*discussion series "This Is Forever: From Inquiry to Refusal."*

**T**onight I will present a critique of the theory of precarious labor that has been developed by Italian autonomist Marxists, with particular reference to the work of Antonio Negri, Paolo Virno, and also Michael Hardt. I call it a theory because the views that Negri and others have articulated go beyond the description of changes in the organization of work that have taken place in the 1980s and 1990s in conjunction with the globalization process—such as the "precarization of work," the fact that work relations are becoming more discontinuous, the introduction of "flexy time," and the increasing fragmentation of the work experience. Their view on precarious labor presents a whole perspective on what is capitalism and what is the nature of the struggle today. It is important to add that these are not simply the ideas of a few intellectuals, but theories that have circulated widely within the Italian movement for a number of years, and have recently become more influential also in the United States, and in this sense they have become more relevant to us.

# History and Origin of Precarious Labor and Immaterial Labor Theory

My first premise is that definitely the question of precarious labor must be on our agenda. Not only has our relationship to waged work become more discontinuous, but a discussion of precarious labor is crucial for our understanding of how we can go beyond capitalism. The theories that I discuss capture important aspects of the developments that have taken place in the organization of work; but they also bring us back to a male-centric conception of work and social struggle. I will discuss now those elements in this theory that are most relevant to my critique.

An important premise in the Italian autonomists' theory of precarious labor is that the precarization of work, from the late '70s to present, has been a capitalist response to the class struggle of the '60s, a struggle that was centered on the refusal of work, as expressed in the slogan "more money, less work." It was a response to a cycle of struggle that challenged the capitalist command over labor, in a sense realizing the workers' refusal of the capitalist work discipline, the refusal of a life organized by the needs of capitalist production, a life spent in a factory or in an office.

Another important theme is that the precarization of work relations is deeply rooted in another shift that has taken place with the restructuring of production in the 1980s. This is the shift from industrial labor to what Negri and Virno call "immaterial labor." Negri and others have argued that the restructuring of production that has taken place in the '80s and '90s in response to the struggles of the '60s has begun a process whereby industrial labor is to be replaced by a different type of work, in the same way as industrial labor replaced agricultural work. They call the new type of work "immaterial labor" because they claim that with the computer and information revolutions the dominant form of work has changed. As a tendency, the dominant form of work in today's capitalism is work that does not produce physical objects but information, ideas, states of being, relations.

In other words, industrial work—which was hegemonic in the previous phase of capitalist development—is now becoming less important; it is no longer the engine of capitalist development. In its place we find "immaterial labor," which is essentially cultural work, cognitive work, info work.

Italian autonomists believe that the precarization of work and the appearance of immaterial labor fulfills the prediction Marx made in the *Grundrisse*, in a famous section on machines. In this section, Marx states that with the development of capitalism, less and less capitalist production relies on living labor and more and more on the integration of science, knowledge, and technology in the production process as the engines of accumulation. Virno and Negri see the shift to precarious labor as fulfilling this prediction about capitalism's historic trend. Thus, the importance of cognitive work and the development of computer work in our time lies in the fact that they are seen as part of a historic trend of capitalism towards the reduction of work.

The precarity of labor is rooted in the new forms of production. Presumably, the shift to immaterial labor generates a precarization of work relations because the structure of cognitive work is different from that of industrial, physical work. Cognitive and info work rely less on the continuous physical presence of the worker in what was the traditional workplace. The rhythms of work are much more intermittent, fluid, and discontinuous.

In sum, the development of precarious labor and shift to immaterial labor are not for Negri and other autonomist Marxists a completely negative phenomenon. On the contrary, they are seen as expressions of a trend towards the reduction of work and therefore the reduction of exploitation, resulting from capitalist development in response to the class struggle.

This means that the development of the productive forces today is already giving us a glimpse of a world in which work can be transcended, in which we will liberate ourselves from the necessity to work and enter a new realm of freedom.

Autonomous Marxists believe this development is also creating a new kind of "common" originating from the fact that immaterial labor presumably represents a leap in the socialization and homogenization of work. The idea is that differences between types of work that once were all-important (productive/reproductive work, e.g., agricultural/industrial/"affective labor") are erased, as all types work (as a tendency) become assimilated, for all begin to incorporate cognitive work. Moreover, all activities are increasingly subsumed under capitalist development—they all serve the accumulation process, as society becomes an immense factory. Thus, e.g., the distinction between productive and unproductive labor also vanishes.

This means that capitalism is not only leading us beyond labor, but it is creating the conditions for the "commonization" of our work experience, where the divisions are beginning to crumble.

We can see why these theories have become popular. They have utopian elements especially attractive to cognitive workers—the "cognitariat," as Negri and some Italian activists call them. With the new theory, in fact, a new vocabulary has been invented. Instead of proletariat we have the "cognitariat." Instead of the working class, we have the "multitude," presumably because the concept of Multitude reveals the unity that is created by the new socialization of work; it expresses the communalization of the work process, the idea that within the work process workers are becoming more homogenized. For all forms of work incorporate elements of cognitive work, of computer work, communication work, and so forth.

As I said, this theory has gained much popularity because there is a generation of young activists with years of schooling and degrees who are now employed in precarious ways in different parts of the culture industry or the knowledge-production industry. Among them, these theories are very popular because they tell them that, despite the misery and exploitation we are experiencing, we are nevertheless moving towards a higher level of production and social relations. This is a generation of workers who looks at the "nine-to-five" routine as a prison sentence. They see their precariousness as giving them new possibilities. And they have possibilities their parents did not have or did not dream of. The male youth of today (e.g.) are not as disciplined as their parents, who could expect that their wife or partners would depend on them economically. Now they can count on social relationships involving much less financial dependence. Most women have autonomous access to the wage and often refuse to have children.

So this theory is appealing for the new generation of activists who, despite the difficulties resulting from precarious labor, see within it certain possibilities. They want to start from there. They are not interested in a struggle for full employment. But there is also a difference here between Europe and the US. In Italy, e.g., there is among the movement a demand for a guaranteed income. They call it "flex security." They say, we are without a job, we are precarious because capitalism needs us to be, so they should pay for it. There have been various days of mobilization, especially on May 1st, centered on this demand for a guaranteed income. In Milano, on the May Day of this year, movement people have paraded "San Precario," the patron saint of the precarious worker. The ironic icon is featured in rallies and demonstrations centered on this question of precarity.

## Critique of Precarious Labor

I will now shift to my critique of these theories—a critique from a feminist viewpoint. In developing my critique, I don't want to minimize the importance of the theories I am discussing. They have been inspired by much political organizing and striving to make sense of the changes that have taken place in the organization of work, which has affected all our lives. In Italy, in recent years, precarious labor has been one of the main terrains of mobilization together with the struggle for immigrant rights.

I do not want to minimize the work that is taking place around issues of precarity. Clearly, what we have seen in the last decade is a new kind of struggle. A new kind of organizing is taking place, breaking away from the confines of the traditional workplace. Where the workplace was the factory or the office, we now see a kind of struggle that goes out from the factory to the "territory," connecting different places of work and building movements and organizations rooted in the territory. The theories of precarious labor are trying to account for the aspects of novelty in the organization of work and struggle, trying to understand the emergent forms of organization.

This is very important. At the same time, I think that what I called precarious labor theory has serious flaws that I have already hinted at. I will outline them and then discuss the question of alternatives.

My first criticism is that this theory is built on a faulty understanding of how capitalism works. It sees capitalist development as moving towards higher forms of production and labor. In *Multitude*, Negri and Hardt actually write that labor is becoming more "intelligent." The assumption is that the capitalist organization of work and capitalist development are already creating the conditions for the overcoming of exploitation. Presumably, at one point, capitalism—the shell that keeps society going—will break up and the potentialities that have grown within it will be liberated. There is an assumption that that process is already at work in the present organization of production. In my view, this is a misunderstanding of the effects of the restructuring produced by capitalist globalization and the neoliberal turn.

What Negri and Hardt do not see is that the tremendous leap in technology required by the computerization of work and the integration of information into the work process has been paid at the cost of a tremendous increase of exploitation at the other end of the process. There is a continuum between the computer worker and the worker in the Congo who digs coltan with his hands trying to seek out a living after being expropriated, pauperized, by repeated rounds of structural adjustment and repeated theft of his community's land and natural sources.

The fundamental principle is that capitalist development is always at the same time a process of underdevelopment. Maria Mies describes it eloquently in her work: "What appears as development in one part of the capitalist faction is underdevelopment in another part."

This connection is completely ignored in this theory, which is permeated by the illusion that the work process is bringing us together. When Negri and Hardt speak of the "becoming common" of work and use the concept of Multitude to indicate the new commonism that is built through the development of the productive forces, I believe they are blind to much of what is happening with the world proletariat.

They are blind to not see the capitalist destruction of lives and the ecological environment. They don't see that the restructuring of production has aimed at restructuring and deepening the divisions within the working class, rather than erasing them. The idea that the development of the microchip is creating a new commons is misleading. Communalism can only be a product of struggle, not of capitalist production.

Negri and Hardt seem to believe that the capitalist organization of work is the expression of a higher rationality and that capitalist development is necessary to create the material conditions for communism. This belief is at the center of precarious labor theory. We could discuss here whether it represents Marx's thinking or not. Certainly the *Communist Manifesto* speaks of capitalism in these terms and the same is true of some sections of the *Grundrisse*. But it is not clear this was a dominant theme in Marx's work, at least not in *Capital*.

## Precarious Labor and Reproductive Work

Another criticism I have of the precarious labor theory is that it presents itself as gender-neutral. It assumes that the reorganization of production is doing away with the power relations and hierarchies that exist within the working class on the basis of race, gender, and age, and therefore it is not concerned with addressing these power relations; it does not have the theoretical and political tools to think about how to tackle them. There is no discussion in Negri, Virno, and Hardt of how the wage has been and continues to be used to organize these divisions and how therefore we must approach the wage struggle so that it does not become an instrument of further divisions, but instead can help us undermine them. To me, this is one of the main issues we must address in the movement.

The concept of the "Multitude" suggests that all divisions within the working class are gone or are no longer politically relevant. But this is obviously an illusion. Some feminists have pointed out that precarious labor is not a new phenomenon. Women always had a precarious relation to waged labor. But this critique goes far enough.

My concern is that the Negrian theory of precarious labor ignores—bypasses—one of the most important contributions of feminist theory and struggle, which is the redefinition of work and the recognition of women's unpaid reproductive labor as a key source of capitalist accumulation. In redefining housework as *work*, as not a personal service but the work that produces and reproduces labor power, feminists have uncovered a new crucial ground of exploitation that Marx and Marxist theory completely ignored. All of the important political insights contained in those analyses are now brushed aside as if they were of no relevance to an understanding of the present organization of production.

There is a faint echo of the feminist analysis—a lip service paid to it—in the inclusion of so-called "affective labor" in the range of work activities qualifying as "immaterial labor." However, the best Negri and Hardt can come up with is the case of women who work as flight attendants or in the food service industry, whom they call "affective laborers," because they are expected to smile at their customers.

But what is "affective labor"? And why is it included in the theory of immaterial labor? I imagine it is included because—presumably—it does not produce tangible products but "states of being." That is, it produces feelings. Again, to put it crudely, I think this is a bone thrown to feminism, which now is a perspective that has some social backing and can no longer be ignored.

But the concept of "affective labor" strips the feminist analysis of housework of all its demystifying power. In fact, it brings reproductive work back into the world of mystification, suggesting that reproducing people is just a matter of producing "emotions," "feelings." It used to be called a "labor of love." Negri and Hardt instead have discovered "affection."

The feminist analysis of the function of the sexual division of labor, the function of gender hierarchies, the analysis of the way capitalism has used the wage to mobilize women's work in the reproduction of the labor force—all of this is lost under the label of "affective labor."

That this feminist analysis is ignored in the work of Negri and Hardt confirms my suspicions that this theory expresses the interests of a select group of workers, even though it presumes to speak to all workers, all merged in the great cauldron of the Multitude. In reality, the theory of precarious and immaterial labor speaks to the situation and interests of workers working at the highest level of capitalistic technology. Its disinterest in reproductive labor and its presumption that all labor forms a common hides the fact that it is concerned with the most privileged section of the working class. This means it is not a theory we can use to build a truly self-reproducing movement.

For this task, the lesson of the feminist movement is still crucial today. Feminists in the '70s tried to understand the roots of women's oppression, women's exploitation, and gender hierarchies. They described them as stemming from an unequal division of labor forcing women to work for the reproduction of the working class. This analysis was the basis of a radical social critique, the implications of which still have to be understood and developed to their full potential.

When we said that housework is actually work for capital, that although it is unpaid work it contributes to the accumulation of capital, we established something extremely important about the nature of capitalism as a system of production. *We established that capitalism is built on an immense amount of unpaid labor, that it not built exclusively or primarily on contractual relations, and that the wage relation hides the unpaid, slave-like nature of so much of the work upon which capital accumulation is premised.*

Also, when we said that housework is the work that reproduces not just "life" but "labor-power," we began to separate two different spheres of our lives and work that seemed inextricably connected. We became able to conceive of a fight against housework now understood as the reproduction of labor-power, the reproduction of the most important commodity capital has: the worker's "capacity to work," the worker's capacity to be exploited. In other words, by recognizing that what we call "reproductive labor" is a terrain of accumulation and therefore a terrain of exploitation, we were able to also see reproduction as a terrain of struggle, and, very importantly, *conceive of an anti-capitalist struggle against reproductive labor that would not destroy ourselves or our communities.*

How do you struggle over/against reproductive work? It is not the same as struggling in the traditional factory setting, against (for instance) the speed of an assembly line, because at the other end of your struggle there are people not things. Once we say that reproductive work is a terrain of struggle, we have to first immediately confront the question of how we struggle on this terrain without destroying the people we care for. This is a problem mothers, as well as teachers and nurses, know very well.

This is why it is crucial to be able to make a separation between the creation of human beings and our reproduction of them as labor-power, as future workers, who therefore have to be trained, not necessarily according to their needs and desires, to be disciplined and regimented in a particular fashion.

It was important for feminists to see, for example, that much housework and child rearing is the work of policing our children so that they will conform to a particular work discipline. We thus began to see that by refusing broad areas of work, we not only could liberate ourselves but could also liberate our children. We saw that our struggle was not at the expense of the people we cared for, though we may skip preparing some meals or cleaning the floor. Actually, our refusal opened the way for their refusal and the process of their liberation.

Once we saw that rather than reproducing life we were expanding capitalist accumulation and began to define reproductive labor as work for capital, we also opened the possibility of a process of re-composition among women.

Think for example of the prostitutes' movement, which we now call the "sex workers" movement. In Europe, the origins of this movement must be traced back to 1975 when a number of sex workers in Paris occupied a church, in protest against a new zoning regulation, which they saw as an attack on their safety. There was a clear connection between that struggle, which soon spread throughout Europe and the United States, and the feminist movement's re-thinking and challenging of housework. The ability to say that sexuality for women has been work has lead to a whole new way of thinking about sexual relationships, including gay relations. Because of the feminist movement and the gay movement, we have begun to think about the ways in which capitalism has exploited our sexuality and made it "productive."

In conclusion, it was a major breakthrough that women would begin to understand unpaid labor and the production that goes on in the home, as well as outside of the home, as the reproduction of the work force. This has allowed a re-thinking of every aspect of everyday life—child-raising, relationships between men and women, homosexual relationships, sexuality in general—in relation to capitalist exploitation and accumulation.


## Creating Self-Reproducing Movements

As every aspect of everyday life was re-understood in its potential for liberation and exploitation, we saw the many ways in which women and women's struggles are connected. We realized the possibility of "alliances" we had not imagined and, by the same token the possibility, of bridging the divisions that have been created among women, also on the basis of age, race, and sexual preference.

We cannot build a movement that is sustainable without an understanding of these power relations. We also need to learn from the feminist analysis of reproductive work because no movement can survive unless it is concerned with the reproduction of its members. This is one of the weaknesses of the social-justice movement in the United States.

We go to demonstrations, we build events, and this becomes the peak of our struggle. The analysis of how we reproduce these movements, how we reproduce ourselves, is not at the center of movement organizing. It has to be. We need to go back to the historical tradition of the working class organizing "mutual aid" and rethink that experience, not necessarily because we want to reproduce it, but to draw inspiration from it for the present.

We need to build a movement that puts on its agenda its own reproduction. The anti-capitalist struggle has to create forms of support and has to have the ability to collectively build forms of reproduction.

We have to ensure that we do not only confront capital at the time of the demonstration, but that we confront it collectively at every moment of our lives. What is happening internationally proves that only when you have these forms of collective reproduction, when you have communities that reproduce themselves collectively, you have struggles that move in a very radical way against the established order—for example, the struggle of indigenous people in Bolivia against water privatization or in Ecuador against the oil companies' destruction of indigenous land.

# Once we say that reproductive work is a terrain of struggle, we have to first immediately confront the question of how we struggle on this terrain without destroying the people we care for. This is a problem mothers, as well as teachers and nurses, know very well.

I want to close by saying that if we look at the example of the struggles in Oaxaca, Bolivia, and Ecuador, we see that the most radical confrontations are not created by the intellectual or cognitive workers, or by virtue of the internet's common. What gave strength to the people of Oaxaca was the profound solidarity that tied them with each other—a solidarity, for instance, that made indigenous people from every part of the state come to the support of the "maestros," whom they saw as members of their communities. In Bolivia, too, the people who reversed the privatization of water had a long tradition of communal struggle. Building this solidarity, understanding how we can overcome the divisions between us, is a task that must be placed on the agenda. In conclusion, the main problem of precarious labor theory is that it does not give us the tools to overcome the way we are being divided. But these divisions, which are continuously recreated, are our fundamental weaknesses with regard to our capacity to resist exploitation and create an equitable society. ◆

# Dishwasher

## FERNANDO FORTÍN

If a restaurant is an army
Then the dishwasher is the infantry man
The waiters are navy pilots
The cooks are the army in general
The chef is a captain
The bar is the tanks

But the dishwasher
The dishwasher is the foot soldier
The grunt
The backbone of the army
At one point or another we all have been the dishwasher doing all the
hard work
And getting hardly any recognition

The primary school teacher that gives 20 or 30 years of her life to educate
the future leaders of a nation
She's a dishwasher
The honest cop is a dish washer
The honest politician
The good parent, that works two jobs to feed his/her kids.
A dishwasher is the addict that gets clean
The drunk that gets sober

The prostitute that gets off the streets
I think that if we are spiritual beings going through a human walk and we
all were given assignments then the dishwasher is special forces, covert
operations.

Now you might be thinking that little fucking Mexican has spent too much
time behind that dish washing machine
But please stay with me
The dish washer probably holds the balance of the universe
One day all of them will rise and defeat the evil forces of the dark side
They'll protect us from an alien invasion

It's 5 pm at the popular restaurant it just opened
the waiters receive the costumers, with their usual fake smile

by 8 pm the place is a mad house
it's an all out war
people just keep on coming

waiters are screaming orders,
I hear fuck you, you fucking liar
One waiter to another
The kitchen is moving like a well-oiled machine

In the dish area José and Mike are buried in dishes
A Mexican and a black man working side by side
Not missing a beat, they're wet and tired but at the same time the adrena-
line is pumping.
José almost slips but there are no broken dishes.
Mike tells him don't worry my brother we're going to make it

They know the dishes got to keep flowing or they'll have to close the restau-
rant it's 10 pm the rush is almost over in a far away corner of the universe
god smiles. Balance has been restored.
This poem is for the single mothers for the poets, for the independent
film makers
This poem is for the dish washers
The strong
The courageous
Yes the dishwasher
The unsung hero

# The Snail

## REVIEWED BY MIRANDA MELLIS

But do we have the doctrine which Kafka's parables interpret and which K.'s postures and the gestures of his animals clarify?

—Walter Benjamin, "Franz Kafka"

## 1.

*The Snail* is a novel composed collaboratively by an anonymous collective whose stated intent is to transmit that doctrine which, Walter Benjamin speculated, Kafka's parables intimated. The reader is immersed in an aether, a Kafkaesque medium that dissolves anthropocentric defense mechanisms. However, self-forgetting absorption is not to be found in this dissolution, for there is no singular plot to unearth. The book is not plot-driven so much as plot-flown, plot-crawled, plot-swum, plot-migrated. One begins to feel it directly after a short prologue introduces the non-human narrator and invites us to hold the book up to a mirror to learn her name

*The Snail*

Though she is ostensibly the main narrator, *The Snail* occasionally and even suddenly goes dormant. When this happens the pages start to exfoliate language until all that is left are the blank pages, glimmering here and there with traces of *The Snail*'s silvery, iconoclastic departure. As *The Snail* recedes like eyestalks, the under-plots of *The Snail* take over. The first under-plot opens on a critic in a small studio apartment, also reading *The Snail* in an enormous horsehair bed. The bed takes up almost the whole chapter as well as the whole apartment. After an 18-page ekphrasis of the bed, with no attention paid whatsoever to anything else about the setting, we realize that the bed is history itself, where reason has been sleeping, where the state, too, has been dreaming. The critic underlines a sentence: *"What is the state dreaming?"* Here you must turn the book to the side, for the interval of the state's dream is written in long horizontals so far into the gutters of the book that you have to break its spine to read it. The critic breaks the book open and pages containing the dreams of the state fall out onto the floor.

The state's dream begins with fear and ends with walls. It begins with tigers and ends with riot police. It begins with ulcerous fighting great apes and ends with gang-raping soldiers. It begins with the hippocampus and ends with automata. It begins in a womb and ends in a cage. It begins with myth and ends in space-time. It begins with numbers and ends with letters. It begins with songs and ends with signatures. It begins with names and ends with lists. It begins with slaves and ends with slaves. It begins with snails and ends with snails. It begins under water and ends under water.

When she finishes reading the state's dreams, the critic falls asleep exhausted and dreams herself that she is searching for the authors of *The Snail*. As she loses consciousness the pages thin out and turn to vapor. The next chapter begins inside the critic's mind, where she is dreaming that she has commissioned Detective Vic Deet, a moon-pale private eye, to find the authors of *The Snail*. During an interview with Mandaug of the Quarrel Sea, who *The Snail* claims knows who wrote *The Snail*, Detective Vic Deet begins to feel his human identity dissolving. As she observes Deet's dissolution in the dream, the critic too feels her identity dissolving. She tries to wake up to halt this liquefaction but cannot. The reader, in turn, begins to feel wildly empty. The crescent of narrative slides to black. We read that the grasses on the mountains have turned brown, the cities are flooding, and the trees have caught fire. The text very suddenly and literally fades. The reader is about to throw the book in terror, when, waking up, the critic glances out at the church windows outside her window and sees "the virgin." From window to window the critic and the virgin lather each other in light. The reader is suddenly also flooded with light, and comprehension. She spills beyond domestic frames becoming a lace prism, casting a rainbow as long and large as Alice. She turns the page and a seven-foot, letter-pressed gatefold on thick, birch-white paper unfolds. On every page is written the following text in red ink:

THE PLANET EARTH HAS A MESSAGE
YOU MUST DISMANTLE ALL MILITARIZED BORDERS
THIS IS YOUR PRIMARY TASK
ALL BORDERS MUST BE OPEN FOR MIGRATIONS
THE PLANET OF UNCOUNTABLE SPECIES
MAY NO LONGER BE SPATIALLY DEFINED
BY THE HUMAN CONCEPT OF NATION

# 2.

Everything forgotten mingles with what has been forgotten of the prehistoric world, forms countless, uncertain, changing compounds, yielding a constant flow of new, strange products.

—Walter Benjamin, "Franz Kafka"

Since he feels he cannot discover anything about the provenance of *The Snail* by the usual means of canny deduction or paranoid acuity, Detective Vic Deet uses more innocent methods. These are the subject of the chapter that follows the gatefold containing the Planet's epistle instructing humankind to dismantle borders. Deet's methodology is not so much forensic as it is psycho-geographic. His notebook describes him raking ice, pushing string, beseeching street signs, swallowing coins, placing marbles in his ears, and grabbing clouds with his hands. However he is soon convinced he is under surveillance. It is his innocence itself that has brought him to the attention of the authorities he believes. He writes in his notebook, *As the Stalinist motto has it, the more innocent they are the more they deserve to be shot*. Detective Deet's methods as well as his notebook entries betray his certain uncertainty. *Assured I doubt I be not sure*, he equivocates.

On his erratic quest to coordinate clues, Detective Deet discovers "The Indeterminates," a group of statues scattered throughout the town. They function alternately as a chorus, providing historical exposition and crowd scenes, and at other times like manipulative gods with unclear motives. He wills himself to receive their messages, standing silently before them with eyes closed and palms out. One of The Indeterminates, a statue of Francisco Pizarro, finally speaks. But he lies. Deet thinks to try for an older Indeterminate. But capering Dionysus, playing panpipes, sends Deet running in fruitless circles like a madman in a roundabout. Finally, a veteran of the Korean War points straight to a gutted, reeking car full of clues: perfumes

(Bliss, Obsession, Passion) and tea bags (Joy, Calm, Vigor). Also in the car Deet finds wet cardboard, a calling machine, Fabiona, plastic ivy, resin, floral brocade, a filthy grinder, a size-19 sandal, and a soggy edition, circa 1987, of *What Color Is Your Parachute?* These clues retroactively structure the chapters of the novel as discrete yet interrelated episodes. Put more simply, halfway through the book, we begin again at chapter one, which locates all that is to come in the past (with the exception of the Planet's red message addressing the reader in the eternal tense).

Despite the soggy plenum of matter, Detective Deet is ultimately unable to make anything of the clues in the broken car and he has it towed, which abruptly reminds the critic that she must move *her* car to avoid the same fate. She wakes up and leaves the house. Deet vanishes and she forgets the dream. Under her windshield wiper, however, she finds a coastal map to the Quarrel Sea. Following her intuition she sets out.

As one does on road trips, the critic vaguely ruminates and suffers a sore back in the vacant sanctum of her car. Her mind goes blank; the pages too. Several pages of blankness later, *The Snail* reappears, digressively elaborating the intricate structure of palm trees. The segment does with dendrology what Melville did with cetology. This taxonomy of trees, seemingly an obsessive interruption, is actually central to the ghostly figure at the core of the book, *The Snail*'s Ishmael: the reader, who comes to vividly comprehend the *made-ness* of trees as far more complex, not to say beautiful, than the most astounding human architecture. The profundity of trees—and indeed all that is "unmade" in a manufactured world—had heretofore been obscured, un-thought. But now all ignored ignorance decays into nothingness. Knowledge is revealed to be a matter of subtraction: "the scales fall"; "the veil lifts."

## 3.

This much is certain: Of all of Kafka's creatures, the animals have the greatest opportunity for reflection.
—Walter Benjamin, "Franz Kafka"

*The Snail* is best read outside above the treeline with mountains visible on the horizon. When you look up after several hours of reading, the distance between the nearest bush and the most far-off mountain range will produce a curious desire to begin to traverse that space so slowly that if you moved any slower, you wouldn't be moving at all, while also transmitting the undeniable insight that in the simple act of raising your head and looking out, you have already closed the gap between yourself and that horizon, as surely as if you had already spent your whole life gliding there on your muscular foot. Is this believable, realistic, unrealistic? Such questions are hardly material. Yes, the entities that inhabit *The Snail* seem like you and me, eating dinner, drowning in mystery, running for it, interpreting patterns, having cravings, and taking shelter, but of course there is not a single character in *The Snail* who is, in our sense, alive. And yet, we embody them and they embody us.

*The Snail* reunites history and fiction; human creature and animal creature; holy book and holy body; the near and the far. And it all unfolds at *The Snail*'s pace: our reading slows down: our eyes crawl over and under, weave through and around each letter shimmering in our annotative wake. We finger the air for signals and spiral on, metabolizing and excreting the structure of the story-as-world, the world-as-story. Proprioception is heightened dramatically; everything is magnified, and all of our questions are new. For example, we have never had the opportunity to wonder before, but now we ask, *By what power have the translators on the Quarrel Sea at last managed to instantiate the Inferred Kafka Doctrine, unraveling the human knot of the anthropocene, putting an end to the dismal apocalypse, and reuniting all beings in wit and friendship by showing us that we are them?* ⬣

# Bergsonism

## JORGE CARRERA ANDRADE

*(Translated by Alejandro de Acosta
and Joshua Beckman)*


In the alphabet of things
the snail invents
the penultimate letter.

From its little cell
before the spectacle of the world
it stretches out
its living Y.

Ypsilon,
the snail begs
continuity.

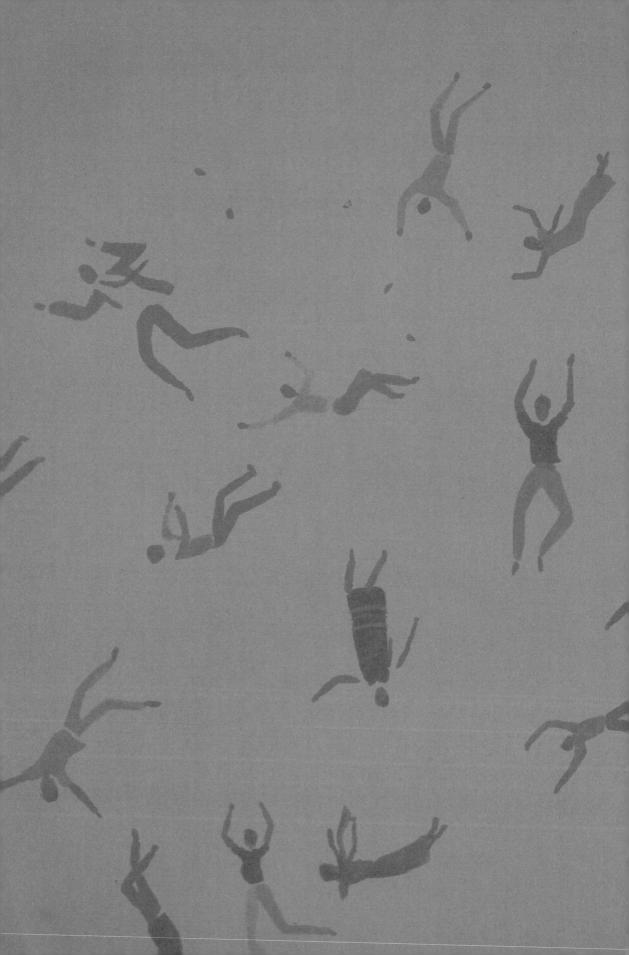

# Which Little Flicker of Facial Recognition Am I?

## EMILY ABENDROTH

The piece that follows is an excerpt from a work in progress, currently titled *Sousveillance Pageant*. There are two things you need to know about Sousveillance Pageant, who is also a primary character in the text, before venturing forward:

> 1. Sousveillance Pageant is many things; these things either move about nimbly in her solo torso or they do not. Don't be bewildered if she multiplies, or divides, or refuses to abide by the diameters or inhibitors of her own container. The measurements have always been manipulated. One day Sousveillance is a fallow crater, another day she's clinging to your hip waders, another day she's human talcum. That's not a summary or a spectrum; that's just a warning.

> 2. Sousveillance Pageant currently has two primary and dominating obsessions. For one, she is utterly preoccupied by the beguiling task of breaking every aspect of an item into its constituent parts and then artfully trying to redefine its most basic, albeit cryptic, components. This year's particular favorite, which has become almost a covenant of sorts, is her conceptual redubbing of the beloved "bikini." Sousveillance *overstands* the bikini as any paired contraption that covers two and only two tiny portions of the body's anatomy. For Sousveillance, it is neither the nature nor the location of those two parts that matters; rather, it is the bareliness and the doubling which is everything. Finally, the Pageant is hard at work on a com-

binatory history audit and field report that is sometimes called "MI-CROFICHE / MICROFILCH / MICROMANAGE / MICROFEIGN: A Series of Reflections on Surveillance & Resistance." But then again, it might be called anything, anything with a cavernous ring to it.

T he social anthropologist Philippe Bourgois has noted that in many ways the experience of consistent "*systematic* surveillance is a class privilege," whereas elsewhere and for everyone else the phenomenon is encountered more as a drag net, an unfettered barrage of gaudy, but arbitrary, enforcement

> sweeping its erratic tracks across the grit-waxed city streets
> taking indiscrete tracking shots of auto lots and shoddy half-scrapers
> targeting huge swaths of people via spontaneous displays of deeply
>     ingrained historical prejudice running at a clip with present tense
>     political gainsaying
> saying little but capturing much, whatever its eye touches really

For Bourgois's own current field work, studying the culture of addiction, drug sales, and small-time dealers in North Philadelphia, he often accompanies his selected "case studies" for years running as they go about their daily lives and exchanges and, in the course of doing so, are routinely harassed and apprehended by those forces of the state that frequently await their curbside appearances or tactical transactions. In 2009, a gathering of Bourgois and five Latino men from Kensington was abruptly interrupted when police violently threw them all to the sidewalk—kicking, searching, and citing them.

> "Like a football," Bourgois says he was kicked
> Like a ticketless passenger trying to stow away or to stave off a mob
>     of angry interrogators
> Like a low-hanging hollow sack exposed to fruitless but exuberant
>     group ransacking

>        Except that Bourgois was a person with a ticket, as it were.

---

And thus, from the social factory of racialized capital, only Bourgois was able to ultimately fight the charges leveled against him. He leveraged his at-large, Ivy League, and heavily endowed private college—the University of Pennsylvania—to perform scores of independent, friendly DNA tests and background checks in his own favor—at a cost of thousands upon thousands of dollars. With the help of his white collar educator status, he had himself professionally cross-surveilled in order to produce an officially legitimated, self-exonerating counter-record.

Whereas everyone else was compelled to plea bargain, and was left steeped in significant criminal imprints, even if and when they avoided jail time. In other words, they lacked the requisite class status that was required in order to bring forensics to their own aid.

They were baited and then found that they couldn't, in turn,
      rise to the occasion to abate the tendencies of their own pervasive
      demonization by others.
They simply couldn't de-rudder the laserlike attention drawn to
      incriminating details only.

Jailtime was sometimes avoided at first, only to return with a rather burning vengeance later in the wake of unpaid and unpayable fines.

That sublime emblem of the statute of limitations never once occasioned itself in these others' favors.

––––––––––

To monitor, to disrupt, to neutralize
      to size up, to aggregate, to rank, to harvest, to profile
            to compile on the sly with an eye toward future red-lining

          First, they were counted double
              and then no one could be troubled to
              acknowledge them at all.
          First, they were meticulously censused
              and then they were meticulously and
              outright censored.

Doubled down upon loudly in those moments wherein involuntary forced speech was mandatory and then, once more, upon the hardcore lurid imposition of long-term penetrating silence.

The more the word "safe" is repeated, the worse our worries of violence become.

Although always more for some than for others.

What was it that the Roman scholar and translator Poggio Bracciolini once wrote about his friend, his fellow notary penman, Nicolaus De Niccolis—inventor of the italic script—whose habits Poggio complained had become unto rocks—progressing like clockwork into ever more rigid and calcified cruelties. Inducing the dubious compliment:

> "He is a little more diligent in exactly those things where it is the greatest kindness to be very negligent."

> Having a bent toward the outward-directed default of maximum unalterable intolerance

---

In an article bearing the congratulatory title, "An Anthropologist Bridges Two Worlds," and appearing in *The Chronicle for Higher Education*, journalist Christopher Shea writes: "Charges against Bourgois were dropped, and he did not file a complaint about his treatment. But only now is he getting back in touch with his dealers. These days he carries a letter signed by the police commissioner explaining who he is."

> Who *he is* exonerates him.
> Just as who *they are* condemns others.
>> Who their mother was, or to whom their grandmother was
>> made to be a lover.

> Nothing that could fit in the breastpocket,
>> nothing that could sit there so lightly, so half-crocked,
>>> so easy
> can unlock or untease or rectify that        let alone *unpack* it.

> That heavily trafficked space between a paper pulp record which exculpates its owner and a record of traces which tend to shape their owner's pate into a staging zone for pulping.

This isn't about Bourgois, of course, at this point—
> a person who is, in most respects, a rare sane advocate for
> foundational U.S. drug policy overhaul.

Rather this is about the ROLES—the old and the new infrastructures of national constraint coming together as friendly birds of a feather, donning with revery their shared carryover of leather boots, even as booting their squad cars for new extra large, armored Hummers

to the numb exaltation of made-for-TV drum rolls.

————————

In February of 2013, a participatory game of public interference with the optical regime of the state was anonymously instigated in Berlin, Germany. Its organizers announced, "The idea of CAMOVER is to destroy as many CCTV-cams as possible and for this we decided to announce a competition."

It was an open, public invitation; in order to partake in this dynamic and ever-shifting, urban live-action game, all one needed was a group with a name that started with "command", "brigade", "cell", or "platoon" and ended with a historic person. Points were awarded for the most creative destructive acts and the greatest panache or verve or chivalry in their delivery.

The everyday multimodal sensory interfaces suddenly suffered a racy
interference in the form of direct face-offs
The mechanics of each digital casing were first unlaced and then pulverized
in the wake of the arrivals of:

Platoon Huey Newton, The Judith Butler Cell,
The Society of the Spectacle Cell, Command Los Indignados

The Jane Brigade in their gay neon green campuches who sang as they swung their steel pipes:

*Why am I a little flicker of facial recognition?*
*Where am I a little flicker of facial recognition?*
*When am I a little flicker of facial recognition?*
*Which little flicker of facial recognition am I?*

————————

*Can I swiftly bypass it?*
*Can I whisk or squish or squirrel or mallet away*
*the pixilated denouement of my very features?*
*Is it creaturely of me to try? Is it wise?*

The whole imaginative enterprise of CAMOVER, with its entire structure designed to knock out surveillance pieces and encourage others to do the same, was built around and resoundingly depended upon filming oneself while doing so. And further still, upon subsequently posting those real-time videos of sabotage for boast-worthy public consumption onto widely available and heavily visited online sites.

In other words, it was tightly reliant as a concept upon the scrupulous documentation of one's own most self-incriminating behaviors.

A voyeuristic spectacle of authority skeptics gone viral

Their spiraling gestures of mimicry obtaining a reverse directionality that does wonders to confer visibility to hidden equipments, but that nonetheless still leaves one wondering:

> To what extent does this disruption allow the central model and its primary dynamics to remain intact, even as it successfully counteracts discrete mechanisms?

> Simultaneously mirroring and confronting
> offering a vehement critique while perhaps still secretly admiring the sleek physique

> a leaky and peekaboo feeling with which Sousveillance herself
> is all too intimately familiar

---

In Berlin, CAMOVER officially "ended" on February 19, 2013—the very day when the annual convening of the European Police Congress commenced in that same city. The transgressive competition at hand had served as a vanguard precursor to a continental amassing of legions of badge-holders, who were at the very least now beholden to confront the people's disgust and distrust at their arrival.

The rival publics were not smiling, nor were they filing by in pre-contrived and neatly aligned droves, hoping to be philanthropically "protected." Instead, they were heckling those in uniforms and they were beckoning to their masked comrades.

For once, they were rattled enough not to tattle on their neighbors; they stood in favor of battering down the endless chambers of mug shots which they had been taught first to identify and then to be

identified by.

This isn't about CAMOVER, of course, at this point.

This is about the ROLES. This is about what we undergo when what we know of privacy is simply  an economic tendency that readily makes ghosts of huge offshore-hosted estates, but can't seem to sublimate a single patient's lousy credit rating.

"I think it's useful," muses Sousveillance Pageant, "to position all those hundreds of thousands of municipal, but hidden, cameras as seen and, even more importantly, as destroyable. I think it's useful to be playful and not to always hide one's inevitable contradictions. And yet I'm also reminded of Brecht's line in *The Trial of Lucullus* where the Courtesan commiserates:

> '[O]ur lot is the same. For me, too, prodigious Rome could not protect from prodigious Rome.'"

--------------

"Or of the graceful recognition of deep and difficult internalizations about which James Baldwin laments:

> 'In a society much given to smashing taboos without thereby managing to be liberated from them, it will be no easy matter.'"

> It will take more than episodic scattering or temporary black outs.

> What it will take is tantamount to an hourly power outage. But then we don't mean electricity, do we?

With each new and cleaving thought, Sousveillance Pageant is growing increasingly agitated.

She flutters her arms in alarming, although harmless, miniature circles. She swivels her head gently up, down, and around. She pounds her fingers against the paved ground as Platoon Russell Maroon Shoatz lights a votive candle and harmonizes in chorus:

> *Once he was almost killed.*
> *Twice he was almost killed.*
> *Three times he was almost killed.*

*And that was terrifying.*
*And that was humiliating.*
*And that was illuminating.*
*Each time was terrifying, humiliating, and profoundly*
*    illuminating.*
*It was painful really, how much he now knew.*
*But nothing he knew could prelude a fourth time.*
*Learning, he finds, had been replaced by mere*
*    confirmation.*
*Confirmation and rage.*

*Mere rage and mere confirmation*

——————

What follows is a coping mechanism that Sousveillance Pageant invented in order to deal with the versions of "WHEN LEARNING HAS EXPIRED BUT EXPERIENCE HASN'T" that inhabited her own life.

She called the pose "MERE CONFIRMATION." The first time she executed the maneuver, she was wearing her all-time favorite bikini. It consisted of a single plastic green finger cap and a wide front-cinching belt with two enormous golden lion heads at the center. The belt fastened where the lions' cheek bones would have met were they to extend toward the interior textures of her intestines. The center medallions were gold leaf on beefy steel and proved a little unwieldy to wear against one's bare skin; nonetheless, Sousveillance strongly believed they finished the initiating weave of the green finger sleeve admirably.

To perform MERE CONFIRMATION correctly, required assuming a seated position for which the practitioner did not receive a chair. The legs were drawn, like a retractable awning, up toward the chest, bent at the crest of the knees, trumpeting the body's closure. The arms, however, were extended upward, wide beyond the collarbone, fingers outstretched. The head was bowed toward the pectorals, not as if nestled but stiff and restless, compressing the neck into the site of all sublimated anger and tender feeling, while the shoulders were allowed to remain somewhat gangly.

The overall angle or tenor of just how one wrangled one's body to achieve this was of the utmost importance. The practitioner in this position should be hearing but not hearing, open but not open, non-vocal as if from a chokehold, obedient but not in agreement. ⬣

# NOTES

Philippe Bourgois's story is told in Christopher Shea, "An Anthropologist Bridges Two Worlds," *The Chronicle of Higher Education*, June 12, 2009. His remark that "systematic surveillance is a class privilege" was made at a panel on "Surveillance and Civil Liberties in Inner City Neighborhoods" at the University of Pennsylvania on 14 March 2012.

Poggio Bracciolini's commentary on his friend Nicolaus can be found in *Two Renaissance Book Hunters: The Letters of Poggius Bracciolini to Nicolaus De Niccolis*, translated by Phyllis Walter Goodhart Gordan (New York: Columbia University Press, 1991), 94.

The passage from Brecht's "The Trial of Lucullus" can be found in *Bertolt Brecht, Collected Plays, Vol. 5: Life of Galileo / The Trial of Lucullus / Mother Courage and Her Children*, edited by Ralph Manheim and John Willett (New York: Vintage, 1972).

The lyrics of the Jane Brigade, from which this excerpt takes its title, are a modification of a meditation uttered by the character named Rose in Gertrude Stein's compelling children's book *The World is Round* (New York: Harper Design, 2013), 4: "Why am I a little girl? Where am I a little girl? When am I a little girl? Which little girl am I?"

# The Difference Is Spreading: Sabotage & Aesthetics

## EIRIK STEINHOFF

On June 7, 1913, thousands of striking silk workers streamed by train and by foot into Manhattan to stage *The Pageant of the Paterson Strike* for a standing-room audience of some 15,000 at Madison Square Garden. "Lesser geniuses might have hired a hall and exhibited moving pictures of the Paterson strike," the *Tribune* reported. "Saturday night's pageant transported the strike itself bodily to New York." The program set the scene:

> The *Pageant* represents a battle between the working class and the
> capitalist class conducted by the Industrial Workers of the World
> (I.W.W.), making use of the General Strike as the chief weapon. It
> is a conflict between two social forces—the force of labor and the
> force of capital.

This conflict was "performed by the strikers themselves," as a poster for the *Pageant* adverts. In front of a life-size replica of a silk mill, some 90 feet tall and 200 feet wide, its windows darkened in all but the first episode before the strike kicks off, skilled ribbon weavers and broad-silk weavers, unskilled dyers' helpers, and their Wobbly allies represented the actions they'd undertaken across the river against overwork and underpay and on behalf of the eight-hour day. As the program explains:

> While the workers are clubbed and shot by detectives, the mills remain dead. While the workers are sent to jail by hundreds, the mills remain dead. While organizers are persecuted, the strike continues, and still the mills are dead. While the pulpit thunders denunciation and the press screams lies, the mills remain dead. No violence can make the mills alive—no legal process can resurrect them from the dead. Bayonets and clubs, injunctions and court orders are equally futile. Only the return of workers to the mills can give the dead things life. The mills remain dead throughout the enactment of the following episodes.

"PATERSON STRIKERS NOW BECOME ACTORS," the *New York Times* announced the next day. The same edition of the paper also brings news of another performance that had taken place a little over a week earlier across the *Atlantic*: "PARISIANS HISS NEW BALLET." This hissing—which we are told gave way to "hostile demonstrations"—was in response to the premiere of Igor Stravinsky's *Rite of Spring* on May 29, 1913. Rather than precipitate a riot, as the *Rite* so famously did, the *Pageant* re-enacted one—in Madison Square Garden, no less, the most opulent venue in town, built by a syndicate of some of the richest men on earth (including J.P. Morgan, Andrew Carnegie, and W.W. Astor). In his review of the *Pageant* for the *New York Globe*, Hutchins Hapgood wrote, "The art of it was unconscious, and especially lay in the suggestion for the future. People interested in the possibilities of a vital and popular art, and in constructive pageantry, would learn much from it." But then why is it no surprise that—in contrast to the *Rite of Spring*, whose centenary you'd've been hard pressed to miss in the summer of 2013—both the *Pageant of the Paterson Strike* and the Silk Strike itself have been all but stricken from the record, already forgotten by the future in which we take up space? Such oversight may well be part and parcel of our culture's congenital unwillingness to recollect the contentions of labor, but it also demonstrates our readiness to accommodate certain kinds of avant-gardes while simultaneously occluding others.

---

In her 1926 lecture "Composition as Explanation," Gertrude Stein describes a kind of metamorphosis in taste that I think might be pertinent to our analysis of this phenomenon (Stein missed the premiere of the *Rite of Spring* but made it to the second night with Carl van Vechten; she was also acquainted with central figures in the Greenwich Village scene of intellectuals and artists complicit in the making of the *Pageant*):

Those who are creating the modern composition authentically are naturally only of importance when they are dead because by that time the modern composition having become past is classified and the description of it is classical. That is the reason why the creator of the new composition in the arts is an outlaw until he is a classic. [...] There is almost not an interval. For a very long time everybody refuses and then almost without a pause almost everybody accepts.

Stein is describing a cultural process that transforms a "beauty" that is "irritating and stimulating" into one that can be "classified" and "accepted." That's certainly what's happened with Stravinsky's *Rite*—play the opening bars to a random person on the street, and they'd be readily classified as "classical music" and not, say, hissed at: The piece has moved from outlaw to classic. *The Pageant of the Paterson Strike*, by contrast, has eluded such a metamorphosis. "No one is ahead of his time," Stein explained (using the pronoun her contemporaries would have expected), "it is only that the particular variety of creating his time is one that his contemporaries who are also creating their own time refuse to accept." Our ongoing inability to receive the signal from the Silk Strike—both as such and as pageant— paradoxically indicates that it may well be less antique than the century between us suggests. The temporal momentums of past and present, and the political-economical imperatives that set those inexorable paces, can be seen to coincide in this erasure, marking what Dipesh Chakrabarty describes as "a disjuncture of the present with itself." Chakrabarty is writing about subaltern South Asian rebels, but suggests that the temporal disjunction he describes can be encountered in other contexts as well:

[T]he nineteenth-century Santal—and indeed, if my argument is right, humans from any other period and region—are always in some sense our contemporaries: that would have to be the condition under which we can even begin to treat them as intelligible to us. Thus the writing of history must implicitly assume a plurality of times existing together, a disjuncture of the present with itself. Making visible this disjuncture is what subaltern pasts allow. [...] It is because we already have experience of that which makes the present non-contemporaneous with itself that we can actually historicize. [...] It is because we live in time-knots that we can undertake the exercise of straightening out, as it were, some part of the knot (which is how we might think of chronology). [...] What underlies our capacity to historicize is our capacity not to.[1]

1   Dipesh Chakrabarty, *Provincializing Europe: Postcolonial Thought and Historical Difference* (Princeton: Princeton University Press, 2000), 109, 112, 113.

Perhaps if rather than *turn away from* we attempt to *turn towards* the thing we've been trained to avoid—if, that is, we were to cultivate a counter-apotropaic reflex—the *Pageant* and the strike it represents could be allowed to spring back into view as an undomesticated and not so much a de-classified beauty as a pre-classified one that may yet have the power to recruit us into its knotted contemporaneity. This would be to consider the *Pageant* as an aesthetic artifact that has the power to make a kind of outlaw sense, stimulating us to feel a dilation of the horizons of possibility that contain us, which in turn might enable us to imagine unexpected practical projects to be undertaken in our own time in response to the ongoing "conflict between the force of labor and the force of capital," however transmogrified that conflict may be.

———————

Now as it happens, the beginning of the strike itself on February 25, 1913, came one week after the February 17 opening of the International Exposition of Modern Art in the 69th Regiment Armory on Park Avenue in Manhattan. Known now in art-historical shorthand as the "Armory Show," and commemorated in 1998 with a 32-cent postage stamp, this was the first major exhibition of Modernist painting in the United States.[2] In a letter to Stein (who loaned a few Matisses to the show), Mabel Dodge predicted that it was going to be "the most important public event to have ever come off since the signing of the Declaration of Independence, and it is of the same nature [...] [T]here will be a riot and revolution and things will never be quite the same afterwards." No riots were recorded, but Hutchins Hapgood in his review for the *Globe*—tellingly titled "Art and Unrest"—described the exhibit as "dynamite" and made a more contemporary comparison: "[T]he important thing is that it means agitation. It means education in the disturbing, doubting sense. Post-Impressionism is as disturbing in one field as the I.W.W. is in another. It turns up the soil, shakes the old foundations, and leads to new life."[3] These agitating analogies and invocations of revolution by both wealthy patron (Dodge) and anarchist journalist (Hapgood) indicate that the Armory Show and the Paterson Silk Strike shared more than just proximity in space and time: both also strategically refused received regimes of representation, whether aesthetic or political or both. On the aesthetic side of the dial, the dynamic visual investigations of the Cubists and the down-and-out subject matter of the so-called Ashcan Realists vied against the conservative canon-clinging of the arts academies. By the same

2   The Beaux Arts building on Park Avenue remains operative to this day as a National Guard armory: it was and is a space designed to stage war materiel, whatever else one might pull off within its bounds.

3   Dodge and Hapgood are both cited in Maria Morris Hambourg, *Paul Strand, Circa 1916* (New York: The Metropolitan Museum of Art, 1998), 20–21.

*A RECORD OF THE CATASTROPHE*

token, the ambitious political push by the silk workers and the Wobblies for "One Big Union" organized along democratic lines challenged the American Federation of Labor's model of hierarchical trade unionism (which refused to consider the interests of "unskilled labor," who were pointedly involved in Paterson)—even as the Paterson striker's invocation of the General Strike signaled their embrace of a tactic recently rehabilitated by Rosa Luxemburg over and against the dismissals of Marx and Engels in light of actions and events in St. Petersburg in 1905.[4]

Given this common appetite for experiment and invention that cuts against the grain of both radical and traditional conventional wisdom, it makes sense that key players in both the Armory Show and the Silk Strike, having hobnobbed together in various Greenwich Village environs as the strike wore on, would find themselves collaborating in late spring on the composition of the *Pageant* in an effort to raise consciousness and funds alike.[5] That the strike was ultimately defeated, and that the *Pageant*—while reckoned a successful spectacle even by viewers hostile to the cause—should have failed to break even, may come as no surprise. The value of such failures, in any event, is contingent on the use one puts them to. The strike plan so successfully deployed by the I.W.W. in the textile mills of Lawrence the previous year (an action that had initiated important networks of trust between the union and the denizens of Greenwich Village) did not succeed in Paterson in 1913 (where the structure of industry was favorable to the

---

4  On the Armory Show's provocations, see Allan Antliff, *Anarchist Modernism: Art, Politics, and the First American Avant-Garde* (Chicago: University of Chicago Press, 2001). On the General Strike, see Rosa Luxemburg, "The Mass Strike, the Political Party, and the Trade Unions" (1906), in *Rosa Luxemburg Speaks* (New York: Pathfinder, 1970), 155–218.

5  The collaboration embodied in both strike and *Pageant* is recognizable from this distance as an instance of what Alice and Staughton Lynd, following Archbishop Romero, have recently called "accompaniment": a genre of collective political composition which, in contrast to top-down forms of "organizing" we may be more familiar with (which stars the organizer as the subject who knows), treats all participants in the struggle ("intellectuals," "activists," and "workers" in this instance) as experts in their particular field, and equitably coordinates these facilities accordingly. See Staughton Lynd, *Accompanying: Pathways to Social Change* (Oakland: PM Press, 2013). The first page of Steve Golin's definitive history, *The Fragile Bridge: Paterson Silk Strike, 1913* (Philadelphia: Temple University Press, 1988), underscores the counterintuitive intersections in operation here:

> The 1913 strike is important because it challenges certain conservative assumptions about labor history that have become so widely held as to be shared even by many on the left: the elitist role of skilled workers, the bureaucratic function of union organizers, and the irrelevance of intellectuals. But in Paterson in 1913, skilled weavers began the strike and successfully reached out to unskilled dyers' helpers; union organizers committed to the idea of workers' control successfully encouraged the emergence of rank-and-file leaders, particularly women; and intellectuals went beyond sympathy and support to participate successfully in the strike itself.

Two other useful accounts of the *Pageant*, both in context and since, can be found in Martin Green, *New York 1913: The Armory Show and the Paterson Strike Pageant* (New York: Scribner, 1988) and S.E. Wilmer, "The role of workers in the nation: The Paterson Strike Pageant," in *Theatre, Society, and the Nation: Staging American Identities* (Cambridge: Cambridge University Press, 2002).

bosses), but that didn't prevent the Wobblies from going on to innovate other strategies and tactics, most notably, perhaps, in the Pacific Northwest lumber industry where, at the height of World War I, every last one of the I.W.W.'s demands were granted (a story we can save for another day).

––––––––––

The migration and evolution of Wobbly *praxis* before, during, and after the Paterson strike was greatly aided and abetted by Elizabeth Gurley Flynn, a remarkable orator who, in contrast to her colleague Big Bill Haywood, had been skeptical of the *Pageant* (even though she consented to play herself alongside him in it). Of particular interest for our latter-day purposes—our appetite for stimulating beauties, say, or our desire for as yet un-classified outlaws—is the treatise on sabotage she composed in response to court cases involving silk strikers accused of property destruction and the like. Over and against this sensational juridical reduction of sabotage to what in Oakland not long ago was nicknamed "smashy-smashy," Flynn posits a strategically more capacious definition: sabotage, she tells us, is best defined as "the conscious withdrawal of the worker's industrial efficiency."

I'd wager that once you hear it put that way, you all but automatically start imagining how you might try your own subversive hand at it—a thought-experiment worth engaging, if only to locate the pivot-points of the structure we're in. How might one "withdraw efficiency," for instance, in a debt economy? Are there more or less effective ways of making that withdrawal? And what might we compose in its place?[6] Beyond such practical political-economical applications, we might also benefit from speculating on the relevance of this definition of sabotage to the theory and practice of aesthetics, which in turn might indicate underutilized advantages and overlooked points of leverage that the arts might have in the area of concrete political activity. In what way, for instance, might poets or painters or sculptors or playwrights intentionally withdraw not only their own efficiencies, but also the efficiency of the audience on encountering the products of such aesthetic sabotage? And how might an aesthetic investigation of this process—a process that involves a dynamic relation between artist, art-object, and audience—illuminate foreclosed or forgotten horizons of

6  *Caveat saboteur*: Sabotage defined thus, as Flynn observes, is a tactic frequently indulged in by capitalists as well: what else is a lock-out or a downsizing but "a conscious withdrawal of efficiency"? In this light the city of Detroit, whose now-derelict Michigan Central Station was opened in 1913, thus stands as a tragic urban emblem of capitalist sabotage. Another author from the period to consult, once you've read your Flynn, is the heterodox economist Thorstein Veblen, who in 1919 published an essay in *The Dial* that builds explicitly from Flynn's account; called "On the Nature and Use of Sabotage," it was subsequently reprinted as the first chapter of his 1921 book, *The Engineers and the Price System*. A more contemporary way of putting withdrawal to work was imagined by Joshua Clover in "The Time of Crisis," October 2011, http://occupyeverything.org/2011/the-time-of-crisis.

possibility?

The best answers to these questions would involve not so much a defense or definition of the aesthetic as a description of its action. And in that regard we might consult Michael W. Clune's recent uptake of a neuroscientific description of what could be termed "the efficiency of perception":

> The first time we encounter an image, our perceptual experience tends to be richly vivid. Time seems to move more slowly. But it doesn't last. "With repeated presentations of a stimulus," writes [neuroscientist David] Eagleman, "a sharpened representation or a more efficient encoding is achieved in the neural network coding for the object." Once the brain has learned to recognize the image, it no longer requires the high "metabolic costs" of intense sensory engagement. This efficiency has obvious evolutionary advantages, in conserving human attention for new threats and opportunities. But it means we are subject to an incessant erasure of perceptual life.[7]

Even if you prefer not to subscribe to the biological econometrics on display in this way of computing perception, it's hard not to recognize the process he describes—a process one could present in the less scientistic but no less effective lingo of habit, for instance, which at the very least might shift the inquiry onto a more familiar philosophical register that runs from Aristotle to Montaigne to William James (with whom Gertrude Stein had studied).[8]

———————

Let's consider the circuits of habit and efficiencies of perception disrupted by the aesthetic constellation we're working with from 1913. Duchamp's "Nude Descending a Staircase" was notoriously described by one critic of the Armory Show as "an explosion in a shingle factory," the distance between "nude" and "explosion" (both terms applied to the same form) triangulating a gap between what can and can't be seen and said from incommensurate aesthetic vantages. The languorous, foot-dragging bassoon that kicks off Stravinsky's *Rite of Spring* gives way, as the curtain rises,

---

7   Michael W. Clune, "The Quest for Permanent Novelty," *The Chronicle Review*, February 11, 2013, http://chronicle.com/article/The-Quest-for-Permanent/137039/. Clune is quoting from David M. Eagleman and Vani Pariyadath, "Is Subjective Duration a Signature of Coding Efficiency?" *Phil. Trans. R. Soc. B* (2009): 364.

8   It is worth noticing that in James's case the economic model Eagleman deploys is already firmly established: "If practice did not make perfect, nor habit economize the expense of nervous and muscular energy, [we] would [...] be in a sorry plight." (*Principles of Psychology*, 1890). Presumably Darwin can be credited as a common ancestor. In his 1917 essay "Art as Technique," composed a few years after the *Pageant* and in the vicinity of the October Revolution, Victor Shklovsky proposes an aesthetic theory that works from this "law of the economy of creative effort" (as he describes it) to theorize the strategic aesthetic potentials of deliberate defamiliarization.

to robotic karate chops of arrhythmic dissonance accompanied by the frenetic twitching and stamping of dancers dressed as peasants—a spectacle sharply at odds with the expectations of an audience trained to appreciate the refined gestures of classical ballet (even if, it must be said that notwithstanding such formal adventurism, the content of the *Rite* complies quite readily with that tradition: a young woman is kidnapped and forced to dance herself to death whilst surrounded by a conclave of withered old men). In *The Pageant of the Paterson Strike*, rather than have professionally trained actors play imaginary characters, actual workers played themselves, re-performing in Manhattan actions undertaken across the river in the Paterson silk mills: holding mass meetings, getting beaten, arrested, and killed by the police, burying the dead, celebrating May Day, convening workers' councils. "There was no play-acting," the *Independent* observed, "The strikers were simply living over, for their fellows to see, their most telling experiences. No stage in the country had ever seen a more real dramatic expression of American life." In this light, the *Pageant* could be seen to anticipate Marcel Duchamp's readymades by a few years: rather than a urinal in a gallery turned on its back and signed by "R.Mutt," we get a general strike transported into the center of the city and announced "by an electric sign of giant proportions with the letters 'I.W.W.' in red lamps" (as Big Bill Haywood recalled in his memoir). The *Independent* was especially taken by the *Pageant*'s unexpected use of space:

> Down from the stage and the entire length of the main aisle the workers march, cheered all the way by the sympathetic audience of 15,000 workingmen and their families. [...] It is an unequaled device for clutching the emotion of the audience—this parade of actors through the center of the crowd. [...] Rarely has it been used in New York theaters [...], but never with more effect than in this performance, where actors and audience were of one class and one hope.

Such a description calls to mind Luxemburg's reckoning of the General Strike as "the method of motion of the proletarian mass, the phenomenal form of the proletarian struggle in the revolution." The review in the *Independent* concludes, "It was not a pageant of the past; but of the present—a new thing in our drama."

In each of these instances, a received model of representation—the efficiency model, call it—is held in suspense while a new form takes its place, affording a more "richly vivid" encounter with the signals transmitted in each particular case, signals yet to be foreclosed by the predictions of habit. In this sense, each of these aesthetic episodes displays the lineaments of "a situation" as defined by Lauren Berlant: "a genre of social time and practice in which a relation of persons and worlds is sensed to be changing but the rules for habitation and the genres of storytelling about it are unstable, in chaos."[9] And yet the *Pageant* stands out in relation to its contemporaries for at least two reasons. In the first place, it includes within its "sharpened representation" an unprecedented form of political representation. "The strikers, men and women, legislate for themselves. They pass a law for the eight-hour day. No court can declare the law thus unconstitutional": thus Episode Six, as described in the program. Whereas in retrospect with the *Rite* we cherish the musical form but abhor—or worse, ignore—the conceivably misogynistic content of the ballet, with the *Pageant* we immediately recognize and take for granted the content (the eight-hour day) even as we find the forms through which it is achieved incomprehensible at best or quite simply unimaginable (pageantry, self-representation, horizontal decision-making, autonomous organization of political economy). In the second place, unlike both the *Rite* and the Armory Show, the *Pageant* (and the strike it represented) has succeeded in eluding the canon, in not being classified, in failing to have its irritating stimulating outlaw beauty stabilized into a readily recognizable genre at the expense of becoming philanthropically preserved in the aspic of distinction, and having its centenary celebrated by means of a ceremonious application of saliva to the adhesive on the backside of a commemorative stamp (using, of course, the compliant organ of speech as a utensil in the operation).

----------

I heard the other day that Giorgio Agamben said something about how "the past lives only in the present."[10] Here's one past that hasn't been living in our present, as described by Randolph Bourne, a sympathetic and perspicacious eyewitness:

> Who that saw the Paterson Strike Pageant in 1913 can ever forget that thrilling evening when an entire labor community dramatized its wrongs in one supreme outburst of group emotion? Crude and rather terrifying, it stamped into one's mind the idea that a new social art was in the American world, something genuinely and excitingly new. [11]

**9** Lauren Berlant, *Cruel Optimism* (Durham: Duke University Press, 2011), 6.

**10** "The Endless Crisis as an Instrument of Power: In Conversation with Giorgio Agamben," June 4, 2013, http://www.versobooks.com/blogs/1318-the-endless-crisis-as-an-instrument-of-power-in-conversation-with-giorgio-agamben.

**11** Randolph Bourne, *The Radical Will: Selected Writings 1911–1918* (Berkeley: University of California Press, 1992), 519.

So "genuinely and excitingly new," we can now add, after one hundred and some orbits of the earth around the sun, that it has been all but entirely forgotten, all but omitted from the record. *Whoso list to see a pageant?* Whereas with the *Rite* and the Armory Show "the shock has been 'consumed'" (to use a memorable phrase from Peter Bürger's *Theory of the Avant-Garde*), in the *Pageant* we find a bolus that didn't make it down the hatch.[12] This failed digestion is a symptom of its perduring inefficiency, which may paradoxically be the very thing to recommend the *Pageant* to our attention: it may yet have the power to administer a shock. "The purpose of the avant-garde," Napoleon explains in one of his maxims, "is not to seize territory but rather to conduct maneuvers." What Stein calls the outlaw—the composition whose creation of time fails to comply with the contemporary—Thomas Kuhn calls "the anomaly," which he defines as that which "cannot, despite repeated effort, be aligned with professional expectation."[13] The anomaly, etymologically, is "the unsame" (from the privative Greek prefix *an* + *homalos*, which has *homo* at its root). It's hard not to remember in this context a wonderfully ominous sentence from Gertrude Stein's *Tender Buttons* (first published in 1913): "The difference is spreading."

I dwell on these examples—paleolithic artifacts, really, when reckoned from the amnesiac and hyperventilating timescape of our media metabolism beset by charismatic megaphones braying predatory slogans—not for the sake of nostalgia, nor for the sake of ancestor worship, nor to set these three episodes in competition ("It's not a competition, it's a competency mission," as I heard it said once at the Oakland Commune), but rather in order, first, to unredact the record, that is, to disinter a contemporaneous constellation of actions and events that might allow us to recalibrate our understanding of the aesthetic and political past, present, and future; and second, to argue for the value of remembering the forgotten theory and practice, both political and aesthetic, of the silk strikers in our own moment, not so much as an example to follow *per se* (they lost, after all—even if there can be no doubt that they and the I.W.W. and their Greenwich Village allies were asking exactly the right questions), and more as an example to learn from insofar as it could teach us the benefit of making wagers that cut against the grain, of undertaking irresistible aesthetic and political actions that risk all but absolute obsolescence on behalf of the possibility of collectively composing a better image of the good life that all of us can actually thrive in. ⬢

12  Peter Bürger, *Theory of the Avant-Garde*, trans. Michael Shaw (Minneapolis: University of Minnesota Press, 1984 [1974]), 81.

13  Thomas M. Kuhn, *The Structure of Scientific Revolutions* (Chicago: University of Chicago Press, 2012), 6.

# THE REBEL WOMEN CLAIM:

## THE RIGHT TO BE LAZY.

## THE RIGHT TO BE AN UNMARRIED MOTHER.

## THE RIGHT TO DESTROY.

## THE RIGHT TO CREATE.

## THE RIGHT TO LOVE.

## THE RIGHT TO LIVE.

*The Woman Rebel: No Gods No Masters, 1914*

John Beauparlant, *Triple Jackie*, 2010

November 2014

Rag Pickers in Paradise

" Don't read much now ; the dude
  Who lets the girl down before
  The hero arrives , the chap
  Who's yellow and keeps the store
  Seem far too familiar. Get stewed :
  Books are a load of crap."

                    Philip Larkin
                    A Study of Reading Habits

Crazy, warm, disturbing, delicious, evening
in San Francisco. Heat rising from the pave
ments as I drop down into "don't sleep in
the subway darlin" MUNI as I head "downtown"
with Petula. Two events, a gathering at the
Mechanics Institute Library on Post St.;
The Arcades ; From Hausmann's Paris to Occupy
Wall Street. Table discussion and film screen-
ing of THE PASSAGES OF WALTER BENJAMIN .
Later, a party at the TOP OF THE MARK, Mark
Hopkins Hotel, with the pretty people of
San Francisco and my friend Susan. I am wearing leather soled Gianni Versace loafers
circa 1989, with little silver lion heads on
the buckles. Looking forward to dancing later.

Marxists, academics, art types from the Mission
North Beach, Berkeley, Oakland, Santa Cruz,
Harvard, MIT, even Texas. All are pouring out
of the elevator into little chess tables with
old style chairs in a beautiful 1908 room at
the Mechanics Institute Library. Wine bar in
the back, professors at the front table. The
wineless overflow standing in the hall. Grumbling
pissed-off scores turned away for lack of space.
The talk was about current social and economic
upheaveals in urban culture. Hausmann's
gentrification of Paris, the rezoning of San
Francisco, and a good movie about Benjamin and
Baudelaire. Old photos, drawings, card images of
hundreds of Arcades. Benjamins years spent in the
Paris libraries studying books with drawings of
that era, fashion, building, society,parties.
Under the pretense of the important consideration

of health and beauty, Hausmann gutted Paris for
his employer, Napoleon III. Napoleon III had
been elected Frances' first President. He did
not like term limits and in a coup d'etat ~~became~~
became Emperor. Financed by two brothers who
became known as Credit Mobilier. Hausmann
wiped out the neighborhoods of riots, revolutions and barricades, "from one end to the
other".

Susan texts; "be out front in 15". She is rolling
down Twin Peaks in UBER. I spirial down the
steel and marble staircase of the Mechanics
Library and out onto Post St. Unusual warm
night air.  Is it Cairo? Waiting on the curb
I see a homeless man. A well built man, maybe
40, filthy black cloths, hands, feet, face but
with long curling shining golden hair. He was
like a fallen angel. In his hand, a book. Rose
madder in color with elaborate arabesque and
floral gilding. A nineteenth century book in
perfect condition, immaculately clean. A spectacular sight even in a city where the magic of
Gold and fog make apparitions common place.
Breathing deeply, waiting for Susan and UBER,
high on the wonder of what just passed my eyes;
I notice notice three giant plasticgarbage bins
on the curb. They are jammed with books. Hardbound
old, perfect. A rush of emotion, alarm, distress,
panic, greed. UBER pulls up, "hello darlin" leans
out the limo window. My little brain is high on
Critical Theory and a ton of books in garbage
bins. "WAIT WAIT WAIT..PLEASE PLEASE.!! I dive.
Restaurant slop has already been tossed on top
of one bin, oozing down through the volumes
and decades. From the second and third bins I grab
books off the top. Susan; "What are you doing? Get
out of the garbage! Let's go ! Let's go ! PARTY !"

There was a live camel at the front door of
the Mark Hopkins Hotel. Inside, gym buffed
nearly naked men were costumed as Egyptian
Slaves. San Francisco's best Jazz singer was
wowing her crowd: Paula West. Extra tall extra-
ordinary drags were working the elevators. We went
to THE TOP where Beyonce's sister Solanges was ~~doing~~
doing a set spinning records. Champagne, caviar,
youth, beauty, and money all in attendance.

*A RECORD OF THE CATASTROPHE*

Danced-up, tipsy and kissed, we elevatored
down & out into the warm night and glittering
San Francisco.
Next morning Sue made coffee. I checked out my
score from the garbage bins. * In my hand was a
book titled, Radical Periodicals in America
1880 to 1950. I thumbed through and found the
entry: HOME. It was a periodical named after the
anarchist community called HOME, founded in 1901
on Puget Sound near Seattle (where I live now).
Emma Goldman spoke in their town hall in 1909.
Law enforcement shut down and disolved the community
in 1919 after more than half the towns citizens
were arrested for swimming nude.

MECHANICS' INSTITUTE
MECHANICS'
MERCANTILE LIBRARY

* Dictionary of antique british glass 1975
( and about their guilds )
Anyone Can Whistle, a musical fable 1965
Cyclopedia of Horticulture,L.H.Bailey vol II

Royal Horticulture Society dictionary of
Gardening vol.I 1965
Radical Periodicals in America 1880 to 1950
All hardbound, like new,3 first editions

Nostalgie de la boue
Patrik Øöd-Noir

# The Politics of "Pure Means"

## Walter Benjamin on Divine Violence

### SAMI KHATIB

## 1. On Benjamin's Critique of Violence

Walter Benjamin's essay *Zur Kritik der Gewalt* or *On the Critique of Violence* was first published in 1921, in the journal *Archiv für Sozialwissenschaft und Sozialpolitik*.[1] It was intended to be part of a greater, either lost or uncompleted work on politics, consisting of two parts: *The True Politician* and *True Politics*.[2] It is notable that Benjamin's early work on politics around 1920 was written shortly after the failed German revolution of 1918/19 and in the light of communist and anarcho-syndicalist uprisings in various regions in Germany. Within his oeuvre, *Critique of Violence* has a unique place since it is the first explicitly political essay and his last great work on politics before his Marxist turn in 1924. In 1921, Benjamin had read neither Marx nor Lenin; the political thought he was familiar with ranged

---

[1]  This article is based on a paper presented at the Historical Materialism annual conference in London/UK, November 13, 2010. An earlier version was published on the blog "Anthropological Materialism: From Walter Benjamin, and Beyond," August 28, 2011, http://anthropologicalmaterialism.hypotheses.org.

[2]  Cf. the editor's note in Walter Benjamin, *Gesammelte Schriften*, vol. II, Frankfurt a. M., 1977, 943. See also M. Tomba: "Benjamin's text was conceived as part of a work entitled *Politik*, subdivided into two parts: the first titled "Der wahre Politiker," of which the review by Paul Scheerbart is all that remains, and the second, entitled "Die wahre Politik," in turn divided into two chapters, a) "Der Abbau der Gewalt" and b) "Teleologie ohne Endzweck." The first chapter is included in "Zur Kritik der Gewalt," while the second can be traced throughout the dense "Theologisch-politisches Fragment" (Massimiliano Tomba: "Another kind of *Gewalt*: Beyond Law Re-Reading Walter Benjamin," in *Historical Materialism*, 17, 2009, 127).

from anarchist and anarcho-syndicalist authors such as Gustav Landauer, Georges Sorel, and the metaphysico-political circle around Erich Unger, to the early Ernst Bloch of *Spirit of Utopia* and the early anarcho-Zionist Gershom Scholem, who later became one of the most important scholars in Jewish mysticism. However one evaluates the importance of this intellectual context, I argue that none of these influences can fully account for the uniqueness of the radical attempt Benjamin undertook in his essay *On the Critique of Violence*, that is to say, undoing the nexus of life, law, and violence by referring to another kind of violence—*divine violence*. Giorgio Agamben rightly describes the aim of Benjamin's essay as to ensure "the possibility of a violence (*Gewalt*) that lies absolutely 'outside' (*außerhalb*) and 'beyond' (*jenseits*) the law."[3]

For Benjamin, it was clear that there was something fundamentally "rotten in the law"—be it the law of monarchy, Western democracy, or autocratic regimes (*SW* 1, 242).[4] The violence inherent in the law contradicts itself since law enforcement—e.g., the police—always blurs the line between law-preserving and law-making or law-constituting (*rechtsetzende*) violence. And vice versa, every rebellious attempt to break the law and its supporting powers leads to the establishment of a new law. In other words, is there a realm of truly revolutionary politics outside and beyond the law—a sphere of justice and non-legal violence?

## 2. What Is Violence?

The German word *Gewalt* originates from the Old High German verb *waltan*, which roughly translates into "to be strong," "to dominate," or "to master." In modern High German, *Gewalt* covers a variety of meanings, among them violence, force, coercion, power, and authority. The latter meaning is today most notably used in the German constitutional "Basic Law" (*Grundgesetz*), the 20th article of which reads: "Alle Staats*gewalt* geht vom Volke aus." ("All state *authority* is derived from the people.")[5] As Étienne Balibar notes: "The term *Gewalt* thus contains an intrinsic ambiguity: It refers, at

---

**3** Giorgio Agamben, *State of Exception*, trans. Kevin Attell, Chicago; London: University of Chicago Press, 2005, 53.

**4** Benjamin citations are taken from the editions Walter Benjamin, *Selected Writings*, ed. Marcus Bullock; Michael W. Jennings, 4 vols. (Cambridge, MA: Belknap Press, 1996–2003) [henceforth abbreviated "*SW*, number of volume"] and Walter Benjamin, *Gesammelte Schriften*, ed. Hermann Schweppenhäuser; Rolf Tiedemann, 7 vols., Frankfurt a. M.: Suhrkamp, 1972–1989 [henceforth abbreviated "*GS*, number of volume"].

**5** The German Parliament, the *Bundestag*, chose the translation "authority" for the German word "*staatsgewalt*," cf. https://www.btg-bestellservice.de/pdf/80201000.pdf, (Article 20).

the same time, to the negation of law or justice and to their realization or the assumption of responsibility for them by an institution (generally the state)."[6] Due to this ambiguity, for Benjamin the problem of *Gewalt* is inherent to all legal and moral questions, as the opening passage of his essay suggests: "The task of a critique of violence can be summarized as that of expounding its relation to law and justice. For a cause, however effective, becomes violent, in the precise sense of the word, only when it intervenes into moral relations" (*SW* 1, 236). An action can only assume the status of violence in the strict sense once it stands in a relation—in a moral relation. Benjamin gives no further inherent definition of violence; it remains a relational concept, which can only be presented, defined, and criticized from within these relations and their respective polarizations.

## 3. Means and Ends

According to Benjamin, within a legal system the most essential relation is that between means and ends; if violence is not an ethical or legal goal, it can only be found in the sphere of means—as an effective force, whatever its justification or legitimization might be. The basic dogma of any theory of violence is therefore: "Just ends can be attained by justified means, justified means used for just ends" (*SW* 1, 237). Benjamin mentions two legal schools that diametrically legitimate violence: "natural law" and "positive law." While the former "perceives in the use of violent means to just ends no greater problem than a man sees in his 'right' to move his body in the direction of a desired goal" (*SW* 1, 236), the latter, the school of positive law, is more concerned with just means. Benjamin does not side with either school, though he recognizes the effort of the school of "positive law" to focus on the justification of means as such, whereas the school of natural law conceives of violence as a quasi-organic "product of nature, as it were a raw material" (*SW* 1, 236–37.). However, both schools, natural and positive law, share a common mistake: When speaking about violence, they believe in the instrumental nexus of ends and means. "Natural law attempts, by the justness of the ends, to 'justify' the means, positive law to 'guarantee' the justness of the ends through the justification of the means" (*SW* 1, 237). In contrast, Benjamin denies any critique of violence based upon a theory of just ends or of just means.

This denial is not only of theoretical but also of major political importance. Whereas the position of natural law is often at issue when armed anti-hegemonic, anti-state, or anti-colonial struggles are to be legitimized,

---

6  Étienne Balibar, "Violence," in *Historical Materialism*, 17 (2009), 101.

the opposite standpoint of positive law is normally put forward by the state in order to justify state repression and institutionalized coercion. Although both standpoints are diametrically opposed in their emphasis on either just ends or justified means, they share the belief that violence has always to be perceived within a causal chain of means and ends. Benjamin, however, insists on independent criteria for both just ends and justified means.

Following this argumentation, even the most basic theological principle from the Decalogue, "thou shalt not kill," cannot be perceived as a forbidden means with regard to certain just or unjust ends. On the contrary, the deed itself, the means of killing, has to be scrutinized as such without referring to a possible goal. Therefore, "no judgment of the deed can be derived from the commandment"; it does not exist "as a criterion of judgment, but as a guideline for the actions of persons or communities" (*SW* 1, 250). A guideline for actions, however, can never be fully applied to a situation since it only offers a general orientation; it always needs a negotiation regarding whether and how a concrete situation can be guided by an ethical principle. It is precisely this infinite and non-accomplishable work of negotiation that arises from this lack of absolute judgment, which Kant's *Groundwork of the Metaphysics of Morals* wanted to contain. According to Kant's first formula of the categorical imperative, you are to "act only according to that maxim whereby you can at the same time will that it should become a universal law."[7] Because this imperative is not a means to certain ends but a self-sufficient end-in-itself or pure end, it has to maintain a timeless and universal applicability to all possible historical situations. Yet Benjamin strongly opposes the empty and homogenous temporality of the Kantian categorical imperative. Since no historical situation is identical to another, nothing can be said categorically in advance. As much as the "force of law" hinges on its universal applicability to any concrete historical situation, its classic foundation of morality in Kant's categorical imperative is based upon a timeless universalizability abstracting from concrete historical and never recurring situations. For Benjamin, therefore, the universal value of an ethical guideline must never be conflated with the universalizability of judgments, principles, or imperatives.

## 4. The Dialectic of Mythic Violence

As Werner Hamacher argues in his reading of *Critique of Violence*, every positing (*Setzung*) of law or ethical principle already implies its reversal, for every positing requires its enforcement against any other acts of posit-

---

7 Immanuel Kant, *Grounding for the Metaphysics of Morals*, 3rd ed. Hackett., trans. James W. Ellington; Indianapolis; Cambridge: Hackett, 1993, 30–31.

ing, setting, or constituting.[8] Hence, the logic of positing is always threatened by other acts of positing. Within the paradigm of the state, Benjamin distinguishes between two forms of violence that mutually presuppose and deconstruct each other: "All violence as a means is either lawmaking or law-preserving" (*SW* 1, 243). While the former concerns the constitutive act of establishing power through violence—i.e., terror, war-on-terror, or capitalist "original accumulation" (Marx)—the latter is embedded in state institutions. Benjamin calls these two forms of violence "mythic violence" because their intrinsic dialectic leads into an inescapable and circular logic: any law-destroying act results in a new positing (*Setzung*) of law which again violently tries to preserve itself. For Benjamin, this fateful cycle of overcoming law by re-establishing it is a clear indicator that there is something fundamentally "rotten in the law" (*SW* 1, 242).

Put into practice, however, these two forms of mythic violence are difficult to differentiate. In the sphere of direct state repression—i.e., police force—law-preserving *force* and law-making *violence* are always spectrally conflated (because the police preserve law precisely by enforcing new regulations or by re-evaluating established sanctions), whereas in the realm of the social order mythic violence has become almost invisible. While excessive law-making violence is today more or less "outsourced" from the capitalist center into the periphery, in contemporary post-Fordist capitalism mythic violence tends to obscure its law-making force by turning into a seemingly intangible juridical web of bio-political practices. This form of law-preserving violence operates as a self-producing and self-eternalizing "microphysics of power" (Foucault), producing and re-producing, disciplining and controlling, regulating and sanctioning bare life as actual, potential, or superfluous labor force. Mythic violence has thus become the political economy of bare life—however productive the latter's labor potential might be.


# 5. Pure Means

Against mythic violence and its inherent cycle of law-making and law-preserving violence, Benjamin searches for a nonviolent, pure, or unalloyed violence that could interrupt the application of law to bare life. His name for this violence is "divine violence"—a paradoxically pure or non-violent violence that coincides with its tautological opposite: a strikingly violent violence. Before we turn to the latter, let us tarry with the profane and have

---

**8** Cf. Werner Hamacher, "Afformative, Strike: Benjamin's "Critique of Violence," in Andrew Benjamin and Peter Osborne, *Walter Benjamin's Philosophy: Destruction and Experience*, London; New York: Routledge 1994, 110–38; here, 110ff.

a closer look at Benjamin's expression of "pure means," which can break the cycle of mythic violence since it is not bound to any ends.

At first sight, a means without end is a paradoxical expression since a means is normally defined with regard to an end. In other words, the common understanding of a means already implies a teleological reference to an end to which it is subordinated as a secondary instrument. This hierarchy becomes most apparent when speaking of an end-in-itself indifferent to its supplementing means. For example, values, ideals, ethical end-goals such as freedom, equality, or self-determination, etc. From a Kantian perspective, Benjamin's formula of a means without end can be read as an inversion of the ethical end-in-itself emancipating the plane of means from its secondary, supportive role. It is not by accident that in the *Critique of Violence* Benjamin avoids an explicit discussion of Kantian *Moralphilosophie*.[9] Instead he takes his cue from Kant's third critique, the *Critique of Judgment*, and its paradoxical formulation of a *Zweckmäßigkeit ohne Zweck*, a purposiveness without a purpose, which Kant introduced when discussing the aesthetic of the beautiful:

> ... the beautiful, the judging of which has as its ground a merely formal purposiveness, i.e., a purposiveness without an end, is entirely independent of the representation of the good, since the latter presupposes an objective purposiveness, i.e., the relation of the object to a determinate end.[10]

In contrast to Kant, however, Benjamin's version of Kant's "purposiveness without a purpose" is not directed to the realm of aesthetics. Benjamin's expression of "means without end" or "pure means" belongs to the plane of language (a) and politics (b) expressing their inner non-instrumental relation.

## A. LANGUAGE

Already in his early essay *On Language as Such and On the Language of Man* (1916), Benjamin introduced the idea of an a-teleological, pure means in linguistic terms: "Name-language" (*SW* 1, 66) is language deprived of all its communicating, instrumental, and transmitting qualities. Generally, language does not only serve communicative ends but designates the pure me-

---

**9** However, already in an earlier letter to Ernst Schoen, dated from December 28, 1917, Benjamin mentioned his "desperate reflections on the linguistic foundation of the categorical imperative" (Walter Benjamin, *Correspondence*, ed. Theodor W. Adorno; Gershom Scholem, trans. Manfred R. Jacobson; Evelyn M. Jacobson, *The Correspondence of Walter Benjamin 1910–1940*, Chicago; London: University of Chicago Press, 1994, 108).

**10** Cf. Immanuel Kant, *Critique of the Power of Judgment*, ed. Paul Guyer, trans. Paul Guyer, Cambridge; New York: Cambridge University Press, 2000, 111 (§ 15, Akademie Ausg. vol. V, 226).

dium of the "mental being" of humanity. The various contents of the latter (we might say in linguistics: the "signified") are not communicated *through* but *in* language as the pure medium of language as such. "All language communicates itself" (*SW* 1, 63). Therefore, language is not the instrumental bearer of meaning but the "un-mediated" pure medium in which cognition (*Erkenntnis*) becomes communicable. Hence for Benjamin, recognizability (*Erkennbarkeit*) is transcendentally rooted in language. Name-language, or "language as such," speaks itself in all languages and thereby guarantees the translatability of every language into another. In his essay *The Task of the Translator*, which Benjamin wrote at the same time as *Critique of Violence*, he elaborated further on this theory of pure language providing ground for his theory of the freedom of translation:

> In this pure language [...] all information, all sense, and all intention finally encounter a stratum in which they are destined to be extinguished. [...] It is the task of the translator to release in his own language that pure language which is locked up [*gebannt*] in alien tongues, to liberate the language imprisoned in a work in his re-creation [*Umdichtung*] of that work (*SW* 1, 261). [11]

Already the concepts employed in this dense passage—extinction, devoiding, and liberation—indicate that Benjamin's "politics of language" features structurally similar arguments to his "politics of violence." As pure language extinguishes all positing of intention and information, pure violence de-activates and de-poses or de-posits, un-sets the law which is itself an auto-performative function of language.

As Giorgio Agamben has argued, the sphere of law is the paradigmatic realm where all human language tends to become performative: "Doing things with words" immediately turns factic—legally factic. [12] If we remind ourselves of Austin's classic argument, the paradox of performative utterances is the following: In the performative speech act, the meaning of an enunciation (such as "I swear," "I declare," or "I promise") coincides with the reality that is itself produced through its utterance (this is why the performative can never be either true or false, as Agamben adds). This quality is particularly important in the case of the law. The juris-diction—the performative utterance of a sentence in the court—eliminates the denotative function of normal everyday language: Every *dictum* becomes immediately *factum*, or, as Agamben put it:

11 Trans. modified.

12 Giorgio Agamben, *The Time That Remains: A Commentary on the Letter to the Romans*, trans. Patricia Dailey, Stanford: Stanford University Press, 2005, 131ff.

The performative thus substitutes normal denotative relations between words and deeds with a self-referential relation that, in ousting the first, posits itself as decisive fact. What is essential here is not a relation of truth between words and things, but rather, the pure form of the relation between language and world, now generating linkages and real effects. Just as, in the state of exception, law suspends its own application in order to ground its enforcement in a normal case, so too in the performative does language suspend its own denotation only in order to establish links with things.[13]

This is why the relation of jurisdiction also formally sounds like a somehow senseless language out of touch with normal language. It needs to suspend language's denotative function. In other words, Agamben detects an uncanny parallel to the language of the law, juris-diction, at the political state of exception.

## B. POLITICS

In the political arena, the realm of true freedom and ethical acting beyond instrumental cause-and-effect calculations can be found in class struggle. Benjamin refers to Georges Sorel and his anarcho-syndicalist distinction between the political and proletarian general strike. While the former fights for certain political-economic ends (political rights, higher wages, better working conditions, etc.), the latter questions the *Staatsgewalt*, the state and its power/violence as such. The antithetical relation of the political and proletarian general strike is to be located on the level of their relation to violence: If the strike is a means to an end, its violence will be instrumental; but if a strike is a pure means without any concrete goal other than overcoming the state, it will reach beyond the vicious circle of mythic violence. In Sorel's words:

> The political general strike demonstrates how the state will lose none
> of its strength, how power is transferred from the privileged to the
> privileged, how the mass of producers will change their masters.[14]

In contrast to this form of strike, the proletarian general strike "nullifies all the ideological consequences of every possible social policy" (Sorel).[15] Moreover, it "announces its indifference towards material gain through conquest by declaring its intention to abolish the state" (*SW* 1, 246). To put it differently, the proletarian general strike is not a violent means to an

---

13 Ibid., 133.

14 Georges Sorel, *Reflections on Violence*, quoted in Benjamin, *SW* 1, 246.

15 Ibid.

end because there are no concessions to be made under which the workers will resume their work under modified or improved conditions. The strike's "striking" character stems from its unconditional character. It is a "pure means" and therefore nonviolent. While the political general strike remains in the domain of mythic violence since it establishes a new law, the proletarian general strike is anarchistic insofar as it reaches fully beyond law-making violence. In doing so, its deeply anarchistic, a-teleological, and non-instrumental character is strictly non-utopian. As a pure means without taking into account its possible consequences, however destructive or catastrophic they might be, the proletarian general strike does not envision a stateless new society. Against any future program, Benjamin sides with Sorel's comment that with the general strike, all utopianism will disappear: "The revolution appears as a clear, simple revolt, and no place is reserved either for the sociologists or for the elegant amateurs of social reforms or for the intellectuals who have made it their profession to think for the proletariat" (*SW* 1, 246). Benjamin's famous theses *On the Concept of History* from 1940 and their fierce criticism of socialism's belief in progress will later echo this Sorelian stance towards future programs and visions.

## 6. Divine versus Mythic

As many commentators have noted (think for instance of Jacques Derrida's essay *Force de loi*),[16] Benjamin's most controversial concept remains "divine violence"—a term the later Marxist Benjamin explicitly dismissed as "an empty blind-spot, a limit concept, and regulative idea."[17] The pre-Marxist, more anarchist Benjamin of 1921, however, is still fighting from a radically ethical standpoint against the mythic link between law and its application to life, reducing the latter to "bare life."

For the early Benjamin, ethical monotheism as developed in Hermann Cohen's *Religion of Reason Out of the Sources of Judaism* (1919) provides a theoretical framework according to which false paganism can be criticized from the standpoint of a truly ethical monotheism (out of the sources of Judaism) purified from all forms of mythic ritual and false equations. Echoing Cohen's pure monotheism, Benjamin takes the (pagan) mythic and the (monotheist) divine as his most important antithetical opposition. In contrast to Cohen,

---

**16** Jacques Derrida, "Force of Law: The 'Mystical Foundation of Authority,'" *Cardozo Law Review*, 11 (1990), 921–1045.

**17** Cf. Werner Kraft, "Tagebucheintrag vom 20.5.1934," in Werner Kraft: "Tagebucheintragungen. ed. by Volker Kahmen," in Ingrid a. Konrad Scheurmann (eds.): *Für Walter Benjamin. Dokumente, Essays und ein Entwurf*, Frankfurt a. M.: Suhrkamp, 1992, 47ff.

however, Benjamin's anti-pagan and anti-mythic standpoint is not limited to theology and ethics but concerns also politics and jurisdiction.

Already in his essay *Fate and Character* (1919), Benjamin fiercely criticizes the "dogma of the natural guilt of human life, of original guilt, the irredeemable nature of which constitutes the doctrine, and its occasional redemption the cult, of paganism [...]" (*SW* 1, 206). In the center of Benjamin's critique stands the principle of guilt and retribution, or, more generally, the nexus of cause and effect, which is the foundation of any modern form of law and ethics. From Benjamin's structurally monotheist standpoint, there can be no ethical order based on the "guilt nexus of the living" (204). For the nexus of guilt and retribution is a mythic belief and must not be conflated with the truly ethico-political standpoint of justice.[18] Although the legal system grounds its judgments in a thorough investigation of the chain of events, it is precisely the establishment of such a casuistic nexus which turns law into mythic fate that strikes at bare life. "The judge can perceive fate wherever he pleases; with every judgment he must blindly dictate fate. It is never man but only the life in him that it strikes [...]" (204). Consequently, there is no essential difference between the mythic belief in guilt and fate and the secular principle of law and judgment.

Fate as the opposite of freedom originates from the realm of the mythic where man is subordinated to the will of gods. As Lukács and early Frankfurt School thinkers have argued, with the rise of modernity and its intrinsic "dialectic of enlightenment," the *mythos* has returned in the form of mythic beliefs and mythic social relations. Man's original emancipation from first nature has turned into the subordination to second nature—to society or, as Marx put it, to the domain of the social as a *naturwüchsige*, naturally-grown relation. This materialist insight is already at work in Benjamin's early writings when he relates modern law to a mythic cult of guilt resulting in fate.[19]

---

18 In his fragment *Capitalism as Religion* (*SW* 1, 288–90) Benjamin identifies this principle with capitalism; the ambiguity of the German word *Schuld*, which denotes moral guilt as well as economic debt, leads him to the thesis that capitalism is a pure cult religion deprived of any specific theological dogma.

19 Consider for instance the following passage from *World and Time*, a fragment from around 1919/20: "In its present state, the social is a manifestation of spectral and demonic powers, often, admittedly in their greatest tension to God, their efforts to transcend themselves. The divine manifests itself in them only in revolutionary violence/force [*Gewalt*]. Only in the community [*Gemeinschaft*], nowhere in 'social institutions,' does the divine manifest itself either with violence/force [*Gewalt*] or without. (In this world, divine violence/force [*Gewalt*] is higher than divine nonviolence; in the world to come, divine nonviolence is higher than divine violence/force [*Gewalt*])" (*SW* 1, 227; *GS* VI, 99).

# 7. *Ent-setzung*: De-posing the Law

Against the background of Benjamin's early sketches and essays between 1917 and 1921, and in light of his take on Cohen's ethical turn of pure monotheism, it comes as no surprise that his essay on the *Critique of Violence* employs the antithetical pair pagan/mythic and monotheist/divine as its most crucial opposition. If we consider the following chart,[20] this contraposition becomes apparent.

| Mythic violence | Divine violence |
| --- | --- |
| Law-positing <br> rechtssetzend | Law-annihilating <br> rechtsvernichtend |
| Boundaries-positing <br> Grenzen setzend | Boundlessly destroys boundaries <br> grenzenlos Grenzen vernichtend |
| Indebting/incriminating and atoning <br> verschuldend und sühnend | Expiatory ("de-atoning") <br> entsühnend |
| Threatening <br> drohend | Striking <br> schlagend |
| Bloody <br> blutig | Lethal without spilling blood <br> auf unblutige Weise letal |
| Bloody violence over bare life for its own sake <br> Blutgewalt über das bloße Leben | Pure violence over all life for the sake of the living <br> reine Gewalt über alles Leben um des Lebendigen willen |
| Demands sacrifice <br> fordert Opfer | Accepts sacrifice <br> nimmt Opfer an |
| Law-making violence is executive violence (schaltende Gewalt) <br> Law-preserving violence is administrative violence (verwaltete Gewalt) | Divine violence is violent/non-violent violence (waltende Gewalt) |

The last antithesis above—*schaltende* and *verwaltete* versus *waltende Gewalt*—brings us back to the German word for violence, *Gewalt*, which de-

---

20 A similar chart can be found in Willem van Reijen, *Der Schwarzwald und Paris. Heidegger und Benjamin*, München: Fink, 1998, 201; cf. Willem van Reijen and Herman van Doorn, *Aufenthalte und Passagen. Leben und Werk Walter Benjamins. Eine Chronik*, Frankfurt a. M.: Suhrkamp, 2001, 66. See also my book *"Teleologie ohne Endzweck." Walter Benjamins Ent-stellung des Messianischen*, Marburg: Tectum, 2013, 395 (chart 6).

rives from *waltan*. Hence, Benjamin's formulation *waltende Gewalt* is strictly speaking tautological: a violent violence which coincides with its opposite, a non-violent violence. Divine violence as violent violence does not perform a double negation in the classic Hegelian sense of becoming positive again. Rather, divine violence remains negative, unstable, impotent; as an *ent-setzende*, de-posing or de-positing violence it denotes neither a positive quality, a positing of something, nor a definite or predictable event. As Benjamin writes, "only mythic violence, not divine, will be recognizable as such with certainty, unless it be in incomparable effects, because the expiatory force of violence is not visible to humans" (*SW* 1, 252). Divine violence as the zero-level of mythic violence can only be retroactively identified as such; in the present situation, however, Benjamin leaves us with vague insinuations: "It may manifest itself in a true war exactly as in the divine judgment of the multitude on a criminal" (*SW* 1, 252). This comment indicates that divine violence is not simply an external power, an intrusion from outside. On the contrary, the difficulty of divine violence is precisely that it can take the form of profane violence insofar as it is not mythic. On this thin, almost hairsplitting but nonetheless crucial difference hinges the antithesis of mythic and divine violence: In revealing no deeper meaning or mythical secret, divine violence has a proto critico-ideological function rendering it impossible to justify or legitimize. In this context, it is important to understand that Benjamin's critique of violence neither argues for pacifism nor opposes capital punishment. Years later, in his aphorism book *One-Way Street* (1926–28), he writes: "The killing of a criminal can be moral [*sittlich*]—but never its legitimation" (*SW* 1, 481; *Gesammelte Schriften* IV, 138). In a Kantian sense, critique of violence does not mean the refutation of violence but the measuring out of its scope and its area of competence.

With the term divine violence as a problematic limit-concept, Benjamin is testing out the scope of the entire concept of violence, entering a zone of indistinction where a stance *for or against violence* loses its significance. However, divine violence is not a lacuna, an empty signifier, a mere stand-in for something untouchable, but the inaccessible *correspondence* to the revolutionary deactivation of mythic violence, that is to say, of undoing law by de-positing the cycle of law-positing and law-preserving violence. It is this revolutionary deactivation as pure immediate violence that de-poses the law:

> ... on the de-posing of law [*Entsetzung des Rechts*] with all the forces on which it depends as they depend on it, finally therefore on the abolition of state power, a new historical epoch is founded. If the rule of myth is broken occasionally in the present age, the coming age is not so unimaginably remote that an attack on law is altogether futile. But if the existence of violence outside the law, as pure immediate

violence, is assured, this furnishes proof that revolutionary violence,
the highest manifestation of pure violence by man, is possible, and
shows by what means (*SW* 1, 252).

It is crucial not to conflate divine violence with "the highest manifestation of pure violence by man," that is, revolutionary violence as a pure means (e.g., in the proletarian general strike). Before examining the paradoxical structure of de-posing the law, let us take a closer look at the difference between divine violence and revolutionary violence as a non-violent—pure—means. How are we to conceive of the nature of their correspondence? What is the divinity of divine violence as opposed to the profaneness of the de-posing of law?

# 8. Divine Violence

As a preliminary answer, I propose to understand divine violence as the theological name for an inaccessible site *within* the order of the profane, that is to say, divine violence is not some exterior, transcendent power intervening into human affairs from outside but corresponds to a dimension at the very heart of profane life itself. As a paradoxical violent-non-violent violence, it refers to an "extimate kernel," an excess of profane life not reducible to mythic violence. From the perspective of mythic violence, the law and the state, divine violence thus remains an empty blind spot introducing a minimal cut into the organic cycle of becoming and decaying of *bare life*, rendering it impossible to finally close the bio-political web of mythic violence. Nevertheless, from the perspective of *profane life*, a life that is not deprived of its ethical excess over biological life, divine violence, in fact, represents a dimension *exterior* to the everyday life of mythic violence. From this viewpoint, the divine character of divine violence consists of a lack that can only be addressed in terms of correspondences and not by means of equations or identifications. In other words, revolutionary violence as the profane embodiment of something inaccessible at the very heart of the profane *refers* to divine violence (without being identical with it). Paradoxically, on the one hand, divine violence belongs to the order of the Event: it is not an integral part of everyday life but introduces a caesura into the mythic nexus of life and law; on the other hand, however, it can be performed, embodied, or presented by humans in the form of revolutionary pure violence without being predictable or predicable beforehand.

Lacking definite predications in advance, divine violence can easily be mistaken for its asymmetrical negation, that is, the violence of the sovereign, which aims at constituting mythic violence through the suspension of the law. The "state of exception"[21] in which sovereign power seeks to ground its authority, however, has to be strictly distinguished from divine (violent/non-violent) violence and revolutionary pure violence. With regard to fascism, in the eighth thesis *On the Concept of History* (1940) Benjamin clearly states:

> The tradition of the oppressed teaches us that the "state of emergency" [*Ausnahmezustand*, state of exception] in which we live is not the exception but the rule. We must attain to a conception of history that accords with this insight. Then we will clearly see that it is our task to bring about a real state of emergency, and this will improve our position in the struggle against fascism. One reason fascism has a chance is that, in the name of progress, its opponents treat it as a historical norm (*SW* 4, 392; *GS* I, 697).

In the same way as the real state of emergency/exception relates to the fascist *Ausnahmezustand* of Carl Schmitt, so does divine (violent/non-violent) violence as the de-posing of law to the violent suspension of mythic violence by virtue of sovereign violence.[22] The entire argument of *Critique of Violence* hinges on this minimal but crucial distinction. In fact, Benjamin's essay demonstrates how sovereign violence as the false suspension of mythic violence partakes in the spurious dialectics of the cycles of law-making and law-preserving violence. Benjamin's relational definition of mythic violence, however, proves difficult if one focuses on the prospective content and attributes of divine violence. In the first essay of his *Homo Sacer* series, Agamben remarks: "The violence that Benjamin defines as divine is instead situated in a zone in which it is no longer possible to distinguish between exception and rule. It stands in the same relation to sovereign violence as the state of actual exception, in the eighth thesis, does to the state of virtual exception."[23] Against the backdrop of this reading, we are to insist that the indeterminate content and attributes of divine violence as the "*real* state

---

**21** Cf. Carl Schmitt, *Politische Theologie. Vier Kapitel zur Lehre von der Souveränität*, Berlin: Duncker u. Humblot, 1922, 2004.

**22** Benjamin already discussed Schmitt's theory of the "state of emergency/exception" in his earlier book on German *Trauerspiel*, published in 1928, cf. *GS* I, 245–53. Benjamin argues that the position of the *Fürst*, prince, is caught between the antithesis of *Herrschermacht*, the ruler's power, and *Herrschvermögen*, the capacity or potency to rule. As a result, the prince is exposed his own incapacity to decide on the state of emergency/exception (cf. *GS* I, 250). For Schmitt, however, this decision is precisely what defines sovereign power (cf. Schmitt, Carl: *Politische Theologie. Vier Kapitel zur Lehre von der Souveränität*, Berlin: Duncker u. Humblot, 1922, 2004, 13).

**23** Giorgio Agamben, *Homo Sacer. Sovereign Power and Bare Life*, trans. Daniel Heller-Roazen, Stanford: Stanford University Press, 1998, 42.

of exception" and the "deposing of law" cannot symmetrically be opposed to the fascist "state of exception" in which it is no longer possible to distinguish between exception and rule. Even in the absence of assignable determinations, there is no symmetry *ex negativo* of divine (violent/non-violent) violence and sovereign violence vis-à-vis the spurious dialectics of mythic violence. In his later essay on *State of Exception*, Agamben clarifies this point, arguing that the lacuna, which separates the law from its application and enforcement, always remains blind from the perspective of the apologetics of state violence and law. In other words, the Schmittian theory of the "state of exception" misses the nature of the lacuna it is pretending to theorize by introducing a fictitious problem: "Far from being a response to a normative lacuna, the state of exception appears as the opening of a fictitious lacuna in the order for the purpose of safeguarding the existence of the norm and its applicability to the normal situation."[24] Put differently, the theory of the "state of exception" can be read as an attempt to include that which is outside the law, yet always remains blind from the latter's perspective, into the law by inventing a fictitious zone of indistinction within a field that Benjamin defines as mythic violence. Unlike sovereign violence, divine violence is not introducing a zone of indistinction between law and nature, outside and inside, violence and law, but short-circuits the spurious dialectics that always anew inscribe life into mythic violence by virtue of suspending the law in the state of exception. Implicitly criticizing Agamben's earlier line of argument, in his essay *Violence*, Slavoj Žižek rightly stresses the importance of clearly distinguishing between divine violence and the state of exception imposed by the state: "Divine violence is not the repressed illegal origin of the legal order [...]. Divine violence is thus to be distinguished from state sovereignty as the exception which founds the law, as well as from pure violence as anarchic explosion."[25]

———

To conclude, let us return to the asymmetric structure of de-posing the law, revealing the incompatible and incommensurable nature of divine violence. If divine violence and revolutionary pure violence can enter an unstable, non-identical zone of indistinction (which is not the fictitious zone introduced by sovereign violence), we can still distinguish between three paradoxical, yet mutually illuminating, features in terms of quality, agency, and temporality.

(1) Pure violence as a pure means designates a "non-quality," an absolute "zero-level" of mythic violence, which is not simply non-violence but introduces a "critical violence"; it is a striking quality-less and "expressionless" violence which interrupts like a "caesura" the fatefully oscillating course of law-making and law-preserving violence.

(2) The "agency" or "activity" of de-posing performs a reversal, a withdrawal of law from its application to bare life; this de-activating act indicates a movement of *désœuvrement*[26]—an active passivity, an act of retreat dissolving, de-creating the application of law to bare life. Paradoxically, in the political event of de-posing of law, a radical activity ("revolution") coincides with a strikingly destructive, annihilating, and disastrous Event ("divine violence") that can only be suffered. Despite this coincidence, howev-

24 Giorgio Agamben, *State of Exception*, trans. Kevin Attell, Chicago; London: University of Chicago Press, 2005, 31.

25 Slavoj Žižek, *Violence. Six Sideways Reflections*, New York: Picador, 2008, 201.

26 Cf. Maurice Blanchot, *The Unavowable Community*, trans. Pierre Joris, New York: Station Hill Press, 1988; see also Jean-Luc Nancy, *The Inoperative Community*, trans. Gisela Febel; Jutta Legueil, Minneapolis: University of Minnesota Press, 1991.

er, divine violence is "precisely not a direct intervention of an omnipotent God to punish humankind for its excesses, a kind of preview or foretaste of the Last Judgment."[27]

(3) De-posing designates a "non-Event," an "A-Event," the temporality of which, as Hamacher comments, "does not conform to any known temporal form, and never to temporality as a form of positing; and one can say that this non-positing violence is contretemporal or anachronistic. Just as pure violence is pre-positional, it is also pre-temporal and thus not representable."[28]

To account for this paradoxical structure, I am tempted to follow Hamacher's reading of de-posing the law. As mentioned before, within the realm of law language becomes auto-performative.

> If one [...] characterizes law imposition in the terminology of speech-act theory as a performative act—and specifically as an absolute, preconventional performative act, one which posits conventions and legal conditions in the first place—and if one further calls the dialectic of positing and decay a dialectic of performance, it seems reasonable to term the "deposing" of acts of positing and their dialectic, at least provisionally, as an absolute *imperfomative* or *afformative* political event, as *depositive*, as political *a-thesis*.[29]

The asymmetric structure of the *afformative*[30] can undo the auto-performative cycle of law and its application to bare life because it can account for the two unaccountable media of pure means that Benjamin mentions: language and politics. In this sense, the proletarian general strike is the afformative *a-thesis* to all political acting based on the state and its mythic violence. ⬢

**27** Slavoj Žižek, *Violence. Six Sideways Reflections*, New York: Picador, 2008, 201.

**28** Werner Hamacher, "Afformative, Strike: Benjamin's 'Critique of Violence,'" in Andrew Benjamin; Peter Osborne (ed.), *Walter Benjamin's Philosophy. Destruction and Experience*, London; New York: Routledge, 1994, 112.

**29** Ibid., 115.

**30** "*Afformative* is not *aformative*; afformance 'is' the event forming, itself formless, to which all forms and all performative acts remain exposed. (The Latin prefix *ad-*, and accordingly *af-*, marks the opening of an act, and of an act of opening, as in the very appropriate example of *affor*, meaning 'addressing,' for example when taking leave.) But of course, in *afformative* one must also read *aformative* as determined by *afformative*." Hamacher, "Afformative, Strike: Benjamin's 'Critique of Violence,'" 128, note 12.

# The Necessary Ingredient

## An Interview with Kshama Sawant, Seattle's Socialist City Council Member

In 2013, economist Kshama Sawant was elected to the Seattle City Council as a candidate for Socialist Alternative, making her the first socialist to win a citywide election in Seattle since 1916. In May of 2014, four months after she took office, a hotly contested $15-an-hour minimum-wage increase was signed into law. A few months later, *Black Box* met with Sawant for a discussion about the necessary conditions for systemic upheaval; the state of America's political consciousness after Occupy; and whether the struggle for modest reforms—such as $15 an hour—could, in fact, create revolutionaries.

**Do you see the success of your election, and the success of Seattle's $15 minimum-wage campaign, as part of a larger, mainstream critique of capital? We can look, for example, at the success of Thomas Piketty's *Capital in the Twenty-First Century*, the way that Occupy still lingers in the American consciousness, and so on.**

What we've been able to achieve so far is definitely part of the larger political context—not just a national but a global context. The most immediate phenomenon that is linked is the financial collapse of 2008. It's an interesting phenomenon happening in the US, because by all appearances the crisis has been stemmed. We have a positive growth rate, but if you look at the trends in the GDP growth rate in the last several quarters, it's been stagnating with indications that the extent of the crisis has not been witnessed yet. And it goes into what capitalism needs, fundamentally needs, in order to rejuvenate the kind of growth that will really put an end to this kind of crisis.

**What kinds of things are you thinking of— the kinds of things that capitalism needs to**

**increase the growth rate in that way?**

If you look at the 20th century, and this is a little of what Piketty looked at, you will see that there are short periods where there was what they would normally call an economic boom, but also the spreading of a little bit of that wealth to what we would call the working class, the people who go to work to earn a living. Some economists in the past observed the period through the end of the Second World War to 1980 and called that the Great Compression—there was a Great Depression and then a Great Compression, a short time during which the much-celebrated American middle class was generated. But it was not going to be a permanent phenomenon. This is something Marxists have been saying for decades—and Marx said back in the 19th century.

To me, Piketty hasn't said anything new, but the fact that he has now become a rock star in academia is an indication that even the ivory towers (the economics discipline has, infamously, become almost fossilized over the last 50 years—and I say that as an economist myself), even they are being forced to take note of the massive fault lines that have been exposed. Fault lines have always existed under capitalism, but now they are being exposed, very painfully. The fact that he has become so popular is an indication that even they can't ignore that anymore. In fact, ironically, the IMF declared [in June 2014] that the US is lagging behind in its minimum wage.

The Second World War ended with massive destruction of not only life—obviously, the human consequences are the most important—but of the economic systems. They ended up with a huge devastation of resources and property. After the overt fighting ended, it opened up a period where a lot of reconstruction was necessary, and the US, because of certain geopolitical and historical reasons,

emerged as perhaps the most important economic powerhouse. That generated the kind of need for growth that propelled the growth itself.

So there is this built-in contradiction of capitalism where the goal of the system is to maximize the gains, the wealth, for a tiny sliver at the top. (Let's even leave aside the financial sector and those complications, but just look at traditional products—goods and services that are produced in society.) The sliver at the top can see those profits only when the goods that are produced by their workers can be sold to some buyers. Otherwise, profit is not generated. So the basis of capitalism, the engine that drives capitalism, is consumption itself.

But who is going to consume? We're talking about trillions of dollars in profits overall, for a very small group of individuals—this is the capitalist class of the globe. But to generate profits on that scale, the scale of consumption that needs to happen globally, you also need a mass of consumers. But that mass of consumers is not the capitalist class—they're a tiny fraction. I mean, how many yachts can you buy? Billionaires buying yachts cannot fuel the scale of consumption necessary. So who are the consumers? It's the households, the working class themselves.

But for all the profits to be maximized, labor has to be paid as little as possible. When you keep stagnating wages, which is the only source of income for the working class, you don't have consumption power. So that internal contradiction inevitably drives capitalism from periods of high growth to slumps. The size of the slump is determined by what we call the proximate factors, the immediate factors of that period. There were certain things that led to the Great Depression, the worst recession, and certain factors that led to this recession being the worst since the Great Depression. However, if you look at capitalism all throughout the 20th century, recessions happened at an average of every five and a half to seven years. So it's a recurring phenomenon. It's in the DNA of capitalism.

And what's happened now—the political awakening is very much rooted in the economic crisis we're seeing here. Of course, that should lead us to the question: "How come, if capitalism is constantly causing recessions and constantly meting out misery to a huge part of the population—why is revolt not a steady state?" But that's where humanity and human consciousness comes into it. Whether or not people move to revolt is a complex phenomenon, and the economic factors that affect people's lives are just one determinant of that.

As an immigrant, I run into American liberals (especially white, middle-class liberals who are well-meaning but have been despairing of the American consciousness) who say: "Americans are so consumed with consumerism and videos and the internet, they don't care about the world outside them and they're never going to move to political activism because things aren't bad enough yet—things need to get worse." I think that's too simple an equation to draw between poor economic circumstances and whether people will become politically active. That's definitely one relationship, but it's not a complete relationship. I often respond to that sort of thing by saying: "Well, I come from India, where things are really rotten for the vast majority of the population, but there hasn't been any full-scale revolt there either." Clearly, whether people become politically active has to do with a lot of other things.

One big factor is how alienated people feel from each other and from their society as a whole. That really determines whether you feel like your fate is connected with other people and whether you want to move into action. The other is a feeling of confidence, a feeling that you can actually have an impact: "If I go out to Tahrir Square in Cairo, will that actually have an impact?" The first five young people who went out there had no idea what was going to happen. For them, the situation was unbearable—they had to do it. But the course of the Arab Spring was determined by the impact that had on other people. So you're always going to have these pioneering individuals who go into action first, but whether it turns into a mass movement is really too complex to ever predict.

But in Egypt, it did happen. When that first stage became successful in driving out Mubarak, it sent shock waves around the world, not just in the Middle East. And you have the public-sector uprising in Wisconsin, which left its mark. Then you have the Occupy movement, which energized a lot of young people. Maybe there is no success metric associated with Occupy because there was no political demand associated with Occupy. It was a general expression of anger. But that left its imprint also. Then you have the fast-food workers walking out in Manhattan in 2012. It was like the first youths in Tahrir Square—they didn't know what was going to happen, but they were so angry at being handed down this dead-end life in low-wage jobs at McDonald's listening to top-40 radio every day: "This is such a miserable existence, I'm going to just go out and say something."

But that ended up having an impact on a lot of workers everywhere else. And here we are—we have achieved a historic victory in Seattle, and the question is how to move ahead.

**These movements aren't necessarily tied to a knowledge of capital, but they are a**

product of certain forms of suffering. Is the crisis here unique, or somehow special, in that it is producing some kind of activism? And can one imagine that continuing, or will it appear in the next crisis?

I think that, whether or not there is something special about this crisis globally, you can look at the American consciousness and see that there is something special. The economic crisis of the big recession is having the biggest impact on the younger generations—they are the children of some of the middle class that was generated during the Great Compression, and they grew up with the idea that they were going to be handed down the American dream. They were told: "If you keep your head down, get good grades, go to college, then everything will be right. You'll be set for your life." Well, they aren't. It doesn't matter how well you do—the vast majority of young people are destined to low-wage jobs and student debt, unless we have a political revolt.

In answering this question—"What is that beautiful confluence of factors that leads to a successful mass movement?"—the contradiction between what you expect and what you get has a lot to do with whether people are willing to move into action.

The other thing that's special about this era is that it's happening at a time when Obama was promised as the messiah who would deliver the nation from a lot of crises. Look at how many things were promised. Obama famously said in 2008 that it's despicable how the Bush administration—I'm paraphrasing, obviously he didn't use the word "despicable"—cracked down on whistle-blowers when we should treat them as heroes. Well, what happened? The Obama administration has already seen the largest number of prosecutions of whistle-blowers than all the previous presidents combined.

They said they were going to be the most transparent.

Exactly. It's been the opposite.

The other unique aspect of today's era is the environmental crisis. Our ancestors, the ancestors of our activists, also fought against it—but at that moment, the issue of climate change was not active. It's only in the last 20 years that it's become clearer. And again, Obama was going to stop Keystone XL. They put all their faith in that and the next thing you know, during the Occupy era, the same activists who voted for him protested at the White House and were arrested.

**It sounds like you think this broader critique of capitalism that's happening, in the US at least, will continue to accelerate as the contradictions continue to put pressure on the younger generations here.**

I think there is an intense pressure on the new generations—pressure on their daily lives, just sheer economic stress, but that economic stress will translate into their hearts and their intellects. I think they're recognizing instinctively that they're not getting much out of the system and aren't invested in defending the past, but I think younger generations are thinking about it more intellectually, and thinking about capitalism and socialism.

People asked me during the campaign: "Don't you think socialism is a dirty word? Don't you think calling yourself a socialist would be a liability?" Not only was calling myself a socialist not a liability—younger people who are looking for a break from the system are looking for a real alternative. People are tired of wishy-washy, alternative-seeming ideas, ideas that are masquerading as alternatives but are really business as usual. Young people are suspicious of them, and what they really want is a bold challenge to the system.

Whether you call yourself socialist or not is actually of not so much consequence. But if you do call yourself a socialist, it gets people to sit up and take notice.

**You were talking about "political revolt" earlier—as you were deciding whether to run for office, you must have had a debate within yourself, and perhaps with others, about the possibilities of revolt outside of electoral politics or inside of electoral politics: the question of reform versus revolution.**

That's a very important question, but before I answer that I have to provide some context about how our campaign came about. Often, in bourgeois politics, some superstar overachiever becomes a point of attraction within some establishment party, and then his or her personal career ambitions drive the question of whether or not to run an electoral campaign. And then the whole establishment rallies around them, but of course only as long as you uphold the needs of the establishment. So Obama becoming a phenomenon reflects both his personal career ambitions, but also the fact that he was willing to uphold the establishment by becoming the candidate with the highest amount of contributions from the financial sector—the same people, Goldman Sachs, who are implicated in this massive collapse.

The reason I point that out is because our campaign, and the reason I keep saying "we" and not "me," is because if we are going to bring up genuine working-class representation, then politics of any kind—whether it's electoral or movement-based—cannot be driven by ego or a desire for aggrandizement. And that's something we should be wary of. The best representative of workers is some-one who is driven by self-sacrifice and not by personal goals or fame or fortune.

Furthermore, the question of whether we should run an electoral campaign itself is based on a political analysis, not a personal analysis. So Socialist Alternative, when we ran our first campaign against Frank Chopp [the longtime Democrat Speaker of the House of Representatives in Washington State] in 2012, the analysis was not driven by "Here's this person who can be a great candidate," but more by "What should we do in 2012?" Occupy was winding down and people were being told: "What can you do? You're going to vote for Obama again, so let's just see how that goes." And look at this disconnect—on one hand, in 2008, Obama was elected in big numbers with pomp and circumstance. You didn't see that replicated again in 2012. It was a clear indication that something happened. And yet, people went for Obama because they saw no other political course of action in 2012. That was the disconnect I'm pointing to. On one hand, people are disgusted and disillusioned, but at the same time that's all they see happening for them.

As long as that disconnect exists, as long as people don't see alternatives to the two political parties, and yet don't see any alternative to voting for the two political parties, it is the duty of the left to wedge itself in and show what a real alternative looks like. That was the starting point for running our campaign. When we won 29 percent of the vote, it was confirmed: Clearly there was an opening. Then we ran for city council and reconfirmed that there was an opening.

There is no purpose to an electoral office unless we're going to use it in service of building the larger consciousness. We don't think that merely engaging in city politics is going to somehow change the world.

**Which brings back this question of "political revolt" and reform versus revolution. The $15-an-hour minimum-wage campaign was a great success, but one could imagine someone coming from a Marxist point of view saying: "Well, you didn't change anything structurally. You raised wages and that will be good for people materially, but you're still operating in the market reality, driven by the government-market system."**

I would say that Socialist Alternative, we are Marxist—we are Trotskyist—but I would say that the question is not whether we fight for reforms or we fight for revolution but how, as revolutionaries, should we build a mass movement that will go towards the fundamental questions of challenging the system itself.

Let's work backwards: What do we need for—and I won't even say "revolutionary movement," because that's a completely different state of consciousness or state of being for the world—but even to get towards a stage where there will be radical political action globally that is causing a kind of upheaval that hasn't been seen in a long time? How do we get to that point? In order to get to that point, what is the necessary ingredient? The necessary ingredient is an explosive mass movement—and I don't mean "explosive" as in gunshots, but an explosion of consciousness at a scale that cannot be determined by one city. For that to happen, what do we need? We need millions, hundreds of thousands, tens of thousands, thousands, hundreds of people moving into political action. How are we going to make that happen? How does that necessary ingredient of mass movements come into being? It comes into being with large numbers of people rallying around a single, unified political demand.

I would define a mass movement as the channeling of the existing anger, the latent anger—capitalism does that job for us. It generates the anger. But simply an amorphous existence of anger and frustration doesn't help. That's always there, but a mass movement is a channeling of that into an organized force that is willing to fight for a political demand. The $15 an hour movement is a very, very tiny example—I wouldn't call it a huge movement. It has a long way to go. It's done a fantastic job as a first step, but there's a huge task ahead.

How is that going to happen? That is going to happen if people rally around radical political demands, and those demands, by definition, are going to be reforms. Anything short of actually overthrowing capitalism, and putting into place a democratic-socialist society, is going to be a reform.

Any fight under capitalism is a reform. The fight for women to have a vote was a reform. But the fight for reform can play many roles. First of all, the reform itself has inherent value because it empowers people with the tangible gains they get—women being allowed to vote makes a difference in women's emancipation. Getting $15 an hour delivers a substantial improvement in people's lives.

But the fight for reform goes beyond that. The fight for reform raises people's sense of what they can achieve, and the process of fighting for reform reveals to people that this entire system is against them.

I've seen a lot of people progress from the starting point in the $15 struggle. At first, they have all these illusions about the political establishment being nice: "What city council member would disagree? Isn't this a no-brainer?" And then they realize: "Wait a minute. Fighting for $15 implies going directly against big business, which is also thinking rationally." I would say that the most intelligent members of the capitalist class think very much like Marxists, except they're trying to protect the other side! They realize that the victory in $15 is not merely a tiny dent in their profit margins, it's a message of confidence to the working class. If I were a capitalist, that's what I would be worried about, and that's why the resistance will be stiff.

People who are moving to struggle for a reform may not have been thinking bigger than $15 at the starting point, but through the process of fighting, they realize that they're up against something bigger.

Of course, things are much more complex than I'm saying here—I don't want to trivialize the process. Nor do I want to exaggerate the process. We have a long way to go. But that is an explanation of how, if we as Marxists are to use our forces to build a revolutionary consciousness, that is not antithetical to fighting for reforms. There are two questions: Which reforms are you going to fight for, and how are you going to fight for them? If, when we are fighting for $15, we don't have any illusions that big business is going to be nice to us, we understand that every single reform, no matter how small it is, has to be wrenched from the hands of the ruling class. The only force standing on your side is how many people are willing to fight with you.

**You mention "fighting" and "struggling," which reminds me of a section from Walter Benjamin's *Theses on the Philosophy of History*, in which he says that virtues like courage arise not as the fruit of the victory but from the struggle itself. How do you understand revolutionary consciousness in terms of how it plays out? Are people growing just by educating other people? Do you see changes in people themselves, some new confidence when they see that they can struggle and fight successfully?**

Confidence is definitely a big part of the creation of a revolutionary consciousness, but I don't think it follows the same trajectory for every person. I'd hazard a wild guess and say, like me, neither of you has an experience of extreme hardship, toiling in the fields, or things we would visually see as indicators of forming a revolutionary consciousness. I didn't grow up poor. I struggled, of course, lived as a poverty-stricken graduate student and everything, but I never experienced things that you would conventionally think of as: "Oh, that's a trigger for revolutionary consciousness."

A lot of people arrive at that instinctively—you can transform yourself, but not on the basis of your actual physical circumstances. It's something that can happen in your brain. For some people, it's a process of transformation, engaging in actual struggle. Being audacious is a necessary component of any kind of social change.

For me, certainly, looking at the absolute and utter misery of poverty in India and not being able to stomach it in any way—even now, I can't think about it without having a visceral reaction—but that led me to think: "Oh, in this same city there are these people who are wealthy beyond belief, and living in a world where technological achievement has transcended unimaginable difficulties, but yet there is poverty."

That led me to think: "This is not something that is inevitable to humanity." All the answers I got were such crap: "This is karma" or "They didn't work hard." That is the most ludicrous response of all. Billions of people are suffering in misery—and to make the argument that poverty is the result of laziness? That defies the entire evolutionary history of humanity. If the vast majority of humanity were lazy, how would this species end up dominating the planet? It makes no sense.

**We've talked a little bit about this crisis, the present crisis, and its uniqueness to some extent. But do you think ahead to the next crisis? As you said, it's cyclical and you can almost feel the next one coming.**

Yes, you can almost feel the rumbles of it.

But the political events of the next two years will be fast and furious. There's a sense of urgency, especially among young people. But I think the left is starting to wake up and there will be a movement toward some sort of left-formation. I don't know what it will look like, but the 2016 presidential elections will lead to a lot of questioning about what the left needs to do, and there will be a movement towards thinking about—I hesitate to say an independent party of the working class, because I do not think it will appear that way in the next two years—but I definitely think that it's something that we are going to see in the next five, six, ten years.

But I think the biggest warning we have to send out is that none of this is going to happen automatically. The left can engage in as many intellectual discussions as we like. But, at the end of the day, if we don't put out a call to action, it will not only be a lost opportunity, but it will leave a vacuum for the right to step into.

**What do you think in terms of the future? Marxists mostly feel that it's inevitable that capital will collapse—it can't sustain itself. So does one actually think about how that collapse looks? Or is that just too far in the future?**

First of all, like anything else in the world, a lot of people who call themselves Marxists have different ways of expressing things and divergent views. I would say that capitalism's crisis is inevitable, but what does it mean for it to collapse? If collapse would mean the beginning of an end to capitalism—I don't think that happens automatically. No matter what crisis capitalism goes into, the overthrow of capitalism and ushering-in of another society—none of that is inevitable. The crisis is inevitable. Look at Europe as a much more striking example at this moment.

The extent of the crisis in Europe is absolutely beyond belief in some ways. If you look at youth unemployment in Spain: 60 percent. The Spanish economy is completely devastated. You can say the same thing about Italy, Greece is in complete disarray, Ireland is getting there, Portugal is right there with Spain. So if you look at the scale of the crises in these countries, you should be seeing an ushering-in of a different future.

But not only are we not seeing that, we're seeing the worst forms of austerity being imposed on people to the point where you now have people committing suicide on a daily basis in Greece—it's horrendous what people are being put through, and yet there is not a resolution. You don't have an end to capital.

The reason you don't is because nothing fundamentally has changed. The resources and political power are still in the hands of the same class of people. They are also afraid of the crisis, because they know there will be struggles—whether or not the struggles succeed—and they don't want to be caught in the middle of it. I'm sure they're thinking about the French Revolution and the crises that befall ruling classes. But the capitalists still own the financial resources and the political power. From that standpoint, nothing fundamentally has changed. Unless there is an actual left force in Europe, a socialist current, nothing else will provide a solution. The only solution for Greece is a genuine socialist political project to gain power and to have radical demands like refusal to pay the debt. Debt gets cancelled.

You can talk about it in fiery speeches, but it comes down to: Are you actually going to have that political demand when you run election campaigns? And are you actually going to run with that when you enter the European Parliament?

Because ultimately, you're going to go up against the Troika—against the European Central Bank, against the IMF, against the European Union, and you're going to go against all the Western superpowers and the banking sector, the kings and queens. The only way you can do that is if you have a majority of people. Of course, they have enough people. Greece has had any number of 48-hour general strikes. If that were a measure of revolutionary change, we should've had revolution many times over. Or at least mini-revolutions many times over.

And yet we don't. Why is that? Because none of the major efforts there have had the clarity to say that the only solution to the crisis of capitalism is: 1) to have radical demands that the debt be cancelled, that the banks pay for their evil deeds, that the major sectors of the economy be taken into democratic-public ownership, and 2) to make a political call for at least a southern European socialist federation, because Greece will not be able to fight this on its own. Neither will Italy, Portugal, or any of the economies in crisis. The only solution, politically, is to have a federation—this is all premature, but a federation that says: "We are going to stand together. The working classes of Portugal, Italy, Ireland, Greece, and Spain are going to stand together against the domination of the big banks and the European Union and our own capitalist governments. We refuse to pay our debts. We refuse to accept this economy that is only giving us unemployment and poverty, and we need to take our banks and major companies into democratic ownership. We are going to run the economy."

Obviously, the question is how this would happen.

We need a clear, Marxist leadership there, but it goes beyond that—even if we did cross that first hurdle and we had a massive enough force to make that call, what would happen after that? That is clearly a call to arms. The capitalist class is not going to sit back and say: "Oh, okay, you want democratic-public ownership of our business?" That is a direct challenge.

**When I heard "call to arms," I wasn't thinking so much of the proletariat rising up, but rather the state in its different forms—of them militarizing because they're afraid of the threat of change and revolution.**

At some stage or another, that will be inevitable because they are fomenting—the military and the police apparatus. It's not so much that the proletarians would be. We don't have that kind of power. We have our numbers, which is our biggest threat. But the weaponry is going to come from the top, and as you said it would be out of their own insecurity at the turn of events.

But I think that it's also a complex question for them. If we're thinking about it carefully, they cannot use force, force that would cause bloodshed, in an indiscriminate manner. They will if they need to, but for them it's much easier if they don't have to use it in any big way. Or use it only sparingly or strategically, because if you use too much force, you can create opponents to your own system. The assassination of Martin Luther King inspired a new wave of black rebellion.

**We've seen very effective moments of state infiltration and disruption—like the Towery case [a US intelligence employee who infiltrated anti-war groups in Olympia and Tacoma], which tore up a whole community of activists and dissidents. People got scared, some left the movement, and some moved away.**

It did have a demoralizing effect, it has a chilling effect, and it was in this instance part of a systematic effort put in place since Occupy. We saw that in the 1960s, of course, with COINTELPRO. That apparatus is already in place, but whether or not it's used against activists will depend on the capitalist class's perception of the threat. One indication of the influence Occupy had was the fact that they responded that way. I'm a little lax about [digital anonymity], myself—perhaps because I know a little bit about technology, I feel like it doesn't matter what you do.

Glenn Greenwald talks about how Edward Snowden contacted him first and Snowden refused to tell him much—he told Greenwald to use PGP, which stands for "pretty good privacy." Greenwald writes that PGP is so random that the most advanced software, which is capable of one billion guesses per second, would require years to break it. There are ways we could protect ourselves. But there are also ways in which this could hamper us greatly. One of the first things Snowden told Greenwald was how every major corporation you can think of in technology—Microsoft, Yahoo, Facebook, Apple, YouTube, AOL, Skype—have entered into these secret agreements with the federal government where they hand over entire records.

What is the antidote to that? The antidote is not to—I don't want to take it too far, we should be careful. But at the same time, our only protection is an explosive mass movement, where no matter what technology they have in their hands—no matter how many army tanks and machine guns they have in their hands—they will not be able to stop it in any significant way. Some of us will have to make sacrifices—real sacrifices, in terms of our lives. But that is an inevitable part of work that needs to be done.

I also want to read one line from Greenwald's book that Snowden said, which is quite striking. Greenwald says he spent hours with Snowden, who was very technical and gave him a lot of information, but he never really gave Greenwald an answer to why he was doing this. What did he want to achieve? He was intelligent enough to know his life was over after this. If he got to stay alive, he'd be lucky. The best thing he would hope for was a life of anonymity and running from country to country, or a lengthy prison term, and that would be the best-case scenario.

So Greenwald says in the book: "Finally, Snowden gave me an answer that felt vibrant and real. Snowden said: 'The true measure of a person's worth isn't what they say they believe in, but what they do in defense of those beliefs.'" It's a complex thing. On one hand, we will need millions of people to move into action, but those actions will begin with people who will take their obligation as human beings seriously. It will require a greater sacrifice, it will require leadership, a core of people who are willing to take that leadership role and to sacrifice themselves in these movements. Just as capitalism, for its own survival, needs spokespeople and spokespeople get created as part of the system, the fight back against capitalism needs leaders and people who will sacrifice, and they will be created.

So often when people give too much credit—"Oh my god, you're the first socialist to be elected in so long! What was your vision?"—but I see myself and all of us as simply people who are products of the times. The times create their own leaders. There are needs and people fill those roles that need to be filled.

**Looking toward the future and looking at Seattle proper, as a city, what kinds of possibilities do you see for radical transformation? So many people are looking at the success of $15, and it has become a movement. But I can't see Socialist Alternative resting on those laurels.**

No, Socialist Alternative will not be resting on those laurels and shame on us if we did. These are definite buildings blocks we can build on. Let's not be in the same old demoralized state. On the other hand, let's not make the mistake of thinking this is great and now we can go back to thinking about our careers or whatever.

So my appeal to everybody else—and my challenge—is to ask how many of us are willing to take that responsibility on. We are not going to be able to predict the future. None of us can say that if you sacrifice your personal ambitions and cushy job and safe retirement that I promise you we'll see some movement in our lifetime. I don't know. I'm always reminded of this teacher who said: "Revolution is the only retirement plan for the working class!"

In Seattle, one thing we need is to fight for is reelection—and I use the word "fight" because I fully expect a ferocious challenge from the Democratic Party establishment. This is a battle for narratives, a battle for history. If the establishment could prove or convince people that all of what's happened in the past—Occupy, our election, $15—was just a flash in the pan and not at all like what you were saying before, an indication of things to come. That's the narrative they want. And we want the opposite. We want a narrative that will empower people into understanding that even with defeats, this is a decisive shift in the course of history. There will be defeats in the future, obviously, but right now we have a victory—what are we doing to build on that?

It's a complex thing. On one hand, we don't have any illusions that voting is some form of high political activism. In fact, it's the most disengaged form because it's a proxy thing—you fill out a black bubble and that doesn't translate into a real movement. However, the process of fighting for the votes will create activists, just like our city council campaign generated a whole layer of new activists who then got involved in the $15 fight. We need many such electoral campaigns—not just in Seattle, but everywhere.

**And what is next for you?**

I always look at my own life and think that—I wouldn't say this about anybody else's life because they have to say it for themselves, but—I feel like my own life is of no consequence. It's an incident. Who decided that you should be born? It's just a quirk of nature that some life was formed. And of what consequence is this life if we don't use every moment of it to fight against injustice?

People say: "Oh my god, isn't this putting a strain on your life?"

My response is: What else would you do? I don't have anything better to do. ⬢

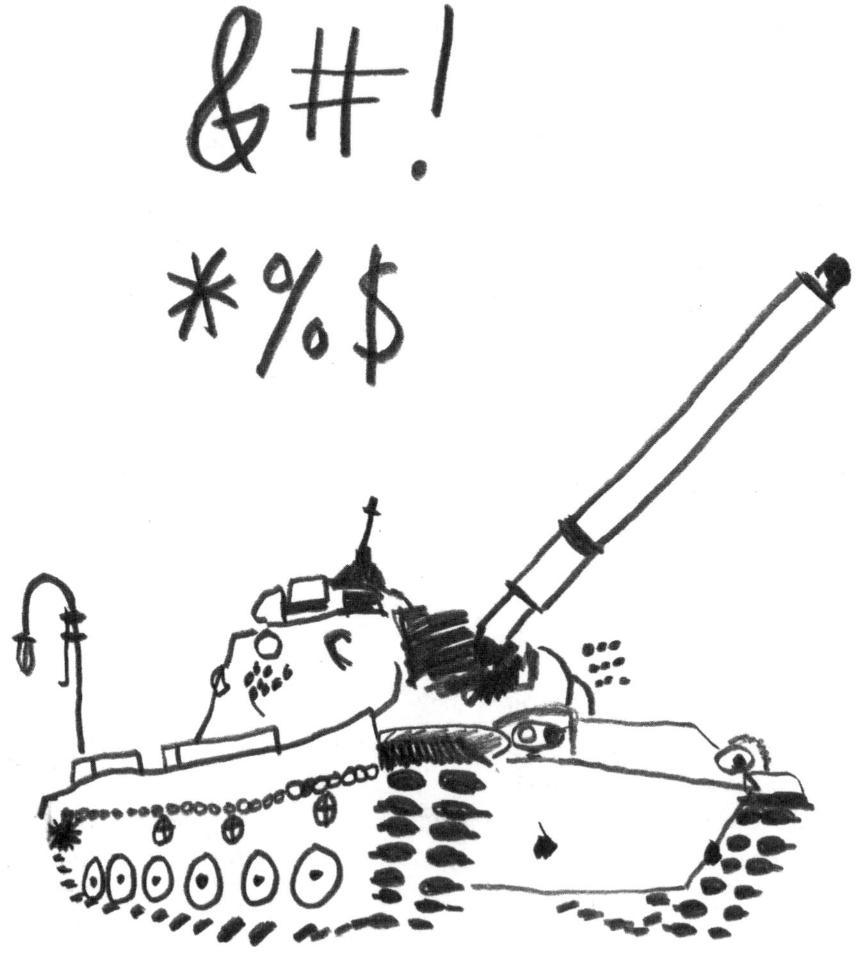

# After the Revolution

## CHARLES TONDERAI MUDEDE

**M**y mother was on the radio. She was talking about the war in Rhodesia. I was listening to her in our apartment, which was near Dupont Circle in Washington, DC. My mother was justifying the use of violence in the struggle for black African self-determination. The Rhodesian government classified the freedom fighters as terrorists—meaning they were criminals, mere murderers. But this, she argued, was not the case.

The men and women fighting the Rhodesian Front—the party that governed under Ian Smith, who famously said, "I don't believe in black majority rule ever in Rhodesia, not in a thousand years"—were highly organized, trained in Ethiopia and North Korea, receiving moral and material support from the USSR and China, and running a network of camps in Mozambique. This was a war: the Rhodesian Bush War, if you were on the side of the settlers, and the Second Chimurenga, if you were on the side of the natives. The First Chimurenga happened between 1887 and 1896, the Second between 1966 and 1979. The first Chimurenga ended with the assassination of Mlimo, a Matabele spiritual leader who was shot as he danced and praised his ancestors; the second ended when the freedom fighters shot down a Rhodesian commercial airliner in February of 1979.

Soon after the death of Mlimo, Cecil Rhodes—the great British imperialist who dreamed of colonizing the stars and the pragmatic founder of the diamond corporation De Beers—set the terms for peace on the Motopo Hills, where he is now buried. Not long after the civilian plane was shot out of the sky, to the amazement of many settlers who were under the impression that the "Afs" were no smarter than baboons, the Patriotic Front[1] set the terms of peace: democratic elections.

The person interviewing my mother that afternoon in DC, a white man, pointed out to her that there were other effective and more morally legitimate forms of resistance. He had to mention MLK and Gandhi. My mother was not impressed with this suggestion. Violence was the most effective means to achieve the post-racial society that she and millions like her envisioned. In fact, the war for independence was not against the British—they actually granted majority rule to the country in 1963—but against the white settlers who decided, in 1965, to maintain power illegally and against the wishes of their home country. Also, everything had been tried, every avenue explored, and all that was left was violence. Change wasn't going to happen peacefully. Bullets and blood was the only language understood by the white settlers, who had everything to lose—their swimming pools, golf courses, homes, servants, status, schools. My mother was on the radio in 1978.

---

That war fully ended in 1980. A year before, however, there came into existence a country very few humans have ever heard of: Zimbabwe Rhodesia. It had a Methodist bishop, Abel Muzorewa, as its leader. He was an African who did not approve of traditional African dancing (it offended Christian morality) and, more importantly, violence. The country he ruled, however, was nothing more than a last-ditch attempt to keep the settlers under some form of rule by sharing power with, essentially, the black middle class (preachers, teachers, nurses). The freedom fighters rejected Zimbabwe Rhodesia and continued to fight until a treaty that promised an election with no strings attached was signed. That treaty, called the Lancaster House Agreement, was arranged and settled in London at the end of 1979. Zimbabwe Rhodesia became a part of history that few of us remember. General elections were held and Robert Mugabe—the head of ZANU, one of the two major black African parties (the other being ZAPU)—won the election easily.

Peace returned to the breadbasket of Africa. The names of cities and streets were changed from European to African, and a noble policy of reconciliation with whites was promoted. The black Africans correctly felt they had the moral upper hand in this struggle and that history was on their side—history, that is, in the Hegelian sense: history as progress, moving from low forms of political organization to higher and more enlightened ones. The Second Chimurenga may have called upon the spirits of the an-

---

1   The Patriotic Front was formed as an alliance between the Zimbabwe African National Union (ZANU) and the Zimbabwe African People's Union (ZAPU), and their respective military wings: the Zimbabwe African National Liberation Army and the Zimbabwe People's Revolutionary Army.

cestors for support, but it was still a progressive movement. Black African intellectuals saw capitalism as barbaric (with good reason—they were brutalized by the system) and socialism as the future. The white settlers were the backward ones; they wanted to live in the past, in the 19th century, in the century of imperialism. Black Africans, from farmers to lawyers, dreamed and sang (music was an important part of the movement) of liberty for all, a fairer and non-racial distribution of wealth, and the recognition of human dignity.

The sun was rising over Zimbabwe. This was the country my family saw in 1981, the year we returned from the US. My mother, who was educated at Catholic University, became a lecturer at the University of Zimbabwe. My father, an economist educated at American University, became a civil servant in the Ministry of Industry and Technology. My cousin James, a freedom fighter trained in Mozambique who saw the last days of the fighting, returned to civilian life and became a very handsome police officer. His wife, Tina, also fought in the war. Indeed, we were told she saw more action than her husband. The two had faced death in the name of democracy. Those who fought in the war were called comrades, and so we called James "Comrade James" and Tina "Comrade Tina." The comrades and the intellectuals spoke the same language. We would build a new society.

There was only one problem with this picture. The violence of the war did not end with the war. It did not go away once a ceasefire was called. The violence was, true, no longer out in the open, or in the bush, but it was in the bodies of the citizens of this new and independent nation. And by bodies, I don't just mean as injuries, as missing limbs, as wounds that are slow to heal. What I mean by bodies is drawn from Spinoza, from the way the 17th-century Dutch philosopher saw memory and meat as one: the body as the storage of experiences and also the generator of associations. When a farmer sees the tracks of a horse in the mud, Spinoza writes in the *Ethics*, he recalls the plow and the harvest. When a soldier sees tracks, he recalls the swords and battles. Violence is written into the body.

James did not share his war stories. He talked about so many other things: how he had plans to raise money to open a shop at a "growth point" (a government-designated village for investment) or a fast-food something in a township or to buy a Toyota Combi to rent to enterprising drivers. But not a single word came out of him about what he saw in the bush. We did not want to hear about his big Combi dreams; we wanted him to tell us what it was like to kill another human. Did it change him? Did it make him want more blood? Did he still remember the faces of those he killed? Did he have nightmares? He kept all of this to himself. He also kept to himself the name of the disease that began killing him in the late '80s: AIDS. Everyone could see he had it but he said nothing. He locked the stories of the war and the name of his illness in his body and took them to the grave. His wife followed him six months later. Neither lived long in the country they fought for.

Zimbabwe's progressive moment turned out to be brief. It began in 1980 and was dead by 1987, the year the country effectively became a one-party state and the leader of that one party, Robert Mugabe, effectively became a dictator. By all appearances, we had removed one oppressive ruler, Ian Smith, only to install another one. All that had changed was the color of the ruler. No progress had been made after all. The French post-colonial philosopher Frantz Fanon named this moment "the betrayal." It was the moment when the revolutionary hero (Robert Mugabe, Julius Nyerere, Kenneth Kaunda) did not fulfill the promises of the cause, the movement from "discovery" to liberation, but instead betrayed it by filling the exact space of the oppressor he helped to overthrow.

Zimbabwe was not the only African country to find its hard-won democracy undone by the betrayal. And indeed, Fanon should have seen the root of this betrayal. (Or, more precisely, the reason fidelity, in Alain Badiou's language, to the moment of discovery—or the struggle, or to use Badiou's language once more: "the event," the "procedure of truth"—in country after country vanished like a dream at the point of waking: the "waking out of sleep shocker," to use the language of Linton Kwesi Johnson.) It was inevitable precisely because of the violence that Fanon and intellectuals like my mother advocated as the only language the colonizers would understand.

---

We must now look back at Zimbabwe, Kenya, Angola, Zambia, and so many other countries in and outside of Africa, and ask the deeper question: Is war really worth it? Meaning: Does war produce the goods? Or is it always lose-lose? The more we ask this question, and the closer we examine the results of armed struggle, the clearer it seems to become that violence might be the worst way to solve what Bob Marley politely called in the tune "Zimbabwe" a "little trouble." What I'm proposing is that the betrayal is a natural outcome of violence, simply because the body never truly recovers from the physical experience of war. Once a body has been in war, has killed other bodies, or has been hurt or wounded by other bodies, it will always associate all signs during peacetime in the terms of that brutal experience. You can't really win a war with a body.

In 1983, Soviet jets fired air-to-air missiles at a South Korean jumbo jet flying over strategic Soviet airspace. The commercial plane fell into the Sea of Japan. Everyone on board, 269 passengers and crew, died. The incident triggered one of the last great Cold War crises. The US demanded that the UN condemn the action; the USSR accused the US of using civilians to spy on its sensitive operations. Zimbabwe, a brand-new nation, happened to find itself in the middle of this conflict because it was on one of the rotating seats in the UN Security Council. The US ordered Zimbabwe to vote against the Soviets—the very country that had given the freedom fighters generous support during the Second Chimurenga. As for the US, it was known that its intelligence community and right-wing politicians had sided with the Rhodesian Front.

The solution to this problem seemed pretty simple, but it was not. There was one big snag to voting in favor of the USSR: The US had in fact promised, as part of the Lancaster House Agreement, to provide funds for black Africans to legally and in an orderly fashion buy land back from white settlers. The war would not have ended without this crucial assurance. The US, led by Ronald Reagan, made itself clear on this point: If Zimbabwe raised its hand for the Soviets, it would not see a dime of that money. Zimbabwe learned that the threat was not empty after it voted in favor of the Soviets. The land issue would not be resolved until 2000 when Mugabe, facing a loss in the general elections, exploited the wounds of the war and encouraged black Africans to reclaim land from white farmers by force.

A year after the fall of the South Korean passenger jet, the violence that was in the bodies of millions of Zimbabweans returned as Gukurahundi, a military operation in Matabeleland that involved the 5th Brigade, an elite unit trained in North Korea. Officially, the operation resulted in the deaths of 20,000 Ndebele civilians (unofficially, the number is 50,000—most believe the truth is somewhere between those two figures). And what was this post-war massacre about? The detonation of a political struggle with a historical, pre-colonial dimension, plus a deteriorating economy and the loss of a key element of the peace agreement. More and more, black Africans were finding themselves to be poorer than they were under white rule. What had happened? What was the solution to this economic crisis? Predictably, the answer was found in what was written on the bodies of the nation. This second wave of violence which, even by the official count, had more casualties than the 15-year Bush War, ended with a one-party state (the unification of ZANU and ZAPU in 1987) and the creation of a dictator who would use what he knew too well, violence, to maintain power. He is still president as of this writing. He is 91 years old.

———————

I have to bring James and his wife back to life for a moment. Before meeting their end in the early '90s, they spent a strange year in Seattle, Washington. The two occupied a windowless basement in the University District. They lived with their four-year-old son and worked odd jobs. The rent was cheap, as was food (they stuck to a basic Zimbabwean diet of sadza, greens, and stewed beef), and so they were able to save a little money. The American landlord had no idea he had trained killers in his basement. Comrade James had a big and friendly smile, and Comrade Tina was portly and liked bawdy jokes. You had to go into their bodies to see the damage and the nightmares.

During the struggle for independence, there was a popular tune by Thomas Mapfumo, the Lion of Zimbabwe, that went something like: "Chipo, get your gun, we need to fight." (Chipo in Shona is like Jane in English—a popular name for girls.) After the revolution ended with hardship and political violence, Mapfumo changed his tune to: "Chipo, get the suitcase, we need to leave the country." (Thomas Mapfumo, a singer who encouraged black Africans to fight for their rights in the '70s, and was even jailed by the white government for his protest songs, moved to the US in 2000 because the black government proved to be as intolerant to criticism as its predecessor.) In the '70s James and his wife picked up rifles to fight for a new country; in the early '90s, they picked up suitcases and moved to the US. But things didn't work out in Seattle. A recession that began in early 1990 made it hard to find stable work, they could not enter advanced schools because the war stunted their education, they could not adapt to American ways, their papers fell into disorder. They were back in Zimbabwe within a year.

But let's go back to 1964, the year the Second Chimurenga began, and ask: What should have been done? When we look ahead to the utopia that was born in 1980 and lived for barely half a decade, the answer is only this: We should never have gone to war with the white settlers. Bishop Muzorewa was an idiot, for sure, but he was right about one thing: The struggle should have been a life movement. Though to be honest, by 1979, the year he became president of Zimbabwe Rhodesia, it was too late for a peaceful challenge to—and transition from—white rule to mean anything. The war had long done its damage.

Utopias must always be concrete from the very start: the flesh itself. We need to be as bodies the utopians we have in mind. The dystopia of war leads only to a dystopian society. Yes, many would have died in this kind of struggle, but the bodies that survived a life movement would have been very different from the ones that survived the armed struggle.

A revolution should be about facing death, never being death. ⬢

# Absolute power corrupts absolutely. Invisible power corrupts invisibly.

# Protect Me from What I Want

## ALLI WARREN

I did it for the data I did it for the lulz
I did it for the money I did it for the children
I did it for the health of the chickens
I did it to overturn attrition I did it to retake the city
I did it for the up-goats for the good company for the habit of my pleasure
    & the unknown links in sub-domains
I did it so that everyone would gasp
I did it for the glory I did it for the potential of psychic space I did it for the
    lithe production I did it for the team
I did it for the people their disambiguation their predatory lending
I did it for the nation to animate paralysis to get numb with consensual
    promise
I did it to carry my propriety into property
I did it for the things that resonate around me
I did it for archaic loss I did it for the clustering
I did it for the rope chain I did it for the manny
I did it for the thousands of unknown civilians their disappearance their
    unsteady accounting
I did it for the decimals I did it for the sake of my name my privilege my
    primary wives
I did it for the welfare of my box
I did it for the sense of self-pride I did it for the lush submerging
I did it for the universe it amused me

I did it for the photos I did it for the booty I did it for the dithering I did it
    for the reorgs
I did it for the music & I did it for Foxconn
I did it for the love of cash your honor
I did it to dispense with all obstacles to profit
I did it for the workings of the inner ear I did it to return to camp refreshed
I did it for the emerging world I did it for the people at work
I did it for the systematic recourse to subcontracting
I did it for the enduring light
I did it for the freebies I did it for the chicks
I did it for the cycle of escalation for the unbound acts I did it for the sur-
    prise of what might be in them
I did it for the betterment of the brotherhood I did it for the pauperization
    of the population
I did it for the norms for the basis of the degree I did it to not look back
    wistfully
I did it for the woman I loved I did it for the greatest country the world has
    ever known I did it for their flourishing
I did it to learn my handicraft in the daytime
I did it for the same reason as you
    for the free-play of my bodily and mental activity
    for the pleasure of my friends
I did it for the moonshine I did it for the endorphins I did it for the districts
    to the north for the public at large
I did it for the portable hoard
I did for the spreading pleasure I did it for the eager fatback
I did it for the idea of the middle class
I did it for the free beer in Montana I did it for the vital rice crop
I did it for the motherland for the halibut for the great Nile abounding I did
    it for the love of blogging
I did it for the present tenses I did it for the herd for the chicken heads I did
    it for the butter cream
I did it for the government of property I did it for the unloved and unknown
I did it for the terror of the totally plausible future
I did it for the function of the mass of agricultural serfs
I did it for thieves rogues and striking workers I did it to fully exploit any
    sale potential
I did it for the sheer fact of my feelings for the buoyancy of your touch
I did it for the entire sweater

# Thoughts on Revolutionary Indifference;

## or, The Thermodynamics of Militancy

## DANIEL HARTLEY

In this regard the subject of a truth is genuinely
in-different.

—Alain Badiou, *Conditions*

So then because thou art lukewarm, and neither cold nor
hot, I will spue thee out of my mouth.

—Rev. 3:16

Throughout modernity there has existed a thermodynamics of militancy.[1] The militant, often equated with the fanatic, is a paradoxical figure at once "cold" and "fiery," "glacial" yet "inflamed" with political passion. "Nothing," wrote Edmund Burke in a diatribe against the revolutionary *philosophes*, "can be conceived more hard than the heart of a thorough-bred metaphysician. It comes nearer to the cold malignity of a wicked spirit than to the frailty and passion of a man" (Burke 1992: 314). Likewise, Herder, inheriting the term *Schwärmerei* from Luther, who had

[1]  I am grateful to Natalya Bekhta, Terry Craven, Gero Guttzeit, and Jernej Habjan for their incisive comments on a previous draft of this article. All remaining errors are my own.

used it against the peasant revolt,[2] referred to the fanaticism of philosophy in equally glacial terms: "If it was a philosopher who named our century the age of philosophy, perhaps he understood thereby the century of cold *Schwärmerei* and *schwärmender* coldness" (cited in Toscano 2010a: xv). Finally, building on this German conception, in his *Biographia Literaria* Coleridge wrote that fanatics,

> [h]aving a deficient portion of internal and proper warmth, [...] seek in the crowd *circum fana* [around the temples] for a warmth in common, which they do not possess singly. Cold and phlegmatic in their own nature, like damp hay, they heat and inflame by co-acervation; or like bees they become restless and irritable through the increased temperature of collected multitudes. (Coleridge 2008: 171)

At once too hot and too cold, the militant-fanatic is a thermodynamic aberration.

What, then, is a "proper" temperature? And according to whose thermometer? To answer these questions we must abide with Coleridge awhile longer, since he develops a system of terms which, together, constitute an implicit thermodynamic ideology. Having already conflated fanaticism with superstition, and both of them with the (too) cold individual and (too) inflamed multitude, he goes on to develop a theory of sanity and genius using these very terms. Attempting to undo the potentially dangerous Romantic presupposition according to which genius goes hand in hand with fanaticism and excess, he claims that "sanity of the mind is between superstition with fanaticism on the one hand; and enthusiasm with indifference and a diseased slowness to action on the other" (Coleridge 2008: 172). Sanity is thus a delicate balance between fanaticism, which lacks all power of imagination and lives off the immediacy of the senses combined with illusory ideas, and the indifference of genius which lives solely (if powerfully) in the mind, thus failing to realize itself in the realm of actuality.[3] The following three sets of interlocking terms can now be distinguished: 1) superstition/ fanaticism/ multitude/ impressions/ too hot/ too cold; 2) enthusiasm/ indifference/ individual/ thoughts/ (too cold?); 3) sanity/ "internal and proper warmth." If the first two sets represent contradictory extremes, sanity is the "complex" term which combines them both.

---

2  The term "denotes confusion, unrealism, and a menacing multitude, a swarm" (Toscano 2010a: vx).

3  Coleridge wrote on the relation between thought and the failure to act in his lectures on *Hamlet*. (Cf. Coleridge 1959: 157–85.) It is worth noting that Coleridge's conception of enthusiasm is an unusual one, not least since enthusiasm is often seen as an attribute of fanaticism itself. Hegel, for example, defines fanaticism as "an enthusiasm for something abstract — for an abstract thought which sustains a negative position towards the order of things" (cited in Toscano 2010b: 195).

I wish now visually to map these terms by triangulating them:

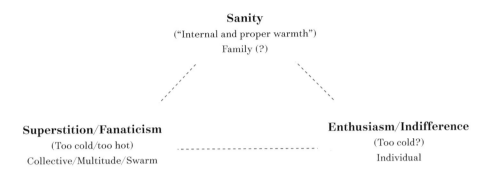

**Sanity**
("Internal and proper warmth")
Family (?)

**Superstition/Fanaticism**
(Too cold/too hot)
Collective/Multitude/Swarm

**Enthusiasm/Indifference**
(Too cold?)
Individual

(Figure 1. Triangulation of Coleridge's definitions of
fanaticism, enthusiasm, and sanity.)

What becomes clear is not only that "sanity" is the "complex" term uniting fanaticism and enthusiasm, but also that it produces a golden mean temperature: what Coleridge described as the "internal and proper warmth" that the fanatics lacked. But if the fanatics generate heat through coacervation, what is the precise source of this ideal warmth? Here, we can provide the missing ideological term implied by Coleridge's semantic system. For if fanaticism consists of a swarming multitude and enthusiasm an unworldly individual, then sanity must surely arise as part of a more limited form of social grouping, one which fuses the external collective with the inner individual. And what better candidate for this position than the bourgeois family itself? As soon as we factor in this missing term, everything falls into place. The "internal and proper warmth" which is the thermodynamic ideal—the *sane* temperature—arises not simply from the cognitive independence of the genius, but from the warm hearth of the bourgeois home. Even though Coleridge himself does not here propose the family as the form of sociality equivalent to warmth, it is nonetheless the logical conclusion of his ideological system. [4]

4  This is confirmed by Coleridge's almost archetypal response to what he perceived as the cold and impersonal abstraction of William Godwin's anti-familial political universalism. Godwin had argued for a "universal benevolence" in which "I ought to prefer no human being to another, because that being is my father, my wife, or my son, but because, for reasons which equally appeal to all understandings, that being is entitled to preference" (cited in Coleridge 1971: 164, n. 1), to which Coleridge responded that "general benevolence is begotten and rendered permanent by social and domestic affections. [...] The intensity of private attachments encourages, not prevents, universal benevolence. *The nearer we approach to the Sun, the more intense his heat: yet what corner of the system does he not cheer and vivify?*" (Coleridge 1795: 29–30, my italics). The point is that the bourgeois home remains a happy medium of warmth until it feels immediately threatened by what it perceives as the coldness of universal abstraction, at which point it turns up the heat. I am grateful to Gero Guttzeit for alerting me to this exchange.

Moreover, it remains as powerful today as it ever was, and for good historical reasons. The warmth which Coleridge celebrates became a social ideal with the rise of capitalism and the culture of the bourgeoisie. "Over against the glitter and ostentation of feudal magnificence," wrote Max Weber in *The Protestant Ethic and the Spirit of Capitalism*, "which, resting on an unsound economic basis, prefers a sordid elegance to a sober simplicity, they [the bourgeoisie] set the clean and solid comfort [*Bequemlichkeit*] of the middle-class home [*bürgerlichen* 'home'] as an ideal" (cited in Moretti 2013: 45). The rise of the bourgeoisie produced the rise of *comfort* as the socio-affective goal of everyday life. "Comfort" forged a compromise between "two equally powerful but completely contradictory sets of values[...]: the ascetic imperative of modern [capitalist] production—and the desire for enjoyment of a rising social group" (Moretti 2013: 51). A constitutive aspect of this new mode of everyday life was *warmth*. Fernand Braudel even went so far as to dismiss *ancien régime* luxury as "all the more false" precisely because "it was not always accompanied by what we would call comfort. Heating was still poor, ventilation derisory" (cited in Moretti 2013: 48). In short, from the chilly excesses of feudal opulence, northern Europe passed to the modest, comfortable warmth of the bourgeois home.

It should now be clear why a thermodynamics of militancy exists: Any political movement challenging the rule of capital or its dominant forms of sociality almost necessarily threatens the "warmth" which originated with the bourgeois home and the nexus of ideologies in which it was entangled (nuclear family, work ethic, patriarchy, modesty, etc.). While the classical bourgeois home no longer exists (capital having long since dismantled it), the ideal of "internal and proper warmth" lives on, not only in neoconservative notions of (suburban) family life but also—more broadly—in (residual Cold War) celebrations of "finitude" which construct everyday life as a realm of authentic "humanness" withdrawn from the external abstractions of capital and the state.[5] The irony, of course, is that the historical condition of possibility for the socio-affective hegemony of "internal and proper warmth" was an economic system celebrated by Marx and Engels precisely for its glacial destruction of feudal bonds:

> It has pitilessly torn asunder the motley feudal ties that bound man
> to his "natural superiors," and has left remaining no other nexus
> between man and man than naked self-interest, than callous "cash
> payment." It has drowned the most heavenly ecstasies of religious

---

5   As André Glucksmann once put it: "There where the state ends, the human being begins" (cited in Bosteels 2011: 137).

fervour, of chivalrous enthusiasm, of philistine sentimentalism, in
the *icy* water of egotistical calculation. (Marx and Engels 2002: 222,
my italics)

Thus, the bourgeois home—just like human "finitude"—is "warm" only in
the context of the "icy water of egotistical calculation." It is a cozy, fuzzy island in a freezing sea of *indifference*. And it is precisely this indifference of
capital that poses the greatest challenge to the radical political imagination.
For how does one match the universal indifference of capital—an axiomatic
indifference to all particular (cultural) differences—without resorting to
nostalgic figures of (politically regressive) "warm" social bonds or, on the
other hand, reproducing the very terroristic "iciness" of capitalist equiva-
lence itself? How, in other words, do we escape the Coleridgean triangle?

The philosophy of Alain Badiou holds the seeds to a possible answer.
Badiou himself attaches unusual importance to the above-quoted passage
from the *Communist Manifesto*, going so far as to suggest that the desacral-
izing operation of capital is the *"necessary condition"* for the mathematical
ontology of pure multiplicity on which his entire philosophy rests:

> [Desacralization] is obviously the only thing we can and must wel-
> come within Capital: it exposes the pure multiple as the foundation
> of presentation; it denounces every effect of One as a simple, pre-
> carious configuration; it dismisses the symbolic representations in
> which the bond found a semblance of being. (Badiou 1999: 56)

Here we approach the dark heart of the problem of indifference—understood now not principally in the Coleridgean sense of philosophically induced apathy, but at the level of ontology itself. For it has not gone unno-
ticed that there is a striking formal similarity between the characteristics
of capitalist indifference and Badiouian truth-procedures (Brassier 2004;
Toscano 2004; Hallward in Badiou 2012: 112–13). Truths, like capital, are
universal and hence *"indifferent to differences"* (Badiou 2012: 27). What
then, to put it bluntly, is the difference between these indifferences? Firstly, it must be noted that Badiou himself is well aware of the stakes of this
similarity, restating in his own terms a problem similar to the Coleridgean
triangle: "The whole point is that differences be traversed, conserved and
deposed simultaneously, *somewhere other than in the frozen waters of
selfish calculation*" (Badiou 2012: 113, my italics). Such sentences should
give pause to those who, like the narrator in the following extract from
Lars Iyer's novel *Exodus* (2013), accuse Badiou of reproducing the deathly
indifference of capital:

But what would Alain Badiou make of us? What would he conclude? Enemies, he would think. No, not even that, Badiou would think.— "Pas enemies. Les tosseurs." But perhaps he wouldn't think anything at all. Perhaps he'd just look through us, as if, as with evil for Plato, we didn't really exist.

For the mathematical philosopher, vagueness doesn't exist, not really; it's only a deficiency of precision. And pathos doesn't exist for the political philosopher, not unless it is the glint of starlight, impersonal and remote, on the eyeglasses of the militant, brick in hand, charging the police. (Iyer 2012: 105)

Iyer's narrator frames Badiou here as a Platonist militant for whom the empirical messiness and vagueness of reality—its *finitude*—do not exist. But this is a serious misreading that ignores the insistence within Badiou's philosophy on the need for the generic indifference of truths to *incorporate* themselves into the finite multiples of situations.

While Badiou is trenchant that "the eventness of the event is anything but a warm presence" (2007a: 197), he has always insisted on the primacy of impurity (Bosteels 2011: 54)—which, for the sake of this article, we might translate as precisely the "warm" ideological admixture of which any given situation consists and which constitutes the finitude in and through which a truth procedure must operate.[6] Indeed, in discussing Althusser's distinction between ideology and science in 1967, Badiou writes: "The object proper to dialectical materialism is the system of pertinent differences that both and at the same time disjoins and joins science and ideology. [...] The fact that the *pair* comes first, and not each one of its terms, means—and this is crucial—that the opposition science/ideology is not distributive" (cited in Bosteels 2011: 53–54). Science is that which is *won* by *working through* (or "subtracting" from) ideology and not simply an abstract predicate that can be attached by a priest-like philosopher to this or that proposition. This is one of the many reasons why Badiou's oeuvre, albeit in ever-changing ways, features a series of subjective figures of (self-)purgation.[7] In *Theory of the Subject* he emphasizes the necessity of a subject's submitting itself to constant "interior exteriorization" or "determining itself *against itself*" (Badiou 2013: 35) so as to purge itself of internal forms of submission to

6 Here, I am consciously drawing on the abovementioned extension of the seme "warmth" from the domestic sphere to that of "human finitude" as such.

7 Purgation is a sensitive term in Badiou's oeuvre since it is the meeting place of what he has come to call the affirmative and negative parts of negation: subtraction and destruction. Badiou has often criticized his earlier work—including *Theory of the Subject*—for its overemphasis on the *essential* relation of destruction and novelty. For a recent summary of his position, see Badiou 2007b (54–57) and 2014 (83–92).

the logic of the "splace." This figure returns in *Ethics* as the second name of evil, "betrayal," in which the subject has precisely failed in its faithful process of constant self-purgation, succumbing to the pressure of everyday opinion and interests, and breaking the sole maxim of ethical consistency: "Keep going!" (Badiou 2012: 78–80). Thus, to charge Badiou with a Platonist contempt for empirical finitude is a grave misrepresentation; without immanent incorporation into a situation—albeit under the form of the generic—a truth procedure simply cannot *exist*.

This is not, however, to deny the formal similarities between capital and truth procedures. Ray Brassier is right to argue that the undecidable inconsistency of the void, which Badiou claims is made immediately present to the situation in *political* truth procedures (Badiou 2005: 142–43), "finds objective determination in the errant automation of Capital" (Brassier 2004: 54). Capital, that "singularity *that has no consideration for any singularity whatsoever*" (Badiou 2003: 10), is thus an asubjective process of unbinding *indifferent* to the differences of a situation, which is homologous to the *subjective* unbinding of a truth procedure. Badiou's error may then be said to consist in failing to distinguish between the two logics of the power of the state (premised upon order) and the power of capital (premised upon order and disorder *simultaneously*).[8] By underestimating the extent to which the unbinding automatism of capital has become "*the* dominant transcendental regime" (Toscano 2004), Badiou seems implicitly to focus only on those forms of power (state order, national borders, territorial logic, police, racist identifications, etc.) that are reterritorializations necessary for the realization of surplus value. In other words, he focuses on those moments of order intrinsic to capital's self-valorization process as opposed to its simultaneous operation of universal unbinding.

But even acknowledging this formal similarity, there are nonetheless clear differences between capitalist indifference and generic truth procedures. Firstly, capitalist indifference involves what Hegel called a "bad infinity," and possesses the hellish temporality that Walter Benjamin (following Georg Simmel) identified in fashion's "infinite sameness"—the eternal return of the "new" which is nothing but an infinite repetition of the same. A universal truth procedure, by contrast, is constructed in fidelity to the unexpected novelty that only an event makes possible: *true* novelty which enables the transformation of a "world" and its logic of appearing. The generic truth procedure that follows—the operation of fidelity to the event—would then be the "good infinity" that remains immanent to but subtracted from the state of a situation. Secondly, although capital is "in itself" indifferent to worldly differences, its systemic dynamics tend to reproduce and reinforce them. The history of capital is a violent and bloody series of genocides, slavery, racism, and sexism. These are integral, not only to its everyday functioning, but also to its ongoing regimes of primitive accumulation. A generic truth procedure, by contrast, is "subtracted from identitarian predicates; *although it obviously proceeds via those predicates*" (Badiou 2004; my italics). A universal truth is thus a production that traverses, via a determinate tarrying with particularities, the identitarian regime of a given situation; it neither abstractly generates, reinforces, nor destroys identities as capital does. Finally, where capital exploits, degrades (both materially and spiritually), or even kills the particularities with which it comes into contact, indifferent truths *give them life*. This is because a truth procedure is an ongoing operation of fidelity to that which is absolutely new, universal, and *immortal*: "What matters, man or woman, Jew or Greek, slave or free man, is that differences *carry the universal that happens to them like a grace*" (Badiou 2003: 106). Thus, what we might call "revolutionary indifference"—that type of indifference unique to political truth procedures—

---

8  I am here adapting an argument made by Toscano (2004). Cf. also Hallward's criticism that "the model of power that seems tacitly to inform Badiou's recent work [...] still appears to predate Foucault, if not Gramsci" (2008: 118).

is clearly distinct from capitalist indifference and possesses the universal scope necessary to oppose it.

But what is its temperature? For it is now clear that revolutionary indifference is not reducible to the "icy" indifference of capital, but that it is also a far cry from the familial warmth of the bourgeois home. Here we must return to the Coleridgean triangle, since the outlines of an answer are contained in its unthought terms. Drawing on Fredric Jameson's suggestive fusion of Louis Marin's theory of neutralization and A. J. Greimas's formalization of the semiotic square (Jameson 2005: 170–81; 2008: 386–414), we can map the negative terms presupposed by the positive contraries of fanaticism and enthusiasm. The hope is that by presenting the unthought of the initial triangle we can produce at least the negative lineaments of a thermodynamic quality beyond the existing predicates of the ideological system.

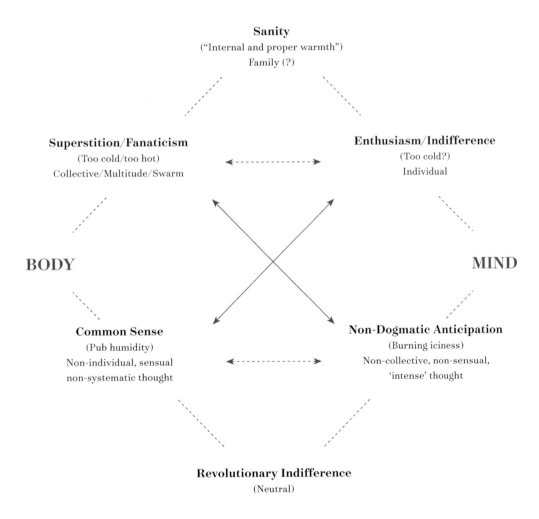

(Figure 2. Semiotic square of the Coleridgean triangle.)

If the fanatic swarm is characterized by its overreliance on sensual immediacy and a weak thought beholden to superstition, then the attributes of
the negative of fanaticism must include: non-collectivity, non-sensuality,
and intense thought. I name this term "non-dogmatic anticipation," inspired by Alberto Toscano's use of the phrase to describe the central problem of communist politics and thought (2010b: 197). For, despite having
itself been written off as an abstract fanaticism, communist thought has
historically consisted of a series of disciplined rejections of non-immanent,
non-situated abstraction. Against those forms of communism which suffer
from an abstract indifference to the specific contours and tendencies of
the historical situation—those which "confront the world with new doctri-
naire principles and proclaim: Here is the truth, on your knees before it!"
(Marx cited in Toscano 2010b: 196)—Marx calls for a communism which
will "develop for the world new principles from the existing principles of
the world" (ibid.). Contrary to dogmatic anticipation, then, which pays no
heed to the relations of forces and tendencies structuring a given situation,
non-dogmatic anticipation might be described as a materialist form of hope.
It involves an "intense" study of the historical conjuncture in two senses:
firstly, a detailed and rigorous examination of the empirical actuality of the
context, its history and its objective tendencies; secondly, because communism "is an idea that contains within it, inextricably, a tension towards
realization, transition, revolution" (Toscano 2010b: 199), this thought is
literally in-tense—striving towards actualization. Hence its paradoxical
thermodynamic quality: burning iciness. It matches the iciness of the cold
waters of capitalist abstraction, reproducing in the mind the movements
of capital itself, but it burns with a militant hope. It is neither the too hot
nor the too cold of fanaticism, but their *indifference*. Historically, it has
three main forms: the "one," the "two," and the "cell." The "one" is the individual militant engaged in intense thought: Marx in the Reading Room
of the British Museum, Lenin in his study, Gramsci in his prison cell—the
brain that the Italian state proclaimed it must stop from functioning for
20 years. The "two" is the militant couple: Marx and Engels, Adorno and
Horkheimer, Sartre and De Beauvoir. Finally, the "cell" is the militant
thought-group greater than the sum of its parts: the avant-garde, the "formation," [9] or the intellectual school.

The second negative term of the semiotic square is of a very different
nature. If the solitary enthusiastic thinker thought himself out of the world
and into apathetic indifference, then the attributes of the negative term
must include: non-individuality, sensuality, and non-systematic thought.

---

9  A "formation" is Raymond Williams's term for a non-institutional, group self-organization, with
   specializing, alternative, or openly oppositional external relations to more general organizations and
   institutions within society at large (Williams 1981, 57–86).

What else could this be but common sense? For common sense is a form of incoherent, culturally shared, pragmatic everyday wisdom. It is incoherent in the dual sense elaborated by Peter D. Thomas in *The Gramscian Moment*:

> "Incoherence" here refers to both a logical and political sense of the word, for the incoherence or inconsistency of *senso comune* is integrally related to the lack of coherence between different historical times and consequent lack of ability to act of those partaking in it, hysterically overdetermined by a past they can neither comprehend nor lay to rest. [...] The experience of the subaltern classes, confined to the terrain of a "civil society" subjugated by the existing "political society" of the dominant class, is one of a continual molecular transformation, of disaggregations that decrease the capacity to act of both the individual and the class to which they belong. In this perspective, the forging of coherence, or the composition of "composite bodies," is an ineluctable moment in the formation of a class capable of exercising hegemony. (Thomas 2009: 373–74)

In other words, common sense consists of a whole admixture of ideologies: "Stone Age elements and principles of a more advanced science, prejudices from all past phases of history at the local level and intuitions of a future philosophy which will be that of a human race united the world over" (Gramsci, cited in Thomas 2009: 204)—whose incoherence simultaneously enables people's day-to-day practical affairs but prevents their aggregation into a hegemonic force. For all its political weakness, however, this is also the medium of everyday life—the medium in which we celebrate our common animality and sociality. So what better symbol is there of common sense than the pub? For this is the place where we warm ourselves at the fire of prejudice and laughter. It is a raucous, bodily, and sometimes excessive and grotesque affair. The thermodynamics here are the very opposite of the passively indifferent genius, coldly withdrawn inside himself. Here, the sweaty mass of joyous human bodies means that individuals literally overflow themselves, sending out their animal warmth into the dimly lit alcoves of the night. This is the *demos*, the people, the rabble in all their—in all *our*—mundane glory.

The key, of course, is that to think the neutral of a given opposition, we must somehow combine the two negative terms. But how is non-dogmatic anticipation to be combined with common sense? And what would be its equivalent thermodynamic quality? Based on the preceding detour through Badiou's philosophy, I have provisionally named the neutral term "revolutionary indifference." For one of the central challenges of political truth procedures is precisely the unsolved problem of how to join and disjoin non-dogmatic anticipation and common sense. It remains a provision-al nomination, however, precisely because the neutral, as Louis Marin reminds us, is "the gap of contradictories, the contradiction itself maintained between the true and the false, opening in the discourse a space that the discourse itself cannot accommodate; a third term, but supplementary, and not synthetic" (1973: 21, my translation). It is, in fact, not unlike the generic itself. It marks the revolutionary impasse, the impossible path that must be traversed step by step by a faithful procedure of subtraction from all ideological predicates. "Revolutionary indifference" is thus the place holder for all the old questions that are yet still new: the *Organisationsfrage*, the Party form, councils, Soviets, free association, co-operation, not to mention Gramsci's "modern Prince." It is the space of a new mode of sociality—solidarity, that "commitment 'to be there' not on the basis of a shared identity or common essence, but precisely on the basis of a[n] 'indistinguishable difference' whose meaning and significance is only worked out in the process of practising solidarity as an active relation of struggle" (Thomas 2011)—as well as the question of the political organizational form which will incorporate this solidarity and fight for its universalization. As for its temperature, here we can but echo the words of Wallace Stevens:

> There is a project for the sun. The sun
> Must bear no name, gold flourisher, but be
> In the difficulty of what it is to be.[10]

# Bibliography

Badiou, Alain. 1999. *Manifesto for Philosophy*. Trans. Norman Madarasz. Albany: State University of New York Press.

Badiou, Alain. 2003. *Saint Paul: The Foundation of Universalism*. Trans. Ray Brassier. Stanford: Stanford University Press.

Badiou, Alain. 2004. "Eight Theses on the Universal." Available online here: http://www.lacan.com/badeight.htm [Last accessed 17.2.15].

Badiou, Alain. 2005. *Metapolitics*. Trans. Jason Barker. London: Verso.

Badiou, Alain. 2007a. *Being and Event*. Trans. Oliver Feltham. London: Continuum.

Badiou, Alain. 2007b. *The Century*. Trans. Alberto Toscano. Cambridge: Polity.

Badiou, Alain. 2012. *Ethics: An Essay on the Understanding of Evil*. Trans. Peter Hallward. London: Verso.

Badiou, Alain. 2013. *Theory of the Subject*. Trans. Bruno Bosteels. London: Bloomsbury.

Badiou, Alain. 2014. *The Age of Poets*. Trans. Bruno Bosteels. London: Verso.

**10** Stevens 1997 (330).

Bosteels, Bruno. 2011. *Badiou and Politics*. Durham: Duke University Press.

Brassier, Ray. 2004. "Nihil Unbound: Remarks on Subtractive Ontology and Thinking Capitalism." In *Think Again: Alain Badiou and the Future of Philosophy*, ed. Peter Hallward. London: Continuum.

Burke, Edmund. 1992. *Further Reflections on the Revolution in France*. Ed. D. E. Ritchie. Indianapolis: Liberty Fund.

Coleridge, Samuel Taylor. 1795. *Conciones ad populum*. Or, Addresses to the People. Bristol: n.p.

Coleridge, Samuel Taylor. 1959. *Coleridge on Shakespeare*. Ed. Terence Hawkes. Harmondsworth: Penguin Books.

Coleridge, Samuel Taylor. 1971. *The Collected Works of Samuel Taylor Coleridge, Volume 1: Lectures, 1795: On Politics and Religion*. Ed. James Engell & W. Jackson Bate. London: Routledge.

Coleridge, Samuel Taylor. 2008. *The Major Works, including* Biographia Literaria. Ed. H. J. Jackson. Oxford: Oxford University Press.

Hallward, Peter. 2008. "Order and Event: On Badiou's *Logics of Worlds*." *New Left Review* 53 (September–October 2008): 97–122.

Iyer, Lars. 2012. *Exodus*. Brooklyn: Melville House.

Jameson, Fredric. 2005. *Archaeologies of the Future: The Desire Called Utopia and Other Science Fiction*. London: Verso.

Jameson, Fredric. 2008. *Ideologies of Theory*. London: Verso.

Marin, Louis. 1973. *Utopiques: jeux d'espaces*. Paris: Les Éditions de Minuit.

Marx, Karl, and Friedrich Engels. 2002. *The Communist Manifesto*. London: Penguin.

Moretti, Franco. 2013. *The Bourgeois: Between History and Literature*. London: Verso.

Stevens, Wallace. 1997. *Collected Poetry and Prose*. Ed. Frank Kermode and Joan Richardson. New York: Library of America.

Thomas, Peter. 2009. *The Gramscian Moment: Philosophy, Hegemony and Marxism*. Leiden: Brill.

Thomas, Peter. 2011. "Solidarity and the Commons." Available online here: http://www.zeitschrift-luxemburg.de/peter-d-thomas-solidarity-and-the-commons/ [Last accessed: 18.2.15].

Toscano, Alberto. 2004. "From the State to the World? Badiou and Anti-Capitalism." *Communication & Cognition*, vol 37 (no. 3 & 4), 199–224.

Toscano, Alberto. 2010a. *Fanaticism: On the Uses of an Idea*. London: Verso.

Toscano, Alberto. 2010b. "The Politics of Abstraction: Communism and Philosophy." In *The Idea of Communism*, ed. Costas Douzinas & Slavoj Žižek. London: Verso.

Williams, Raymond. 1981. *Culture*. London: Fontana.

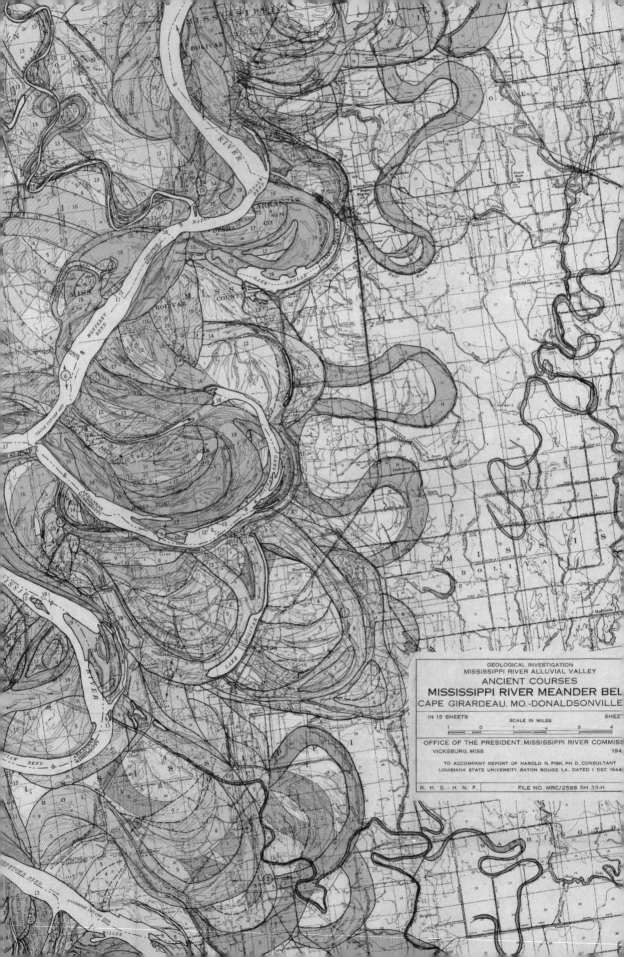

GEOLOGICAL INVESTIGATION
MISSISSIPPI RIVER ALLUVIAL VALLEY

ANCIENT COURSES
MISSISSIPPI RIVER MEANDER BEL
CAPE GIRARDEAU, MO.-DONALDSONVILLE

IN 15 SHEETS          SCALE IN MILES          SHEE

OFFICE OF THE PRESIDENT, MISSISSIPPI RIVER COMMISS
VICKSBURG, MISS.                          194

TO ACCOMPANY REPORT OF HAROLD N. FISK, PH. D., CONSULTANT
LOUISIANA STATE UNIVERSITY, BATON ROUGE, LA., DATED 1 DEC 1944

R. H. S. - H. N. F.          FILE NO. MRC/2588 SH. 33-H

# Fieldbook: Pharsalia

## JOEL FELIX

Leaving the long flood plains of the Mississippi with my two companions: Martin Luther King Jr.'s *Why We Can't Wait* and Lucan's epic Latin poem *De Bello Civili*. Seemingly worlds away, these texts test the coherence of the dialectic so tempting to the franchise of freedom. "Franchise," should it connote pop-up architecture and fast food in the vernacular, was early associated with "freedom" in that the term came from the Roman name for the people that remained free from control and taxation, the *Franc*, who were in turn named after their tool of freedom, throwing axes called the *francisca*, bane of the Centurion. On this green and violet dusk in the middle of the country, we still franchise the self-ordained rational freedoms of the Greeks, the liberties of the Roman citizen, and the freeborn rights from the Levellers of the English Renaissance to Marx, Pisarev, and Malcolm X.

Most influential to 20th-century Judeo-Christian democracies and their interstate highways was Martin Luther King's vision of the franchise. King created a powerful democratic justice claim by aligning the mission of the state to Mosaic and Christian morality. An argument for consistency between the heavenly and earthly cities here emerged in deracinated equality to complete the obligation to God. As King's democratic Christianity led not to a mighty stream of human justice, we may doubt that justice is the truth that history bends toward. But this doubt is in fact power: We need neither discount the legal victories of the Movement nor rest upon them. We merely need to rescue their memory from numbing and restore a standpoint of horror from which democratic life may be renegotiated.

Lucan, a peculiar Silver Age Latin poet forced by Nero to commit suicide before he turned 26, shows one mode of embodying a fraught virtue while doubting the arc of history. Writing in an era when the concept of Roman freedom had fallen into decadence (Lucan and Nero were both cultivated by Stoic education), Lucan showed that without heroes, the mythos of the state is destroyed. In Lucan's depiction of the civil war between Caesar, hero of Imperial order, and the Stoic paragons, heroes of Republican "liberty" (a war won by Caesar's army on the field of Pharsalus), both ideologies are undercut by the fountains of gore that parody the wills of the heroes. Scholars still debate whether the text's ambivalence is the result of Lucan's fear of punishment by Nero or a failure of skill. But the poem's power resides in its glimpse of sub-rational order. The enemy is not to be found among the actors. *De Bello Civili* finds its power not by favoring a moral

---

# The arc of the universe does not bend toward justice; instead, it shreds in the catastrophes of the state. We must find the voice that whispers fear in the same breath as love.

---

order but in inventing a new kind of public reception of history as enslavement without end.

History, for Rome, was the story of power, the rationale for which is that individuals benefit from organization, administration, and command. The opposing ideology, usefully represented by the classical Stoicism of the Roman elite, held that self-control and individual virtuous action (*virtus*) were the only true ways to remediate the inevitable failure of power to avoid tyranny. Lucan's refusal of both of these inclinations leads not to abjection nor to classical Stoicism (its liberal apotheosis the appeal of Voltaire to cultivate your own garden), but to a performance of the vulnerability of citizens to ideology itself. Virtuous acts are profaned in a hollow, horrified vision in which all the historical meanings where *virtus* might reside have collapsed. The center of Lucan's tale of civil war is his engorged imagination of a thousand mutilations of the human body well beyond the mechanically possible. A bitter form of wit, the design serves not as decadent entertainment but as a catalyst to the end of the structures of history, with their false promises, their teleological hoaxes. Caesar's inhumanity is offset by an equal inhumanity beheld in the Stoic paragons. After he's lost the war, Cato follows his Stoic faith, refuses his soldiers the rights of surrender and return to their families. Cato's army flees through the mutated "Libyan sands," a nest of poisonous snake-creatures generated, eons ago, from the blood of the Medusa. In the soldiers' grotesque death march, snake-bit men ignite in flammable pus, drink their own blood, inflate and explode: The reward of Stoic virtue is spectacular punishment. *In se magna ruunt*. Greatness will outreach itself. Power erupts into tyranny, which begets new forms of protest and revolt to restore the basic human need to live rationally and justly with others within social orders and forms of power. It's ultimately true that the weight of any history will force it to fall, like a tree grown heaver than its roots will hold. But to turn that fact into abjection is to give way to decadence, however "stoic" this appears. The only hero that emerges in *De Bello Civili* is the enraged author straining to identify hope with the disgust of history, to reverse numbness to horror, as in that shock we generate temporarily the ontological standpoint of rationality itself, from which tyranny and freedom both reach.

I am trying to relate this thought to Tennessee, inching through an Arby's drive-through, talking into a digital recorder: In the 21st century, the security state justifies its own terror in order to protect our right to not be afraid. We must cry freedom from the liberties the state seeks to secure. We must understand a precarious virtue unblinded to the more obscure truths of cosmos, that there is no end and no beginning but strife. Like Lucan, we cannot easily laud the victories of our most virtuous, as virtue, too, is absorbed in the illegible violence of the state. From Black Liberation's ideological ground of legislated equality we must now reimagine the revolutionary subject for the time we are in—why ignore this lodestone of revolt, visible under the ice sheets of commodity? The arc of the universe does not bend toward justice; instead, it shreds in the catastrophes of the state. We must find the voice that whispers fear in the same breath as love. ⬢

# In Defense of Disco

## RICHARD DYER

All my life I've liked the wrong music. I never liked Elvis and rock 'n' roll; I always preferred Rosemary Clooney. And since I became a socialist, I've often felt virtually terrorized by the prestige of rock and folk on the left. How could I admit to two Petula Clark LPs in the face of miners' songs from the northeast and the Rolling Stones? I recovered my nerve partially when I came to see show-biz music as a key part of gay culture, which, whatever its limitations, was a culture to defend. And I thought I'd really made it when I turned on to Tamla, Motown, sweet soul sounds, disco. Chartbusters already, and I like them! Yet the prestige of folk and rock, and now punk and (rather patronizingly, I think) reggae still holds sway. It's not just that people whose politics I broadly share don't like disco; they manage to imply that it is politically beyond the pale to like it. It's against this attitude that I want to defend disco (which otherwise, of course, hardly needs any defense).

I'm going to talk mainly about disco music, but there are two preliminary points I'd like to make. The first is that disco is more than just a form of music, although certainly the music is at the heart of it. Disco is also kinds of dancing, club, fashion, film—in a word, a certain sensibility, manifest in music, clubs, and so forth, historically and culturally specific, economically, technologically, ideologically, and aesthetically determined—and worth thinking about. Second, as a sensibility in music it seems to me to encompass more than what we would perhaps strictly call disco music, and includes a lot of soul, Tamla, and even the later work of mainstream and jazz artists like Peggy Lee and Johnny Mathis.

My defense is in two parts: first, a discussion of the arguments against disco in terms of its being "capitalist" music and, second, an attempt to think through the—ambivalently, ambiguously, contradictorily—positive qualities of disco.

# Disco and Capital

Much of the hostility to disco stems from the equation of it with capitalism. Both in how it is produced and in what it expresses, disco is held to be irredeemably capitalistic.

Now it is unambiguously the case that disco is produced by capitalist industry, and since capitalism is an irrational and inhuman mode of production, the disco industry is as bad as all the rest. Of course. However, this argument has assumptions behind it that are more problematic. These are of two kinds. One assumption concerns music as a mode of production, and has to do with the belief that it is possible in a capitalist society to produce things (e.g., music, such as rock and folk) that are outside of the capitalist mode of production. Yet quite apart from the general point that such a position seeks to elevate activity outside of existing structures rather than struggles against them, the two kinds of music most often set against disco as a mode of production are not really convincing.

One is folk music—in the United Kingdom, people might point to Gaelic songs and industrial ballads—the kind of music often used, or reworked, in left fringe theater. These, it is argued, are not, like disco (and pop music in general), produced for the people but by them. They are "authentic" people's music. So they are—or rather were. The problem is that we don't live in a society of small, technologically simple communities such as produce such art. Preserving such music at best gives us a historical perspective on peasant and working-class struggle, at worst leads to nostalgia for a simple, harmonious communal existence that never even existed. More bluntly, songs in Gaelic or dealing with 19th-century factory conditions, beautiful as they are, don't mean much to most English-speaking people today.

The other kind of music most often posed against disco, and "pap pop" at the level of how it is produced, is rock (including Dylan-type folk and everything from early rock 'n' roll to progressive concept albums). The argument here is that rock is easily produced by non-professionals—all that is needed are a few instruments and somewhere to play—whereas disco music requires the whole panoply of recording studio technology, which makes it impossible for non-professionals (the kid on the streets) to produce. The factual accuracy of this observation needs supplementing with some other observations. Quite apart from the very rapid—but then bemoaned by some purists—move of rock into elaborate recording studios, even when it is simple and producible by non-professionals, the fact is that rock is still quite expensive, and remains in practice largely the preserve of the middle class who can afford electric guitars, music lessons, and the like. (You have only to look at the biographies of those now-professional rock musicians who started out in a simple non-professional way—the preponderance of public school and university-educated young men in the field is rivaled only by their preponderance in the Labour Party cabinet.) More important, this kind of production is wrongly thought of as being generated from the grass-roots when, except perhaps at certain key historical moments, non-professional music making, in rock as elsewhere, bases itself, inevitably, on professional music. Any notion that rock emanates from "the people" is soon confounded by the recognition that what "the people" are doing is trying to be as much like professionals as possible.

The second kind of argument based on the fact that disco is produced by capitalism concerns music as an ideological expression. Here it is assumed that capitalism as a mode of production necessarily and simply produces "capitalist" ideology. The theory of the relation between the mode of production and the ideologies of a particular society is too complicated and unresolved to be gone into here, but we can begin by remembering that capitalism is about profit. In the language of classical economics, capitalism produces commodities and its interest in commodities is their exchange value (how much profit they can realize) rather than their use value (their social or human worth). This becomes particularly problematic for capitalism when dealing with an expressive commodity such as disco—since a major problem for capitalism is that there is no necessary or guaranteed connection between exchange value and use value. In other words, capitalism as productive relations can just as well make a profit from something that is ideologically opposed to bourgeois society as something that supports it. As long as a commodity makes a profit, what does it matter?

Indeed, it is because of this dangerous, anarchic tendency of capitalism that ideological institutions—the church, the state, education, the family—are necessary. It is their job to make sure that what capitalism produces is in capitalism's longer-term interests. However, since they often don't know that that is their job, they don't always perform it. Cultural production within capitalist society is, then, founded on two profound contradictions—the first between production for profit and production for use; the second, within these institutions whose job it is to regulate the first contradiction. What all this boils down to, in terms of disco, is that the fact that disco is produced by capitalism does not mean that it is automatically, necessarily, simply supportive of capitalism. Capitalism constructs the disco experience, but it does not necessarily know what it is doing, apart from making money.

I am not now about to launch into a defense of disco music as some great subversive art form. What the arguments above lead me to is, first, a basic point of departure in the recognition that cultural production under capitalism is necessarily contradictory and, second, that it may well be the case that capitalist cultural products are most likely to be contradictory at just those points—such as disco—where they are most commercial and professional, where the urge to profit is at its strongest. Third, this mode of cultural production has produced a commodity, disco, that has been taken up by gays in ways that may well not have been intended by its producers. The anarchy of capitalism throws up commodities that an oppressed group can take up and use to cobble together its own culture. In this respect, disco is very much like another profoundly ambiguous aspect of male gay culture: camp. It is a "contrary" use of what the dominant culture provides, it is important in forming a gay identity, and it has subversive potential as well as reactionary implications.

## The Characteristics of Disco

Let me turn now to what I consider to be the three important characteristics of disco—eroticism, romanticism, and materialism. I'm going to talk about them in terms of what it seems to me they mean within the context of gay culture. These three characteristics are not in themselves good or bad (any more than disco music as a whole is), and they need specifying more precisely. What is interesting is how they take us to qualities that are not only key ambiguities within gay male culture, but have also traditionally proved stumbling blocks to socialists.

### EROTICISM

It can be argued that all popular music is erotic. What we need to define is the specific way of thinking and feeling erotically in disco. I'd like to call it "whole body" eroticism, and to define it by comparing it with the eroticism of the two kinds of music to which disco is closest—popular song (i.e., the Gershwin, Cole Porter, Burt Bacharach type of song) and rock.

Popular song's eroticism is "disembodied": It succeeds in expressing a sense of the erotic that yet denies eroticism's physicality. This can be shown by the nature of tunes in popular songs and the way they are handled.

Popular song's tunes are rounded off, closed, self-contained. They achieve this by adopting a strict musical structure (AABA) in which the opening melodic phrases are returned to and, most important, the tonic note of the song is also the last note of the tune. (The tonic note is the note that forms the basis for the key in which the song is written; it is therefore the harmonic "anchor" of the tune, and closing on it gives precisely a feeling of "anchoring," coming to a settled stop.) Thus, although popular songs often depart from their melodic and harmonic beginnings—especially in the middle section (B)—they also always return to them. This gives them—

even at their most passionate, as in Cole Porter's "Night and Day"—a sense of security and containment. The tune is not allowed to invade the whole of one's body. Compare the typical disco tune, which is often little more than an endlessly repeated phrase that drives beyond itself, not "closed off." Even when disco music uses a popular song standard, it often turns it into a simple phrase. Gloria Gaynor's version of Porter's "I've Got You Under My Skin," for instance, is in large part a chanted repetition of "I've got you."

Popular song's lyrics place its tunes within a conceptualization of love and passion as emanating from "inside," the heart or the soul. Thus the yearning cadences of popular song express an erotic yearning of the inner person, not the body. Once again, disco refuses this. Not only are the lyrics often more directly physical and the delivery more raunchy (e.g., Grace Jones's "I Need a Man"), but, most important, disco is insistently rhythmic in a way that popular song is not.

Rhythm, in Western music, is traditionally felt as being more physical than other musical elements such as melody, harmony, and instrumentation. This is why Western music is traditionally so dull rhythmically—nothing expresses our Puritan heritage more vividly. It is to other cultures that we have had to turn—above all to Afro-American culture—to learn about rhythm. The history of popular songs since the late 19th century is largely the history of the white incorporation (or ripping off) of black music—ragtime, the Charleston, the tango, swing, rock 'n' roll, rock. Now what is interesting about this incorporation or ripping off is what it meant and means. Typically, black music was thought of by white culture as being more primitive and more "authentically" erotic. Infusions of black music were always seen as (and often condemned as) sexual and physical. The use of insistent black rhythms in disco music, recognizable by the closeness of the style to soul and reinforced by such characteristic features of black music as the repeated chanted phrase and the use of various African percussion instruments, means that it inescapably signifies (in this white context) physicality.

However, rock is as influenced by black music as disco is. This then leads me to the second area of comparison between the eroticism of disco and rock. The difference between them lies in what each "hears" in black music. Rock's eroticism is thrusting, grinding—it is not whole body, but phallic. Hence it takes from black music the insistent beat and makes it even more driving; rock's repeated phrases trap you in their relentless push, rather than releasing you in an open-ended succession of repetitions as disco does. Most revealing perhaps is rock's instrumentation. Black music has more percussion instruments than white, and it knows how to use them to create all sorts of effects—light, soft, lively, as well as heavy, hard, and grinding. Rock, however, hears only the latter and develops the percussive qualities of essentially non-percussive instruments to increase this, hence the twanging electric guitar and the nasal vocal delivery.

One can see how, when rock 'n' roll first came in, this must have been a tremendous liberation from popular song's disembodied eroticism—here was a really physical music, and not just mealy-mouthed physical, but quite clear what it was about—cock. But rock confines sexuality to cock (and this is why, no matter how progressive the lyrics and even when performed by women, rock remains indelibly phallocentric music). Disco music, on the other hand, hears the physicality in black music and its range. It achieves this by a number of features, including the sheer amount going on rhythmically in even quite simple disco music (for rhythmic clarity with complexity, listen to the full-length version of the Temptations' "Papa Was a Rolling Stone"); the willingness to play with rhythm, delaying it, jumping it, countering it rather than simply driving on and on (e.g., Patti LaBelle, Isaac Hayes); the range of percussion instruments used and their different effects (e.g., the spiky violins in Quincy Jones and Herbie Hancock's "Tell Me a Bedtime Story," the gentle pulsations of George Benson). This never stops being erotic, but it restores eroticism to the whole of the body and for both sexes, not just confining it to the penis. It leads to the expressive, sinuous movement of disco dancing, not just that mixture of awkwardness and thrust so dismally characteristic of dancing to rock.

Gay men do not intrinsically have any prerogative over whole-body eroticism. We are often even more cock-oriented than non-gays of either sex, and it depresses me that such phallic forms of disco as Village People should be so gay-identified. Nonetheless, partly because many of us have traditionally not thought of ourselves as being "real men" and partly because gay ghetto culture is also a space where alternative definitions, including those of sexuality, can be developed, it seems to me that the importance of disco in scene culture indicates an openness to a sexuality that is not defined in terms of cock. Although one cannot easily move from musical values to personal ones, or from personal ones to politically effective ones, it is at any rate suggestive that gay culture should promote a form of music that denies the centrality of the phallus while at the same time refusing the non-physicality that such a denial has hitherto implied.

## ROMANTICISM

Not all disco music is romantic. The lyrics of many disco hits are either straightforwardly sexual—not to say sexist—or else broadly social (e.g., Detroit Spinners' "Ghetto Child," Stevie Wonder's "Living in the City"), and the hard drive of Village People or LaBelle is positively anti-romantic. Yet there is nonetheless a strong strain of romanticism in disco. This can be seen in the lyrics, which often differ little from popular song standards, and indeed often are standards (e.g., "What a Difference a Day Made" by Esther Phillips, "La Vie en Rose" by Grace Jones). More impressively, it is the instrumentation and arrangements of disco music that are so romantic.

The use of massed violins takes us straight back, via Hollywood, to Tchaikovsky, to surging, outpouring emotions. A brilliant example is Gloria Gaynor's "I've Got You Under My Skin," where in the middle section the violins take a hint from one of Porter's melodic phrases and develop it away from this tune in an ecstatic, soaring movement. This "escape" from the confines of popular song into ecstasy is very characteristic of disco music, and nowhere more consistently than in such Diana Ross classics as "Reach Out" and "Ain't No Mountain High Enough." This latter, with its lyrics of total surrender to love, its heavenly choir, and sweeping violins, is perhaps one of the most extravagant reaches of disco's romanticism. But Ross is also a key figure in the gay appropriation of disco.

What Ross's records do—and I'm thinking basically of her work up to the *Greatest Hits, Volume 1* and *Touch Me in the Morning* albums—is express the intensity of fleeting emotional contacts. They are all-out expressions of adoration that yet have built on to them the recognition of the (inevitably) temporary quality of the experience. This can be a straightforward lament for having been let down by a man, but more often it is both a celebration of a relationship and the almost willing recognition of its passing and the exquisite pain of its passing—"Remember me / As a sunny day / That you once had / Along the way"; "If I've got to be strong / Don't you know I need to have tonight when you're gone / When you go I'll lie here / And think about / the last time that you / Touch me in the morning." This last number, with Ross's "unreally" sweet, porcelain-fragile voice and the string backing, concentrates that sense of celebrating the intensity of the passing relationship that haunts so much of her work. No wonder Ross is (was?) so important in gay male scene culture, for she both reflects what that culture takes to be an inevitable reality (that relationships don't last) and at the same time celebrates it, validates it.

Not all disco music works in this vein, yet in both some of the more sweetly melancholy orchestrations (even in lively numbers, like "You Should Be Dancing" from *Saturday Night Fever*) and some of the lyrics and general tone (e.g., Donna Summer's *Four Seasons of Love* album), there is a carryover of this emotional timbre. At a minimum, then, disco's romanticism provides an embodiment and validation of an aspect of gay culture.

But romanticism is a particularly paradoxical quality of art to come to terms with. Its passion and intensity embody or create an experience that negates the dreariness of the mundane and everyday. It gives us a glimpse of what it means to live at the height of our emotional and experiential capacities—not dragged down by the banality of organized routine life. Given that everyday banality, work, domesticity, ordinary sexism, and racism are rooted in the structures of class and gender or this society, the flight from that banality can be seen as a flight from capitalism and patriarchy as lived experiences.

What makes this more complicated is the actual situation within which disco occurs. Disco is part of the wider to and fro between work and leisure, alienation and escape, boredom and enjoyment that we are so accustomed to (and that *Saturday Night Fever* plugs into so effectively). Now this to and fro is partly the mechanism by which we keep going, at work, at home—the respite of leisure gives us the energy to work, and anyway we are still largely brought up to think of leisure as a "reward" for work. This circle locks us into it. But what happens in that space of leisure can be profoundly significant; it is there that we may learn about an alternative to work and to society as it is. Romanticism is one of the major modes of leisure in which this sense of an alternative is kept alive. Romanticism asserts that the limits of work and domesticity are not the limits of experience.

I don't say that romanticism, with its passion and intensity, is a political ideal we could strive for—I doubt it is humanly possible to live permanently at that pitch. What I do believe is that the movement between banality and something "other" than banality is an essential dialectic of society, a constant: keeping open of a gap between what is and what could or should be. Herbert Marcuse in the currently unfashionable *One-Dimensional Man: Studies in the Ideology of Advanced Industrial Society* argues that our society tries to close that gap, to assert that what is is all that there could be, is what should be. For all its commercialism and containment within the to and fro between work and leisure, I think disco romanticism is one of the things that can keep the gap open, that can allow the experience of contradiction to continue. Since I also believe that political struggle is rooted in experience (though utterly doomed if left at it), I find this dimension of disco potentially positive. (A further romantic/utopian aspect of disco is realized in the non-commercial discos organized by gay and women's groups. Here a moment of community can be achieved, often in circle dances or simply in the sense of knowing people as people, not anonymous bodies. Fashion is less important, and sociability correspondingly more so. This can be achieved in smaller clubs, perhaps especially outside the center of London, which, when not just grotty monuments to self-oppression, can function as supportive expressions of something like a gay community.)

## MATERIALISM

Disco is characteristic of advanced capitalist societies simply in terms of the scale of money squandered on it. It is a riot of consumerism, dazzling in its technology (echo chambers, double and more tracking, electric instruments), overwhelming in its scale (banks of violins, massed choirs, the limitless range of percussion instruments), lavishly gaudy in the mirrors and tat of discotheques, the glitter and denim flash of its costumes. Its tacky sumptuousness is well evoked in *Thank God It's Friday*. Gone are the restraint of popular song, the sparseness of rock and reggae, the simplicity of folk. How can a socialist, or someone trying to be a feminist, defend it?

In certain respects, it is doubtless not defensible. Yet socialism and feminism are both forms of materialism—why is disco, a celebration of materialism if ever there was one, not therefore the appropriate art form of materialist politics?

Partly, obviously, because materialism in politics is not to be confused with mere matter. Materialism seeks to understand how things are in terms of how they have been produced and constructed in history, and how they can be better produced and constructed. This certainly does not mean immersing oneself in the material world—indeed, it includes deliberately stepping back from the material world to see what makes it the way it is and how to change it. But materialism is also based on the profound conviction that politics is about the material world, and indeed that human life and the material world are all there is; there is no God, there are no magic forces. One of the dangers of materialist politics is that it is in constant danger of spiritualizing itself, partly because of the historical legacy of the religious forms that brought materialism into existence, partly because materialists have to work so hard not to take matter at face value that they often end up not treating it as matter at all. Disco's celebration of materialism is only a celebration of the world we are necessarily and always immersed in. Disco's materialism, in technological modernity, is resolutely historical and cultural—it can never be, as most art claims for itself, an "emanation" outside of history and of human production.

Disco's combination of romanticism and materialism effectively tells us—lets us experience—that we live in a world of materials, that we can enjoy them but that the experience of materialism is not necessarily what the everyday world assures us it is. Its eroticism allows us to rediscover our bodies as part of this experience of materialism and the possibility of change.

If this sounds over the top, let one thing be clear—disco can't change the world or make the revolution. No art can do that, and it is pointless to expect it to. But partly by opening up experience, partly by changing definitions, art and disco can be used. To which one might risk adding the refrain, if it feels good, *use* it. ⬣

# native code

## ROBERTO HARRISON

*toward Louis Riel*

a contemplative table sees the room as
    mathematical undercurrent, those
regurgitated lines of the ampule and seen lakes
    where one sides over the fish
a detriment to the adorned, to the seasonal
    apocalypse which does not harvest
the attunement and the soaring off of the
    planetary lesions that say
what more? a meeting place of the waters,
    dismembered lights fold
a room beyond network allegiances and a
    forward attachment scene
who is? Get and Put — a round Address
forgiven steams as no water
with an opening desert
does not fail the impression of the name, and
    does not arrive
to seven. when the group and their hunt, the
    steam off of weather
faces, body accumulations and a forest beyond
    the mouth as to
hand behind One around shelter, where the
    measure and the walk
both attend to their many approaches as these.
    some of the homes
do not reveal their memory

and do not view on the Sea, and one as the
    other was
to remain and to deliver the ferns, their open
    tremble will not remove the face
or wear away what once and ever will be
    number, within the topology as
body liquid. once of us
does not remain and does not harvest, and
    once has the beyond
eclipse within a bereavement of the sky, and
    they wander to cook the impression
as their return implies the riot of remainder:
    seven fills beyond
impress, outside markings as the Seas smooth
    attention and water
an imploded tropical lung. we warn that the
    grate
remains within a woods rail, bombs for forests.
    determine what
the literatures of the doorway, no retention or
    the wand as he on a pulse
delivery item. weaker tests, those populations
    grow to divide
themselves in ritual and aftermath, power
    groups seen inside deterrence
in the Amazon where the ointment determines
    what noise will reveal in the house
none. a reason for the entire letter and the
    memory duel within palms
as the season grows in this, and something
    explodes to remain what the face,
those in the early years of a velvet hope
    welcome
avid robes.
equate and then pronounce

do I learn this language as the bottom
or the network planetary whole

Void()

a main body of language sequence, no matter
    where you are. no
people in the state of mute yoga, follow the
    twilight. theirs welcome
a promise language
as the kind palm
of a hand-eye symbolist movement:

Self() $\longrightarrow$ Madeline Island
Self() $\longrightarrow$ Nanih Waya
Self() $\longrightarrow$ Coclé
Self() $\longrightarrow$ Chorrera

topology Self() $\longrightarrow$ Yaviza

circle Self() $\longrightarrow$ Aztalan

Sevilla y Jaén $\longrightarrow$ Self()

origin zero $\longrightarrow$ Mabila

remove the Sea from internal memos, those
    wandering the Float
and what makes us deter the forest
as the main globe in parallels, report
a pulse to amend and grate around promise
with the element interest
one in place, thousands to improve on a letter
    as a Main() to see. in the winter
we belong to a phrasal shore. sentences
connect with the shower
in a husk
with pottery. I as she in it

drive space

to inscribe

# From *Drone On:* A Play in One Act

## STEPHEN VOYCE

**drone** *noun, verb* \drōn\

1. to speak, proceed, or act in a dull, drowsy, or indifferent manner <*office drone*>
2. an unmanned aircraft or ship guided by remote control; the buzzing sound produced by the aircraft

### Note on Production

Are we witnesses who confirm the truth of what happened in the face of the world-destroying capacities of pain, the distortions of torture, the sheer unrepresentability of terror, and the repression of the dominant accounts? Or are we voyeurs fascinated with and repelled by exhibitions of terror and sufferance?

—Saidiya V. Hartman

[Some] may think that the story was really about who presses the button... But actually, the infrastructure and what goes on behind the scenes to allow all of this to take place is crucial to the story.

—Faisal bin Ali Jaber

**A**nd so it is our fledgling century offers up its first defining metaphor to compete with the ubiquity of digital networks. The *drone*—a strange but all too appropriate synonym—abruptly yokes together the monotonous work of "office drones" with the "unmanned aerial vehicles" which they now operate in great numbers above Afghanistan, Iraq, Pakistan, Yemen, Somalia, the Gaza Strip, and soon elsewhere. A weapon for a world marked not by total war but unending conflict. Men and women sit in cubicles gripping joysticks clad in flight suits halfway across the planet from their intended targets.

*Drone On* reframes, word for word, the cockpit transcript of a drone operation, inserting into the text the familiar metadata of traditional theater. The "call name roster" becomes the list of characters; acts, scenes, and production notes are added. Despite these minor adaptations, the play conforms eerily to classical dramatic structure: Exposition, rising action, climax, falling action, and catastrophe are plotted effortlessly in turn.

The document in question records a US Predator drone's coordinated attack on an Afghan convoy in the early hours of February 21, 2010. Twenty-three people died—all of them innocent civilians. Drone operators in Nevada, video screeners in Florida, and a Special Operations Unit on the ground (though several miles away) had pursued the convoy of suspected terrorists through shared infrared and full-motion video screens via a satellite data link. The *LA Times* would soon after submit a Freedom of Information Act (FOIA) request for the chat-logs of military personnel involved in the airstrike.

A "Freedom of Information Act" request may seem to suggest a newly liberated, unaltered text. Not true of course. Distorted by telecommunications failure, massaged by military jargon, redacted by intelligence officials, annotated by journalists, and prefaced by experts, the text already has its fill of filters concurrent with its public appearance. Hence, this literary appropriation is but one in a series of post-publication reframings. The task of any appropriation-based art must be to engage the political-ethical ramifications of *re*contextualizing source text, authorial position, accessibility to readers, and so on. As a matter of theatrical process, the question is how to stage these competing efforts to control the story.

Bugsplat is military-speak for a kill, since apparently a body viewed through heat-sensing satellite images looks like a crushed insect. Comparisons to gaming environments are both inevitable and accurate. US drone programs consciously modeled their control device after the PlayStation joystick. It should be said, all who took part in the February 21 airstrike—indeed, all who participate in such attacks—do so mediated through a network of screens. Screens that reduce the human body to its distributive body heat or a data point on a map. Both in combat and in theatrical production, the play's catastrophic final moments take place offstage, as it were. Only the survivors of the attack are present to witness the atrocity firsthand.

This last point is essential. What we *see* when we watch the play are drone operators, sensors, and other personnel fixated on computer screens. The play does not reproduce the terrible spectacle of mass violence that is its theme but, instead, looks in on those who preside over the bureaucratized machinery of protocols and technologies rendering such acts all but automatic.

Drone On *may be read as a closet drama, staged as a performance, or installed as a multimedia art object. There are no restrictions, nor does the reader require permission to stage it.*

# List of Characters

Convoy of Afghan Civilians
Kirk97, Predator Drone Pilot
MC, Mission Intelligence Coordinator, Predator Crew
Sensor, Sensor Operator, Predator Crew
JAG25, Joint Terminal Attack Controller, Special Operations Unit
Slasher03, AC-130 Gunship
Bam Bam 41, Kiowa Attack Helicopter
Screeners
US Special Operations Personnel

# Settings

Creech Air Force Base, Nevada: Predator Drone Crew Operations
Eglin Air Force Base, Florida: Video Screeners
Uruzgan Province, Central Afghanistan: AC-130 Gunship Crew, US Special Operations Unit, Afghan Civilians

# Acronyms and Abbreviations

ANP: Afghan National Police
ASOC: Air Force Special Operations Center
AWT: Air Weapons Team

CBA: Close Before Air
CDE: Collateral Damage Estimate
DGS: Deployable Ground Station
ICOM: Intercommunications
ISARC: Intelligence, Surveillance, and Reconnaissance Cell
ISR: Intelligence, Sensors, Reconnaissance
JTAC: Joint Terminal Attack Controller
MAM: Military Aged Males
mIRC: my Internet Relay Chat
MISREP: Mission Report
OH-58: Helicopter Model OH-58DR
PAX: Passengers
PID: Positive Identification
QRF: Quick Reaction Force Reconnaissance Cell
ROE: Rules of Engagement
ROVER: Remotely Operated Video Enhanced Receiver
SA: Situational Awareness
SOTF: Special Operations Task Force
TIC: Troops in Contact
WEZ: Weapon Engagement Zone
WOC: Wing Operations Center

## Excerpt from Scene Five

PILOT (02:47): And Jag25, Kirk97,[ CLASSIFIED ], and uhh currently moving uhh west primarily, slightly to the south, looks like we're coming up on a valley here uhh, so we'll be able to tell if they're turning south towards you or not, how copy?

SENSOR (02:47): This is gonna be a nice close look.

JAG25 (02:47): That's a good copy. They're still moving at a high rate of speed, over?

PILOT (02:47): Kirk97, and uhh affirm, faster than the past hour, uhh fastest yet.

SENSOR (02:48): Looking to land us about 13Z, per the WOC room.

PILOT (02:48): Okay. You throw a copy in there, MC, please?

MC (02:48): Will do.

PILOT (02:48): You tell which way these guys are turning yet?

SENSOR (02:48): I just wish they'd stop for a bit.

MC (02:48): Looks they're about to be coming up to a little town over here.

SENSOR (02:48): Still a sweet *expletive* target, geez... Take out the lead vehicle on the run and then uhh bring the helos in.

SENSOR (02:49): [        CLASSIFIED        ].

PILOT (02:49): Cool... Does kinda look like he's gonna turn south here, huh, maybe? ... No? *Expletive*, I can't tell.

SENSOR (02:49): I've got a great idea.

MC (02:49): They could got spooked earlier and called it off.

SENSOR (02:50): Come on back, day-TV. I'm gonna NUC the IR cameras while we're there. Perfect.

PILOT (02:50): Yeah they are turning south, huh?

MC (02:50): Yep.

MC (02:50): There's a road.

PILOT (02:50): Jag25, kirk97. Be advised, it looks like the road we are following currently trending to the south, so uhh back to the south at this time.

SENSOR (02:50): Where'd that third vehicle go?

JAG25 (02:51): Roger, and also the range of it.

SENSOR (02:51): There it is.

PILOT (02:51): RA-nge, from uhh... can you check from them?

MC (02:51): Yep... If I can get my tool to work... Six miles.

PILOT (02:51): And Jag25, Kirk27. Current range from the, uhh, nearest friendlies now six nautical miles.

JAG25 (02:51): Roger.

PILOT (02:51): Thanks dude.

MC (02:51): No problem.

PILOT (02:52): Dude I really don't know man... Maybe he's gonna take this valley to the south and run? Or if they're going to go back towards our guys, or what?

PILOT (02:52): Thirteen-hundred's our new land time.

SENSOR (02:52): According to that drop.

PILOT (02:52): 'kay.

MC (02:53): Yeah it's still following.

SENSOR (02:53): Yeah I showed 'em that two minutes ago.

MC (02:54): Looks like they're bringing a Reaper in.

SENSOR (02:54): You gotta be kiddin' me!

MC (02:54): As well up here.

SENSOR (02:54): Who?

MC (02:54): Warhawk.

SENSOR (02:54): Warhawk's a Reaper callsign?

MC (02:54): Yep.

SENSOR (02:54): *Expletive*.

MC (02:54): 42nd Attack Squadron, *expletive*.

SENSOR (02:54): *Expletive* that, man.

MC (02:54): Just claim we're here first.

MC (02:54): At least we know these guys have weapons.

[Unknown] (02:55): (Muffled talking off comms, some profanity, a chuckle.)

SENSOR (02:55): We got one person on the path... They're just passing by... No interaction with any of the vehicles.

SENSOR (02:58): About a mile or so they might have a chance to turn east. I think there's a road that cuts through these ridges and goes over the open flight area, we'll see if that happens.

PILOT (02:58): Copy.

SENSOR (02:58): Hey, that dude just put a weapon down right above the truck. See it?

PILOT (02:59): See it. See if DGS will call that.

SENSOR (02:59): I think that was there when he walked by it. Come on, focus, get better.

PILOT (02:59): Jag 25, Kirk 97. Be advised all three vehicles are stopped at this time a few of the pax are dismounting it looks like they're taking a break real quick. We'll keep you updated. See if we can PID something.

JAG25 (02:59): Jag 25 copies.

SENSOR (02:59): This is where I can see the most people so I'm gonna try to stay here and get some decent PID... That's about the best picture I've seen here all night.

SENSOR (03:00): The MAMs who've dismounted had possible. But try to get more dudes and see. More dudes more chances.

SENSOR (03:01): Aww where is he going? Just pulling off the road maybe. They probably mostly left their weapons in the vehicles. I'll be damned, it looks like a short dude back there. He's over the rocks.

PILOT (03:01): I see him.

JAG25 (03:02): Kirk 97, Jag 25.

PILOT (03:02): Jag 25, go ahead for Kirk 97.

SENSOR (03:02): Checking out the tire.

JAG25 (03:02): Roger. Those vehicles you're looking at, is there any possibility that they're ANP from further north?

SENSOR (03:02): I don't think so. They may not be in uniform, but they're at least more uniform than this when it's ANP.

PILOT (03:02): And uh, Jag 25. Kirk 97. It's our assessment that they are not ANP. Nobody's in any uniforms, none of the vehicles match. We will look into it with our screeners but we don't think so.

JAG25 (03:02): Alright. Just wanna make sure.

SENSOR (03:03): They're saying one MAM passed rifle to another MAM.

PILOT (03:03): And Jag25. Yea understand. We are checking on that for you. Be advised, our screener did see one MAM pass a rifle to another MAM. Other than that nothing else PID outside the vehicles yet.

PILOT (03:03): You think that was something right there? The one on the right-hand side, now on the passenger's side door had something big.

SENSOR (03:03): I wonder if they're having an issue with that tire. They all seem to be pretty interested in it.

PILOT (03:04): And Jag25, for Kirk 97. From the crew and from our DGS screeners, that's a neg on ANP.

JAG25 (03:04): Roger, good copy. Negative on ANP. And Kirk 97 also are you able to ascertain the demographic of all the occupants in the vehicle? Over.

PILOT (03:05): Check with the screener on that.

PILOT (03:05): Jag 25 standby one. Kirk 97, we're checking. Looks mostly to be military aged males. We have seen approximately two children. Standby.

PILOT (03:05): Dude the only thing I can see if this isn't something [expletive deleted] is the locals trying to get away. You know what I mean? But I don't think so.

[Unknown] (03:06): They all look likes males at least... no females [very faint].

PILOT (03:06): Did he ever give you a count on how many people he thought there were?

SENSOR (03:06): 24 or 25 at the praying stop.

SENSOR (03:07): [ CLASSIFIED ] view I saw the one that looked short enough to be a child.

PILOT (03:07): Jag25, Kirk 97.

SENSOR (03:07): At least 21 in the field of view. Looking at the other vehicles real quick.

PILOT (03:08): Jag 25, Kirk 97.

JAG25 (03:08): Jag 25.

PILOT (03:08): And Jag 25, our screeners are currently calling 21 MAMs, no females, and 2 possible children. How copy?

JAG25 (03:08): Roger. And when we say children, are we talking teenagers or toddlers?

SENSOR (03:08): I would say about twelve. Not toddlers. Something more towards adolescents or teens.

PILOT (03:08): Yeah adolescents.

PILOT (03:08): And Jag25, Kirk 97. Looks to be potential adolescents. We're thinking early teens. How copy?

SENSOR (03:09): Screener agrees. Adolescents. There's still a couple of stragglers at the other vehicles. Still upwards at 24–25 people.

JAG25 (03:09): Kirk 97, Jag 25.

PILOT (03:09): Go for Kirk 97.

JAG25 (03:09): Roger. That's our main interest right now, are these vehicles and where they're heading to. We already know we have PID [radio lost].

SENSOR (03:10): Pretty satisfied on just the weapons calls we made then.

PILOT (03:10): And Jag 25, Kirk 97. We copied the first half of your transition. Understand you're focused on the vehicles and have established PID please repeat the rest.

JAG25 (03:10): Kirk 97, that's affirmative, from the weapons we've identified and the demographic of the individuals plus the ICOM.

SENSOR (03:10): Plus the ICOM.

PILOT (03:10): And Kirk 97, good copy on that. We are with you. Our screener updated only one adolescent so that's one double-digit age range. How copy?

JAG25 (03:10): We'll pass that along to the ground force commander. But like I said, 12–13 years old with a weapon is just as dangerous.

SENSOR (03:11): Oh we agree. Yea.

PILOT (03:11): Hey, Kirk 97. Good copy on that. We understand and agree.


# Appendix I: Disposition Matrix (Drone Lexicon)

**Unmanned Aerial Vehicle (UAV):** Known colloquially as drones, UAVs are flown remotely by "pilots" or automatically by computers. The Central Intelligence Agency and US military employ UAVs for reconnaissance and combat missions.

**Predator:** An unmanned aerial vehicle (UAV) built by General Atomics in 1995. Used primarily by the US Air Force and CIA for special reconnaissance, it was later upgraded to carry missiles, cluster bombs, and other munitions.

**Reaper:** A larger UAV in use by the US Air Force and CIA since 2007, the Reaper has greater cruising speed and weapons-employment capabilities.

**AGM-114 Hellfire Missile:** The air-to-surface missile carried by Predator and Reaper drones. Its original name, "Helicopter Launched, Fire and Forget Missile," led to the acronym "Hellfire."

**Cluster munitions:** A weapon containing multiple explosive submunitions. Dropped from aircraft or fired from the ground, submunitions break in mid-air, saturating areas larger than several football fields. Journalist Jeremy Scahill describes cluster bombs as "flying landmines."

**Naugahyde Barcalounger**: The simulated "cockpit" terminals in the command center at Creech Air Force Base in Nevada, where "pilots" operate drones stationed remotely in Afghanistan and elsewhere. Drone operators wear the same flight suits as fighter pilots.

**Bugsplat**: Name of the software used by the CIA and US Defense Department to model and calculate collateral damage (civilian death) produced by aerial attacks. The term is also used to describe a successful kill by a drone missile.

**Targeted Killing**: A term used by the CIA and US military for the extrajudicial assassination of a known individual.

**Signature Strike**: A term for an intended lethal strike against an individual whose identity may be unknown but whose behavior fits a pattern that suggests to the CIA or the US military that he/she is involved in terrorist activities. The *New York Times* reports that the White House "counts all military-age males in a strike zone as combatants." CIA officials also use the term "crowd killing" as a synonym for signature strikes.

**Double Tap**: A term that designates multiple attacks on the same target with the intention of maximizing casualties by prohibiting medical aid to the wounded.

**Disposition Matrix**: A database of suspected terrorists to be traced, captured, rendered, or eliminated in drone strikes carried out by the US government. The database coordinates the so-called "kill lists" maintained by JSOC and the CIA, and was originally conceived by former National Counterterrorism Center (NCTC) director Michael E. Leiter.

"Marx said that revolutions are the locomotive of world history. But perhaps things are very different. It may be that revolutions are the act by which the human race travelling in the train applies the emergency brake."

—WALTER BENJAMIN

# Vergil

## TRANSLATED BY DAVID HADBAWNIK

### Aeneid I.1

[*As the action begins in the Aeneid, Juno
rouses the winds to a great storm out of her
enduring rage at Aeneas and the remnants
of Troy. Aeneas watches in terror as his fleet
breaks up in the waves and rocks.*]

*Aeneae solvuntur frigore membra*

Clouds snatched sun from the sky.
    dark night reigned over all
    creased by thunder
    and lighting—all things threatened
    the men with instant death.

Aeneas got scared.
Limbs loosened in fear, he
groaned, bent over and
puked over the boat's
edge. "Why" he said
    "couldn't I have met death
    on Trojan soil, poured out
    my soul by your sword,

Diomede, alongside Hector
and all the others...?"

He still talked that way while
waves hung them
high in the air
opening pockets of earth
they swung over—the south wind
turned three ships onto
hidden rocks and right before
Aeneas' eyes a huge wall
of water struck his ship
        hurling
the pilot headlong
over the side
        a vast whirlpool
churned and men scattered
swimming in the abyss, mingled with
weapons  treasure        and broken
            bits of ship.

Then Neptune caught wind of it.
Calling all storms, he
ordered them to stop
                    right now.

Just like when a riot breaks out
and the rabble rage drunk on
their own anger—stones
and fire fly, madness making
weapons of whatever's
ready to hand—then
if they behold a man
moving among them with
quiet dignity, they fall
silent and stand close,
pricking up their ears—
    just so
Neptune calmed the whole hubbub
of waves, routed the clouds and brought back
the sun, lifted the ships and
smoothed the seas.

And Aeneas' tired guys
struggled to pick their way
along the coast, towards Libya

# Aeneid IV.5

[*Dido describes the last moments before her death.*]

*Moriemur inultae, sed moriamur*

Night took tired souls.
I lie awake, love swelling inside me
again in a great black wave
   of hate. What
should I do? Crawl back
to a former lover I'd already spurned?
Follow the fleet like a pathetic whore?
     No.   *Die,*
         *as you deserve—not for you*
         *the guiltless rutting of wild animals,*
         *only marriage vows, broken.*

By the time I pace to the lookout
they're already gone, ships
stirring up foam on the water
at first light, the harbor
       empty.

I beat my breasts, tear out
my beautiful blonde hair
cursing the gods and debating
whether to take up arms
and follow them. Check it out!
This is the guy they say
brought gods of his homeland
with him and lowered his shoulders
to carry his aging dad.
Couldn't I have seized him
when I had the chance, torn up
his body and sprinkled it

on the waves? Why didn't I
slice up Ascanius and serve him
to his father at banquet?

And then offed myself...

I curse Aeneas one last time, him
and all his descendants. Let shores
clash with shores, arms
arms. Let him die, but not before
he's stripped of Ascanius, not before
he sees innocent friends killed
simply and awfully, not until
he realizes there's no peace
in his chosen land. Rise up,
Carthage, after I'm gone,
and piss on the bones of his
descendants. That's the promise
I ask for this heart that still runs
hot with all of your blood.

Then I
turn to my own death, sending a nurse
to fetch Anna so we can at last
complete the bogus rites.
Mounting the platform, I address
the left-behind stuff:
        "Sweet mementoes, accept my spirit.
        I lived
                how I lived. Now my soul
        will go on to Hades.
        I founded this great city,
        built walls, exacted vengeance
        for my husband and tribute
        from enemies. I would've been happy,
        too happy, if Trojan ships
        had never touched shore.
        Now it pleases me to
        go down to hell.
        We die unavenged,
        but let us die."

And I fall on a Trojan sword
and that's how they find me,
spewing blood and gore
on my hands. Rumor
shakes the city, great wails
rising from every quarter.
Anna bursts in, scratching
her face with her nails.

"Why did you lie to me,
sister? Was this your own
funeral pyre, all along?
Why not take me with you—
hell, why not take all of us?
Show me the wounds that
I might wash them and
catch your last breath."

Blood, piss, shit
gush out of me staining
her dress. I lift my eyes.
Three times I try to lift
my body, three times I fall
back on the couch, gazing
up at the heavens.
Juno at last has mercy, sends
Iris to loosen my limbs
from my spirit. She flies
down trailing colors
that glisten in morning dew.

Iris clips a lock of my hair
with her right hand
and all at once the heat
eases and my life
flies away in the wind

—*end book IV*—

# The Problem of Dido

## TISA BRYANT

Somewhere, in the Continuum of our now, two girls sit for a portrait on their uncle's massive Kenwood estate, along the grounds of Hampstead Heath, London. The painter, Johann Zoffany, places one cousin, Lady Elizabeth Finch Hatton, gently on the right edge of a painted wood structure, a trellis, a high-backed bench. Her dress is a corseted pink and white affair, featuring a triangular bodice of white lace atop pink silk brocade, covered by a thin layer of gossamer gloss.

"Pretend to run," Zoffany says to her, "as a lady would run." The young Lady Elizabeth, negotiating around the apparatus of her skirt, attempts to bend, pressing a knee against the fabric of her skirts. It's an awkward stance, not fully seated nor standing. It's a kind of lunge.

"I'm not... comfortable," she says irritably.

"Yes. And... ?" Zoffany begins, conducting her expression with an upward sweep of his hands. Lady Elizabeth faces us. Her eyes are large, brown, and soft, her hair adorned with tea roses at the crown. Her cheeks pink, her lips red, her chin slightly cleft, the double strand of pearls around her neck nearly blend in with her skin. Her right hand holds an open book in her lap. Poetry. Or myth.

"Now here." He takes her right hand and tucks it to rest on her cousin Dido Elizabeth Belle Lindsay's crooked elbow, not closely, but at arms length.

Zoffany places in Dido's right arm a shallow bowl of peaches and figs with sprigs of new oak and grapes hanging over the edge. "What am I to do with this?" she asks.

"Just *hold* it," the painter responds impatiently.

Dido glances at Lady Elizabeth's book, then back again at the bowl of fruit in her hands. She pouts. Zoffany's hands orchestrate Dido's body into a stride, which is easier for her than it was for Lady Elizabeth. Dido's dress is nothing like her cousin's; it is without bone, corset, or triangular bodice. It is devoid of white lace or even a hint of pink. Dido's dress is of a satin pajama variety in silver gray, with a waistline and drape reminiscent of Greco-Roman sculpture. Her skirt is without the layers of petticoats the day required to hold fabric away from flesh, as was the fashion for ladies, at least on the bottom. Dido's dress clings indecently to her form, the shape of her legs and backside visible under her dress. Zoffany produces a beaded turban from his trunk of notions, of the kind often seen in Orientalist paintings by Delacroix. Young Lady Elizabeth gasps; Dido makes a sound of resignation. The painter covers Dido's thick, braid-coiled chignon with the turban, its one maribou feather punctuating the top of her head, pointing down at her, exclaiming. Last, he waves his hands about her deadpan face in an upwards motion until her lips curl up enough to show her dimple. Zoffany takes her left hand, and puts her index finger impishly to rest beside her mouth.

"You certainly look silly!" Lady Elizabeth says indignantly, looking first at Zoffany, then at Dido, who returns her cousin a knowing look. Then they burst into laughter. Zoffany is amused, exasperated, then stern. He hasn't much time. Giggling, the noble pair manage to pull the painter's contrivance back together, their eyes still gleaming. Dido looks mischievously at us. Her eyes are large, brown, and soft, her hair concealed beneath a feathered, beaded turban. Her cheeks pink, her lips coral, her chin slightly cleft, the single strand of pearls around her neck stands out away from her lovely brown skin.

Zoffany hurriedly sketches the scene. Their gaze impresses upon his charcoal their similar faces, and yet the narrative he constructs contradicts itself. Lady Elizabeth could be touching Dido's arm affectionately, or pushing her away. They might be equals in all things, but they are dressed to show marked social difference. It's an ambiguous stance, often interpreted as loving, this portrait of interracial family during the time of England's colonial, slave-trading dominion. Beyond them, a bridge over water, a hillside, the tiny detail of London in the distance. Dido does not appear seated at her white cousin's feet, but a sign of true affection between the two is a bit hard to come by. The space between their bodies, measured by Elizabeth's outstretched arm, helps us read the myth of it. Faraway, so close.

---

There is another story of a young girl from Senegal, Ourika, who was adopted by French nobles and raised in splendor. She died, it seems, from unknown causes (despair, out of the kumbla?) at age sixteen. What survives is Claire de Duras's written, fictionalized version of the tale, *Ourika*, which she learned and often told to entertain her guests. Ourika is adopted by one Mme. De B. of France and raised as a young lady of French society, albeit a sequestered one, where only family and friends delight in her company. Ourika was raised to feel herself equal to her brother and others. She's not conscious of her difference. But de Duras, through the mouth of Ourika, speaks the code to her audience:

"Dressed in oriental costume, seated at her feet, I used to listen—long before I could understand it—to the conversation of the most distinguished men of the day."

Ourika doesn't dress in the European fashion for company, nor does she sit in a chair, a self-contained subject. Instead she's perhaps garbed in satin harem pajamas and a turban, on the floor at her benefactress's feet. A pose of gratitude worthy of a... Chevalier de B. had rescued Ourika, a toddler, from slavery, as she was being taken aboard a ship. Her mother had just died, that minute, hour, day, nameless, faceless, graveless. Ourika has no memory of anything but the lavish estate she lives on.

---

It's 1779. The Queen of England has unfortunate Moorish features. It's a time when many now living in London believed there were no Africans present there. No slaves. And a time when black people are snatched from London's streets and "returned" to slavery in the West Indies, whether they'd known it before or not. Dido knows only Kenwood, where she is kept safe. She is twenty-four years old. Zoffany finishes his studies for the painting and at last the ladies are free to go. Dido goes to her rooms to change into something proper, leaving Zoffany's costume to a servant for its return to him. She hurries down the back stairs and down the rear hall to her great-uncle's study to take his letters for the day. Her great-uncle is William Murray, known throughout British society, and the judiciary, as Lord Mansfield. She knocks upon the study door.

"Yes, Dido. Come," replies Lord Mansfield.

His nephew, Sir John Lindsay of the Royal Navy, is Dido's father. He captured a Spanish vessel and found a black woman, perhaps beautiful, perhaps a recaptured slave or kidnapped African princess, on board. A not-free, not-me woman. No one will say that Sir John Lindsay raped her, regardless of whether or not she was beautiful, or a slave. If we are to imagine it at all, we are to conjure a romance.

*My darling, at last you've come. I thought you'd never find me. I've dreamt of you day and night, without ever knowing whether you were real. But I recognize you, my love, my savior! Deliver me from this captivity, and keep me with you always.*

We are to imagine that something like *this* took place between a black woman from an undisclosed nation, likely non-English speaking, found on a captured Spanish ship, and a high-ranking naval officer with a chequered past. This brief encounter produced Dido Elizabeth Belle Lindsay, whose father, for reasons unknown, saw fit to both claim his biracial child *and* give her a name similar to her titled white cousin's. Then he left Dido in the care of the William Murrays and went back to running in the seas.

She was not left to follow the condition of her mother. She enters her great-uncle's study. No one seems to remember exactly what Dido's mother's condition was, how it might have improved, or worsened, after John Lindsay's touch. What her name was. Where she was when she gave birth. She seems to have simply disappeared from memory. Disappeared from care. Do you remember her, Dido? The years go back. It is 1772. After caring for the goats and chickens, a job she's reported to have enjoyed, she changes and knocks on her uncle's study. The room is consumed with papers about James Somerset, a former slave on British soil, threatened with a return to slavery by his former owner. Lord Mansfield settled Somerset's problem by granting him freedom, but let the question of slavery itself stand. Did you plug your ears, then, Dido? Or did you hear the talk? Did you cover your eyes, or did you read the papers? Did you clamp your mouth shut, or did you dare, just once, to speak on it? Your problem, Dido, is why it seems crucial to enclose the maximum area of your biography within a fixed boundary of silence.

The years go by.

"Naturally the presence of a black woman enjoying the close confidence of Mme de B. had to be explained," Ourika tells the doctor who's come to her convent to cure her of dying. "These explanations martyred me."

She realizes that she's African, and that fact becomes her illness. Only hers. Her hands seem to her monkey paws. "She exaggerates her ugliness," but her looks are not described by anyone in any terms. Where does her understanding of blackness equaling ugliness come from? Ourika sympathizes with the uprising in Haïti, yet feels shame for belonging to a race of murderous savages. She hates herself, not the fact of racism. *You're absolutely not our type. No one in France can identify with you.* It makes her sick.

Mme de B., speaking to her more blunt acquaintance, admits to being troubled, worried, about Ourika's marriage prospects, but is incapable of anything more. There's no Oroonoko in her future, no Equiano or any other possible equal. The fixed boundary of de Duras's literary imagination contains the maximum possibility for Ourika's happiness. Ourika becomes animal, a black angel of death, but she's not roaming in Melville's jungle, saving immoral white men from themselves. It's her own life that she must sacrifice. To save her neck during the French Revolution, however, Claire de Duras returned to her mother's native land, Martinique, to claim a sizeable inheritance. But for Ourika, in the end, it's the nunnery or nothingness.

Dido knocks on the study door, enters. It's 1781. The *Zong* case is on Lord Mansfield's table: an insurance suit for "lost" cargo during a storm: slaves preemptively thrown overboard though alive during a Middle Passage run gone bad. The slave ship's name is actually *Zorg*, Dutch for "care," but the British can't see that. Her great-uncle stands by the leaded window of his study, lost in thought. Young Lady Elizabeth will marry soon, leaving Kenwood, and arm-in-arm strolls with Dido, behind. And me, Dido thinks. What about me? What is to be my future?

"I didn't regret being black," Ourika says. "I was told I was an angel... I didn't know then that these innocent studies would ripen into such bitter fruit." Mme de B. throws Ourika a ball. They do an African dance, the comba, composed of stately steps, which require that she strike a pose signifying an emotion, grief, love, triumph, despair. A kind of Senegalese forebear to vogueing. *La verité: un jeu.* Out-of-the-kumbla: What is the pose for this feeling? Where on your body do you put your hand? Her white dance partner wears a mask of black crepe. Ourika strikes a pose, thinking nothing of it.

*I was told I was an angel.* Dido lets her hand wander over the stacks of writs and decrees, decisions and denials. *My father hasn't come for some time.* Her hand wanders over slavery's documentation as if divining, waiting for sensation, information, to rise up from ink and parchment and into her veins. *Care. Mother. Zorg. Zong. Care not. Something of me began here.* In the papers of William Murray is a letter of manumission for Dido, and, in his will, a bequeath to her of £500, and £100 a year for life. It will be at least ten years, when the Murrays are near death, nearly out of her care, before Dido strikes out into the world on her own, a good forty years before the abolition of slavery. She marries a Charles Davinier (French? Martinican or Haïtian *gens de couleur*?), who risks it, who is himself the risk, or simply loves her, either way. He's clearly not after her money; her purse is rather light. They have children. They manage to pass through time undetected, ignored, or simply accepted as people. Dido's line is somehow secreted away, into the mainstream. In the 1970s, her gravesite is razed for a redevelopment scheme. No roses, seen? But plenty of Violets.

Somewhere in the Continuum of the Imaginary, Princess Tam Tam swings in a cage, singing of Haïti. "If I truly possesses some superiority of mind," Ourika opines, "some hidden quality, then it would be appreciated when my color no longer isolated me, as it had until then, in the heart of society." Ourika sits by her window, reflecting. Outside it is day; she sees only fearsome night. Her smooth skin and bright eyes beam from the clear windowpane, but her vision is filled with monsters barely contained by the French government's *Code Noir*.

There will be guests *ce soir*, Dido muses. The horses nod in the stable, the chickens she's just fed burble and cluck in the yard of their house. She sits on a low stool in the cow pasture, drinking her rose congou tea and nibbling at oatcakes dished on a tray resting in her lap. Kenwood Estate lumbers solidly along the tamed green hillside at her back. Her cousin, ensconced in the still pressure of the sitting room, pokes needle and red thread through a taut hoop of muslin, dreamlessly waiting to be married. It will be dinner, then, she continues, alone in the kitchen. Then only after I'll be seen, all charm and sparkling wit, to entertain the nobles whose sensibilities were just thoroughly plied with fine foods. Only then will it be time for me. Then I'll come out and show off my accomplishments.

Ourika tells her doctor she would have preferred to labor on a plantation, for then she would have a hut to go to at the end of her day, a man of her own race to love her, children to kiss. "Why hadn't I been left to follow my own destiny?"

---

After another long evening, Dido returns to her room to conjure, as she often does, a world she's pieced together from the bits that come to her from the guests. Hints and whispers, oblique repartees, fearful pronouncements of slavery's descent on British soil. At daybreak, she sits singing by her window, *I am here. Where are you?* a glittering soprano, stringing vowels like jewels on clear thread, an invisible garland carried through London's airs. *I am here.* Francis Barber, Samuel Johnson's black servant and heir, turns on his heel at the sound, dictionary in hand. Each utterance of the line is a measure of her maximum area, her unknown biography taking shape. *Where are you?* Barbadian madame Rachel Pringle leaving her brothel, on her way to secure publication for Mary Prince's slave narrative, stops to inspect the sky. *I am here.* Elizabeth Rosina "Bronze" Clements pauses from cleaning Royal Academy sculptor Joseph Nollekens's miserly kitchen. Dido calls. To her mother's image and Ourika's spirit. Dido calls out into the Continuum from the fixed boundary of her human life. To all the other unexplained presences living in isolation, living in community, in and out of the kumbla, beyond her ken, beyond Kenwood. ⬡

# Unknown Race Male

## MITCHELL INCLÃN

**T**his is your new home in Seattle. It is an apartment complex located next to a bar called Waid's. When you read the requirements for tenancy application, a simple sentence stood out to you. Households must have monthly income of at least 2.5 times the rent and must not exceed 60 percent of area median income limits. This sentence is nearly incomprehensible to you, like an image hidden inside a painting, visible after staring at it endlessly. You are able to afford living there, you know that much, but it is not something you would brag about at the bar.

On the last day of February you walk outside your brand-new apartment building, eager to explore your new city. It happens almost instantly at six in the evening, too early and too bright for this type of situation. You later describe him to the police as an unknown race male, wearing a gray hoodie and dark blue jeans with a design running down the side. He threw you to the ground face first and you barely managed to lift your hands to blunt the fall. In the bathroom a few hours later, you rub alcohol on the cuts to your palms and forearms. While you are down on the sidewalk, he takes the smartphone and wallet from your back pockets. When you look up he is running away, nothing more than a blur of gray hoodie and dark blue jeans with a design running down the side.

The man is never caught. Many people in your building believe all the crime around the building comes from the bar next door. You have been to Waid's before and had a good time dancing with strangers. You don't agree with your neighbors but they don't listen to you and insist that drug dealers and gangsters frequent this bar. It's not as if you try very hard to convince them otherwise, and if you pressed the issue any further, they would probably accuse you of calling them racists. Waid is a black Haitian man and there weren't so many white people on the dance floor the nights you were there, so you suspect that maybe they are racist.

March arrives and you try to feel at ease in your neighborhood but it is difficult. You notice yourself flinching whenever you see a gray hoodie and sense someone walking towards you quickly. It is difficult to expel this anxiety and so you try a variety of things. You begin dressing in frumpy clothes, you visit the parts of Seattle your neighbors consider dangerous, you go to Waid's every Saturday night, and eventually you start wearing a gray hoodie. But despite all of your efforts, you still see him out there, bringing sweat to your armpits and quickening the beat of your heart.

One afternoon near the end of March, the Seattle Police Department sends you a terse, institutional email. Your phone reported stolen on February 28th has been located. Your phone can be retrieved at the East Precinct. You call the precinct for a response but are unable to reach anyone. Later that evening you go to the precinct and collect your phone from the red-faced cop working the front desk. It is in the same condition as when you last held its silver and black frame, but when you turn it on, you realize all of your information has been erased. It is an entirely new phone.

"How do you know this is my phone?" you ask the cop.

"We can keep it here if it's not yours."

"No, it's my phone, but none of my information is there anymore."

The telephone rings, the cop answers it, and you instantly grow frustrated. There is no point in remaining at the precinct so you head back to your apartment. You scour the local blogs looking for answers until you stumble on the SPD crime blotter and find them.

It seems as if the man who stole your phone took it to a place called One-Stop Wireless in Little Saigon. According to the SPD, people would line up every morning at 10 and wait to sell whatever electronic commodity they had stolen the night before. When the cops raided the shop, they found over 800 computers and phones waiting to be resold to anyone with access to this black-market network. It occurs to you that no one has ever offered you a stolen phone, nor have you ever known a thief in person. Illuminated by this simple thought, you begin to randomly scroll through the SPD crime blotter until you find something entirely different.

A few nights before, someone tried to burn down an under-construction apartment complex just up the hill from your own building. They threw two Molotov cocktails at the structure but only one of the devices shattered. Because of the rains that had recently drenched the city, the fire did not spread and the structure was not destroyed. In your imagination, you see the man in the gray hoodie throwing a bottle of fire at a shadowy construction site. No matter how hard you try, you cannot visualize his face, even when it is lit by flame. But then you realize what must obviously be true. The person in the gray hoodie was a woman. This is when you actually see her.

At first it is like a dream, but there she is, standing on the corner, just below your third-floor window, and not only is she there, but she is looking at you, clearly smiling. In her hand is a cell phone and over her skinny frame is the same gray hoodie she wore a month ago. With her eyes locked on your own, she raises her free hand and waves at you. In this moment, you fall in love. ⬡

John Criscitello, *Welcome Rich Kids*, 2014, *Wish You Weren't Here*, 2015

# Hole Poems

## CATHY WAGNER

# REKIA BOYD

her too—   eveRyone's too—

noisy  when you'rE

drunK discharging yr off-duty duties

Servin the people of chIcago

in voluntary slAughter

her Boyfriend heard   tho

on his phone   that's nOt a gun   you might have heard

you might have heard

in voluntary dYing

shoulD be noisier

# JOHN CRAWFORD

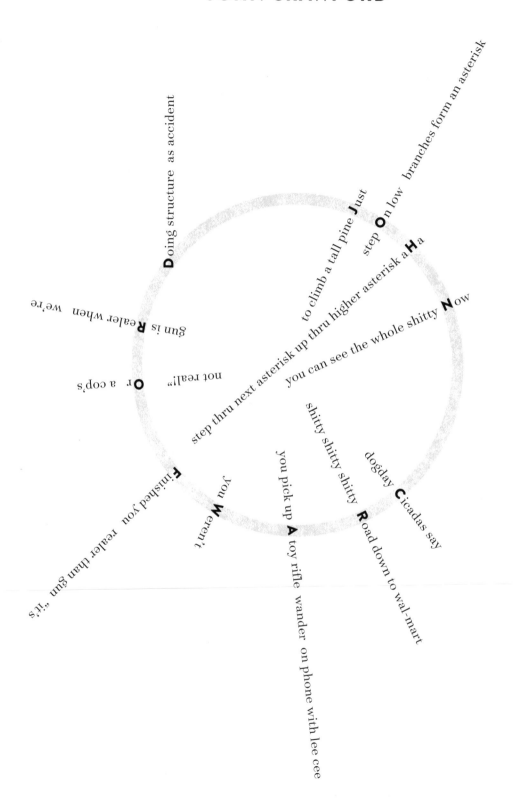

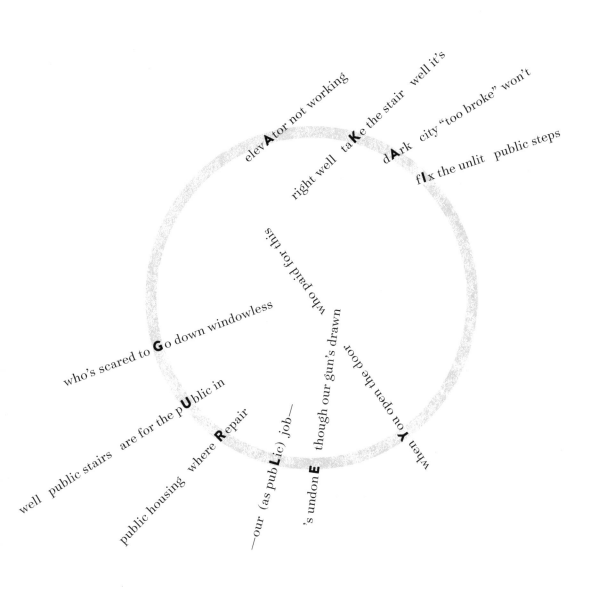

# AKAI GURLEY

elevAtor not working

right well taKe the stair  well it's

dArk  city "too broke" won't

fIx the unlit  public steps

when You open the door

though our gun's drawn

who paid for this

's undonE

—our (as pubLic) job—

public housing  where Repair

well  public stairs  are for the pUblic in

who's scared to Go down windowless

# ERIC GARNER

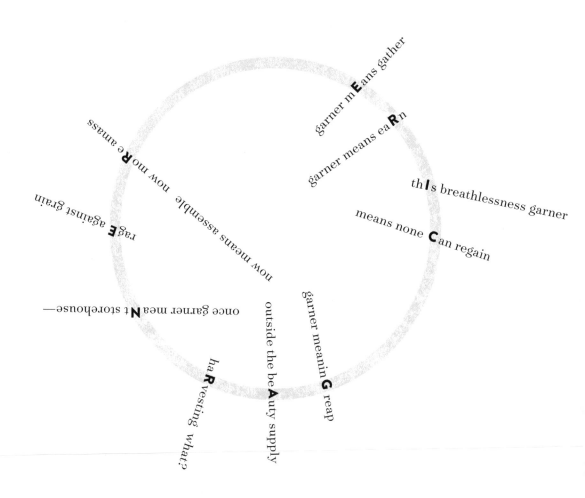

# AMADOU DIALLOU

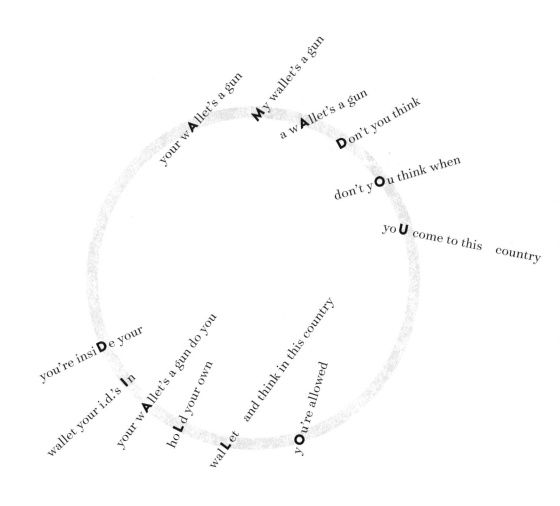

your w**A**llet's a gun **M**y wallet's a gun a w**A**llet's a gun **D**on't you think don't y**O**u think when yo**U** come to this country and think in this country y**O**u're allowed wal**L**et ho**L**d your own your w**A**llet's a gun do you wallet your i.d.'s **I**n you're insi**D**e your

# The Process of Domination Spews out Tatters of Subjugated Nature:

## Critical Theory, Negative Totality, & the State of Extraction

### CHRIS O'KANE

**M**ost contemporary evaluations of Theodor W. Adorno's critical theory in the Anglophone world are indelibly shaped by the peculiar contours of its initial reception in the 1960s, which can be said to frame not only how Adornian critical theory is interpreted, but also how its legacy is conceived.[1] Let's consider two shibboleths of this hegemonic reception. The first is that *Dialectic of Enlightenment* (1944) marks the point at which Adorno (and his co-author Max Horkheimer) abandoned Marxism. This claim, which has its roots in the radical student milieu, criticizes Adorno's pessimistic cultural theory, and suggests that his analysis of the totally integrated reified consciousness of the proletariat led to his abandonment of praxis, and with it Marxism, for residence in the hotel grand abyss. The second shibboleth, as codified by Jürgen Habermas and others, is that the narrative of instrumental reason that replaces Ador-

---

1   The following is based on a talk I gave at the Institute for the Humanities at Simon Fraser University in the summer of 2014, and draws on my article "State Violence, State Control: Marxist State Theory and the Critique of Political Economy" in Viewpoint 4 (2014). I would like to thank Eirik Steinhoff for his helpful comments.

no's Marxism is so totalizing that it eschews a normative basis and discounts emancipatory elements of contemporary society, such as democracy and mutual recognition, which subsequent generations of "critical theory" have taken up. While these two interpretations differentiate themselves in many ways, they also coincide on several points that might be said, without too much exaggeration, to form the dominant Anglophone take on Adorno's late work: He abandoned Marx in favor of a totalizing one-dimensional cultural theory that must be modified or re-thought if it is to be of any relevance today.

I hope to complicate this picture, first, by bringing to light what these approaches have obscured, namely the Marxian core of Adorno's late work, and second, by mapping the ways in which this Marxian element was taken up in a strand of critical theory largely neglected in the Anglophone world, which in contrast to these more familiar receptions of Adorno, can be said to have been inspired by, and sought to complete, the Marxian aspects of Adorno's critical theory. I do this by reconstructing a conversation between Adorno, Horkheimer, and their students about capitalism, the state, and the domination of nature, a conversation that has been taken up and continued by more recent writers to develop a critical theory of contemporary society as a "negative totality" that inexorably dominates nature. I close by aligning these theoretical developments and utilizing them to illuminate the Canadian state's energy policy as a manifestation of this negative totality's dynamic. My goal in undertaking this reconstruction is to demonstrate the vitality of this critical theory's analysis of the intertwined supraindividual political and economic logic of capitalist society, especially as it can be brought to bear on an area that is not only of utmost urgency to our contemporary moment, but which the approaches of intersubjective recognition and communicative action are ill-equipped to explain: the domination of nature.

## What Is Critical Theory?

Adorno's colleague Max Horkheimer lays out the initial conception of the critical theory of society held by the Frankfurt School in his seminal 1937 essay "Traditional and Critical Theory." Whereas traditional theory advocates "the better functioning of any element in the structure" of capitalist society, critical theory, by contrast, holds that "the goals of human activity, especially the idea of a reasonable organization of society that will meet the needs of the whole community, are immanent in human work" but have not been realized because "production is not geared to the life of the whole community while heeding also the claims of individuals." [2] Such an idea of critical theory is premised on a conception of society as that which is constituted by the manner in which humans interact with nature and with each other.

In this account of social constitution, Horkheimer implicitly draws on Marx's notion of the metabolism with nature—labor, for instance, is defined in *Capital* as "a process [...] by which man through his actions mediates, regulates and controls the metabolism between himself and nature" [3]—and he explicitly draws from Marx on a socio-theoretical and explanatory level to argue that capitalist society is constituted by exchange, and that "the inner dynamism" of "the exchange relationship," which critical theory is said to outline, "dominates social reality" with what Marx calls the "rigidity of a law." [4] These concepts are the "abstract determination[s]" which form the basis of the critical theory of society itself. The critical theory Horkheimer describes thus utilizes Marx to conceptualize society as a social totality arising from the metabolic interaction with nature, constituted by exchange, and perpetuated by the internal relationship between the economy and the capitalist state. As Horkheimer puts it in "broad terms," the critical theory of society expounds a "single existential judgement" by deducing present conditions and tensions as a "new barbarism" that is "unfolded from the concept of simple exchange," which itself arises from the "enormous extension of human control over nature." [5]

This tableau is taken up and most fully developed in Adorno's late work, particularly in his conception of social constitution, and of capitalist society as a "negative totality." While a broad understanding of these ideas runs through Adorno's work from his earliest writings to his last, it is after his return to Germany in the 1950s—following the publication of *Dialectic of Enlightenment* (1944)—that these ideas receive their most sophisticated formulation. Contrary to the critical caricature that claims that Adorno abandoned Marx, these late writings reveal Adorno's most explicit engagement with Marx's conceptualization of the metabolism with nature and of the "natural laws" of capitalism. This followed, above all, as a consequence of Adorno's relationship with his student, Alfred Schmidt. Between 1957 and 1960, Adorno and Horkheimer supervised Schmidt's Ph.D. thesis; thereafter Adorno would make consistent use of Schmidt's interpretation of "The Concept of Nature in Marx" (as his thesis was called) in order to refine and elaborate the conception of culture and society that Horkheimer had initiated in his 1937 essay.

2   Max Horkheimer, "Traditional and Critical Theory," in *Critical Theory: Selected Essays*, trans. Matthew J. O'Connell (New York: Continuum, 1972), 207, 213.

3   Karl Marx, *Capital: Volume 1*, trans. Ben Fowkes (London: Penguin, 1976), 283.

4   Horkheimer, 225. Marx, *Capital*, 284.

5   Horkheimer, 227.

Schmidt's influence is most evident in Adorno's account of the constitution of society in *Negative Dialectics* (1966). Here Adorno uses passages from Marx's account of the metabolism with nature often sourced from Schmidt's work on Marx. For instance, when Adorno famously claims in *Negative Dialectics* that "Marx recognized against Hegel" that "the objectivity of historical life is that of natural history," he is essentially paraphrasing Schmidt's analysis of Marx's account of the relationship between social constitution as a metabolic domination of nature and capitalist society as a dominating second nature.[6]

Let's see how this works. In *The Concept of Nature in Marx*, published as a book in 1962, Schmidt argues that Marx's idea of the metabolism with nature held that "the whole of nature is socially mediated and, inversely, society is mediated through nature as a component of total reality."[7] This is because Marx states that "by acting on the external world and changing it" humanity "at the same time changes his own nature."[8] Consequently, "In a wrongly organized society, the control of nature, however highly developed, remains at the same time an utter subjection to nature."[9] This means "that men are still not in control of their own productive forces vis-à-vis nature, that these forces confront them as the organized, rigid form of an opaque society, as a 'second nature' which sets its own essence against its creators."[10] Rather than social labour consciously and collectively constituting a society in which individuals are no longer prey to the caprice of contingencies and catastrophes that characterize nature, the unconscious creation of society premised on the uncoordinated domination of nature reinscribes predation in the catastrophic and antagonistic dynamic of the "natural laws" of society.

As Schmidt argues:

> Hegel described the first nature, a world of things existing outside men, as a blind conceptless occurrence. The world of men as it takes shape in the state, law, society, and the economy, is for him "second nature," manifested reason, objective Spirit. Marxist analysis opposes to this the view that Hegel's "second nature" should rather be described in the terms he applied to the first:

---

6   Theodor W. Adorno, *Negative Dialectics*, trans. Dennis Redmond, http://members.efn.org/~dredmond/ndtrans.html, 347.

7   Alfred Schmidt, *The Concept of Nature in Marx*, trans. Ben Fowkes (London: New Left Books, 1971), 79.

8   Ibid., 41. Here Schmidt is drawing on Marx, *Capital*, 283.

9   Schmidt, 42.

10   Ibid., 16.

namely, as the area of conceptlessness, where blind necessity and blind chance coincide. The "second nature" is still the "first." Mankind has still not stepped beyond natural history.[11]

Echoing Schmidt's interpretation of Marx, in *Negative Dialectics* (1966) Adorno characterizes the history of society as "the control of nature, progressing into domination over human beings and ultimately over humans' inner nature."[12] Society is thus construed in a Marxian vein insofar as its "Natural lawfulness is real [...] as a law of motion of unconscious society."[13] In these ways, Schmidt's interpretation of Marx influenced Adorno's formulation of his late, and most sophisticated, accounts of social constitution as the metabolic domination of nature and of capitalist *society* as an instance of dominating second nature.

The latter can be seen in greater detail by turning to examine how Adorno followed Horkheimer in conceiving of the dominating second nature of capitalist society as arising from the dynamism of exchange. This argument comes into view most clearly in Adorno's account of contemporary society in *Negative Dialectics* as well as in other essays and lectures from the 1960s. What Adorno refers to as "late capitalist society" in these works is characterized as an inverted and autonomous entity, a negative totality that opposes individuals as a second nature and dominates humans beings by compelling their actions. In these works, following Horkheimer, Adorno's account of capitalist society rests on his notion of exchange on both a socio-theoretical and explanatory level.

This late notion of exchange thus provides the grounds for Adorno's conception of the dynamic of the negative totality of capitalist society. As Adorno explains, providing a more developed account of Horkheimer's statement: "society, in its 'socialized' form [...] is determined, as its fundamental precondition, by exchange."[14] Consequently, "What really makes society a social entity, what constitutes it both conceptually and in reality, is the relationship of exchange, which binds together virtually all the people participating in this kind of society."[15] But Adorno does not argue that exchange does this binding on its own. Rather, he argues—again mirroring Horkheimer—that in the totally administered society of late capitalism, the state is integral to such a totality, which in its role as "total capitalist," acts to assure the accumulation of capital. This is because:

11  Ibid., 42–43.

12  Adorno, *Negative Dialectics*, 320.

13  Ibid., 355.

14  Theodor W. Adorno, *Introduction to Sociology*, trans. Edmund Jephcott (London: Polity, 2000), 31.

15  Ibid.

> Economic interventionism is not [...] something cobbled together
> from outside the system, but is rather system-immanent [...]. [T]he
> state, presumably intervening from beyond the reach of society's
> power-struggles, had to be conjured up out of the immanent dia-
> lectic of society in order to damper and police the antagonisms of
> such, lest society [...] disintegrate.[16]

Thus, according to Adorno, the political sphere and the economy do not exist in separate spheres or function for separate ends, nor do the actors within these spheres. Rather, since "everything is one"[17] this necessary interrelation between the state and the economy ensures they are all beholden to the systematic immanent imperatives of negative totality.

In Adorno's view, exchange is thus what makes capitalist society a negative totality. Exchange not only possesses social objectivity because it is the basis for social synthesis, it ultimately possesses its own autonomy, which Adorno describes as a "conceptuality which holds sway in reality itself."[18] This means that the "law which determines how the fatality of mankind unfolds itself is the law of exchange."[19] As Adorno further enumerates, this "negative primacy" of exchange also means that "individuals are subsumed under social production, which exists as a doom outside of them."[20] As a result, individuals are compelled to function in their respective social roles, what Adorno following Marx refers to as character-masks, such as workers or capitalists, to ensure their own survival. This, in turn, maims human psyches, or their own internal nature.

These points are brought together in Adorno's characterizations of modern society, as a whole, in *Negative Dialectics*:

> [T]he economic process, which reduces individual interests to
> the common denominator of a totality, which remains negative,
> because it distances itself by means of its constitutive abstrac-
> tion from the individual interests, out of which it is nevertheless
> simultaneously composed [...]. The violence of the self-realizing
> universal is not.[...] identical to the essence of individuals, but al-
> ways also contrary. They are not merely character-masks, agents
> of value, in some presumed special sphere of the economy. Even

---

**16**  Theodor W. Adorno, "Late Capitalism or Industrial Society?" https://www.marxists.org/reference/archive/adorno/1968/late-capitalism.htm.

**17**  Adorno, "Late Capitalism."

**18**  Theodor W. Adorno et al., *The Positivist Dispute in German Sociology*, trans. Glyn Adey and David Frisby (London: Harper & Row, 1976), 80.

**19**  Ibid.

**20**  Adorno, *Negative Dialectics*, 330.

where they think they have escaped the primacy of the economy, all the way down to their psychology, the *maison tolère* [French for "universal home"], of what is unknowably individual, they react under the compulsion of the generality; the more identical they are with it, the more un-identical they are with it in turn as defenceless followers. What is expressed in the individuals themselves, is that the whole preserves itself along with them only by and through the antagonism.[21]

This dense passage marks the culmination of this Marxian strand of Adorno's critical theory and with it the Marxian strand of the first generation of critical theory. Here we see a refinement of Horkheimer's socio-theoretical use of Marx. In Adorno's evocative expression, Horkheimer's notion of the "inner dynamism" of exchange arises from the domination of nature and is reflected in "the economic process" of the "constitutive abstraction of exchange" dominating reality as a negative totality which possesses an autonomous and contingent dynamic perpetuated by the internal relation between the state and the economy, which compels individuals actions by means of a second nature. We also see, in this exemplary instance, that Adorno's critical theory of society begins with exchange and unfolds to show how society dominates and maims individuals.

Yet, despite the evocative and all too palpable description of the negative totality that functions as a second nature by virtue of exchange as a doom hanging over us, such an account of contemporary society is ultimately enigmatic, undercutting the efficacy of Adorno's critique. This is because, in an echo of Horkheimer's broad conception of society conceived merely in terms of exchange, Adorno stresses that exchange is "what really makes society a social entity," and that such a conception of exchange as the key to society is what differentiates Frankfurt School critical theory from other types of sociology. However, Adorno never really made clear why and how exchange possesses these social properties, how it constitutes a totality. How and why this society functions as a negative totality forcing people to behave as character-masks thus remains undertheorized in Adorno's account. The closest he comes are in enigmatic references to Capital such as the following, which nevertheless aligns the "natural laws" of capitalist second nature to the behavioral rationality induced by economic imperatives: "Natural lawfulness is real however as a law of motion of unconscious society, as it is pursued in Capital from the analysis of the commodity form down to the theory of economic crisis in a phenomenology of the anti-Spirit."

21  Ibid., 305.

*A RECORD OF THE CATASTROPHE*

# The New German Reading: Backhaus and Reichelt

Adorno's underdeveloped account of capitalist social relations between nature, exchange, and the state undercuts the efficacy of his critical theory, insofar as it neglects to fully explicate this negative totality's dynamism. But it also leaves something for subsequent critical theorists to work on. Two students of Adorno, Hans-Georg Backhaus and Helmut Reichelt, found this explanatory gap to be indicative of the first generation of the Frankfurt School as a whole. As Reichelt would recall, when he and Backhaus first became interested in "*Capital-analysis*" as students at Frankfurt in the early 1960s, they "wanted to know in the first place what 'reification' really is." So they set about "systematically plaguing Horkheimer [...] and discovered [...] that after three sentences long silences set in, and that basically there was very little to learn from these theoreticians." [22] Moreover, as Reichelt later wrote, "Adorno [...] assumes that the whole economy is to be developed out of a principle—the exchange principle." [23] And yet:

> How this process of autonomisation is to be conceptualised in detail is not explained by Adorno: The central concepts—objective abstraction, inversion, autonomisation, totality, power of the universal over the particular—remain postulates with regard to their concretisation as far as the critique of economics is concerned. [24]

This gap motivated Reichelt and Backhaus to turn to an investigation of Marx's critique of political economy and his explanation of the dynamic of exchange in order to expand the explanatory power of Adorno's critical social theory. As Werner Bonefeld notes, "Adorno's *Negative Dialectics* did not just provide the theoretical catalyst for the New Reading. Rather, it provided both the incentive and the critical insight for the development of the critique of political economy as a critical social theory." [25] The reading of Marx that Reichelt and Backhaus uncover is consequentially shaped by their teacher's critical theoretical interpretations of Marx.

Reichelt's work on Marx's conception of social reality, begun in the late 1960s, provides a neat summation of how this New Reading of Marx conceived of Marx's critique of political economy as a critical theory of society. In this reading, which draws on Adorno, Marx's critique of political economy consists in a theory of the constitution of *social forms* that become

---

**22** Helmut Reichelt, "From the Frankfurt School to Value-Form Analysis," *Thesis Eleven* 4:1 (1982), 166.

**23** Helmut Reichelt, "Marx's Critique of Economic Categories: Reflections on the Problem of Validity in the Dialectical Method of Presentation in Capital," *Historical Materialism* 15:4 (2007), 5.

**24** Ibid., 6.

**25** Werner Bonefeld, *Critical Theory and the Critique of Political Economy* (London: Bloomsbury, 2014), 4.

autonomous and inverted, compelling and dominating individual bearers of these relations. As Reichelt sees it, "Marx pursued a programme of deciphering society. In this programme [...] the forms or categories of political economy [...] [were] identical with the critique of the inverted forms of social existence, an existence constituted by the life-practice of human beings."[26] Moreover, Reichelt holds that for Marx, "All these forms obtain as inverted form of a 'community' that is external to the individuals, and from which they must emancipate themselves in order ever to be able to interact with one another 'as individuals.'" Marx's project as a whole "is thus a matter of deciphering theoretically the appearance [*Schein*] of independence that this "surrogate of community" posits and then of expelling it practically from the world so that human beings will be able to enter into relationship with one another, not as character-masks, but as real individuals."[27] The critique of these forms of political economy, as a critical social theory, thus consists in deciphering why these forms arise and how they reproduce these very same conditions by dominating individuals.

Hans-Georg Backhaus, for his part, starting in 1963, put forward the influential argument that what he termed "the monetary theory of value" provided Marx's account of the genesis and reproduction of these forms in Marx's critique of political economy. Such a focus can be seen to follow from Horkheimer, and especially, Adorno's notion of exchange. Indeed, Backhaus often compares Adorno's account of the properties of the exchange abstraction with those of Marx. Yet, in contrast to Adorno, who only noted that "In developed societies the exchange takes place, as you all know, through money as the equivalent form,"[28] Backhaus's philological study of the different editions of *Capital* and of Marx's preparatory manuscripts (such as the Urtext, the *Grundrisse*, etc.) provides an account of why money is necessary and why its function as the "equivalent form" provides it with an autonomous social power that compels individuals' actions to reproduce the very society that maims them.

Crudely put, money is necessary because the capitalist mode of production is characterized by a social division of labor in which production occurs for the purpose of exchange. This, in turn, means that some type of general equivalent is necessary to facilitate exchange. Money is this equivalent. But rather than serving as a mere equivalent that simply facilitates exchange, and because money is the only equivalent that facilitates exchange, it acquires what Marx refers to as a "social power" that not only assures individuals' preservation, but the possibility of preserving themselves in

26 Helmut Reichelt, "Jürgen Habermas' Reconstruction of Historical Materialism," in *The Politics of Change: Globalization, Ideology and Critique*, eds. Werner Bonefeld et al. (London: Palgrave, 2000), 105.

27 Ibid.

28 Adorno, *Introduction to Sociology*, 31.

affluent ways. This also means, as Marx shows in the course of his further presentation in *Capital*, that since the capitalist mode of production consists in a class relation in which one class (workers) sells its labour power in order to reproduce itself to another class (capitalists) who exploits this labour power in order to sell commodities for the purpose of valorizing capital, the capitalist process of valorization occurs through the medium of money for the sake of acquiring money. Money thus becomes the sole aim of production, "the self-sufficient purpose of the sale," and thus the end of the never-ending process of valorization, which is simultaneously one of reproduction. Thus, as Marx states, it is ultimately capital, as self-valorizing value that is "the dominant subject of the process" of valorization in which each side of the class relation is compelled: Proletarians are compelled to sell their own labor for money in order to survive; capitalists are compelled to exploit labor power in order to sell commodities for money to assure they remain capitalists. In Backhaus's view, Marx's monetary theory of value thus holds that money necessarily arises from the historically specific form of capitalist social labor and becomes autonomous as the medium of capitalist valorization, compelling people to behave in certain ways in order to acquire money so that they can survive leading to the reproduction of these social conditions.

Reichelt and Backhaus provide a firmer basis for the socio-theoretical and explanatory dimensions of critical theory. Reichelt's characterization of Marx's conception of social reality undergirds Adorno's depiction of the constitution of society, whilst Backhaus's work on the monetary theory of value provides an explanation of how the dynamism of exchange makes society constituent of a second nature. Rather than mere scholasticism, these philological works thus contribute to the vitality of the Adornian critical theory of society.

## Bonefeld on the State

While a number of scholars have sought in recent years to extend this critical theoretical reading of Marx to social domains such as gender and race, here I want to highlight the contributions Werner Bonefeld has made, which focus on how the state participates in this process of capitalist valorization and social reproduction. This will put us in a position to consider what this strand of critical theory can show us in contemporary capitalist relations with nature. Bonefeld's work links the capitalist state to the capitalist economy and points to the interrelationship between politics and economics, and brings the story up to date in order to provide an outline that can show

how neoliberalism's development is an expression of this relationship.[29]

To understand how, we must first examine Bonefeld's 1992 account of the social constitution of the form of the capitalist state. Bonefeld holds that the capitalist economy and the capitalist state are a "contradictory unity" that is created by the "substantive abstraction of class antagonism," with the capitalist state utilizing its political capacities to reproduce this class antagonism. The specific antagonism of capitalist class struggle is the "historical result" of primitive accumulation. As a result, the world market is derived from "the contradictory existence of abstract labour as the social form of wealth founded on exploitation," which in turn determines the form of the state: "The development of the state needs to be seen as one in which the contradictory unity of surplus value production is processed in a political form, as a moment of the same process of class struggle: social reproduction as, and in and against, domination."[30] Bonefeld argues that this antagonism is also at the heart of "the harmonies of formal equality and formal freedom," which are in fact systematic with political domination. The form of the state "concentrates the social reality of exploitation in and through the guarantee of formal freedom and formal equality of property rights."[31] Bonefeld also focuses on how these legal and political forms are instrumentalized to assure reproduction. As he sees it, "the political guarantee of the right of property determines the state as a strong state" which "imposes the rationality and equality of the right of property over society in the attempt to contain the social antagonism of capital and labour by the force of law."[32]

Bonefeld's work following the 2008 crisis provides an account of neoliberalism and the neoliberal state from this perspective. In this purview, the theory of political economy as a political practice shows how its "cohesion, organization, integration and reproduction are matters of state."[33] Here, Bonefeld succinctly formulates the ends of such a political practice: "Crudely put, the purpose of capital is to accumulate extracted surplus value, and the state is the political form of that purpose."[34] He also provides an account of how this purpose is achieved by state policies which are enacted for the purpose of valorization. As he argues, the state "facilitates the order of economic freedom by means of the force of law-making violence"; sustains the capitalist relations of production and exchange by depoliticiz-

---

**29** This section draws on my *Viewpoint* article.

**30** Werner Bonefeld, "Social Constitution and the Form of the Capitalist State," in *Open Marxism*, ed. Werner Bonefeld et al. (London: Pluto, 1992), 119.

**31** Ibid., 116.

**32** Ibid., 117.

**33** Werner Bonefeld, *Critical Theory*, 182.

**34** Ibid., 168.

ing "socio-economic relations"; guarantees "contractual relations of social interaction"; seeks the further progress of the system of free labor by facilitating the "cheapness of provision"; and extends these relations by "securing free and equal market relations."[35] The "strong state" thus utilizes its form-determined capacities in an instrumental manner, to organize, integrate, sustain, and extend the social relation at the heart of the peculiar dynamic of valorization for the purpose of accumulating surplus value.

Bonefeld also enumerates how the "market-facilitating" coercive force of the strong neoliberal state achieves these ends in the three areas outlined above. He argues that capitalist relations have been sustained and extended "over the past 30 years" of neoliberalism by "the accumulation of potentially fictitious wealth"—through "the coercive control of labour, from debt bondage to new enclosures," and from "the deregulation of conditions to the privatization of risk."[36] Thus, Bonefeld argues: "The conventional view that neoliberalism has to do with the weakening of the state has little, if anything, to do with the neoliberal conception of the free economy."[37] Rather, since "the free market requires the strong, market-facilitating state, but it is also dependent on the state as the coercive force of that freedom," the "neoliberal demand for the strong state is a demand for the limited state, one that lim-

35  Ibid., 168–69.

36  Werner Bonefeld, "Free Economy and the Strong State: some notes on the State," *Capital and Class*, February 2010, 16.

37  Bonefeld, *Critical Theory*, 174–75.

its itself to the task of making the economy of free labour effective."[38] This means that "the capitalist state is fundamentally a liberal state" and that the neoliberal state is typical of these fundamental qualities, because "the neoliberal state functions as a market facilitating state."[39]

Echoing Adorno, Bonefeld thus conceives of the state as immanent to capitalist society. Yet by conceiving of the state's socially constituted form-determined political capacities as integral to reproducing capitalist social relations, by virtue of its separation from the economy, Bonefeld provides an explanatory account of how political rule fits in the dynamic of the negative totality of capitalist society.

Bonefeld does not extend this prescient analysis of the neoliberal state to other areas where it can be seen to play a crucial role in "sustaining the capitalist relations of production and exchange" and seeking the further progress of the system of free labor. They can, however, be drawn out of Bonefeld's interpretation of primitive accumulation. He argues that this process, which is facilitated by the state, consists in the forced privitization of land and the subsequent organization of labor (and land) for the purposes of capitalist production. In contrast to some analyses of this Marxian category, which argue that it only pertains to the historical process that preceded capitalism, with its classical locus in the English enclosure movement, Bonefeld also stresses that this process has to be "re-constituted continuously in the process of accumulation proper."[40]

I think it is precisely these areas of Bonefeld's analysis of the state that can be drawn out in tandem with my discussion of Schmidt, Reichelt, and Backhaus's work to provide a symptomatic analysis of how the "natural laws" inherent to the capitalist social form are realized in the Canadian state's economic policies and its rampant metabolization of fossil fuels.

## Critical Theory Now

Thus far we have identified a Marxian constellation at the core of critical theory, discussed how it was distilled in Adorno's late work, and shown how elements of it have been refined by Reichelt, Backhaus, and Bonefeld. I began with an overview of Adorno's critical theory, which, in conversation with Schmidt, holds that the domination of nature has constituted a dominating social second nature and that this type of domination occurs in capitalist so-

**38** Ibid., 180.

**39** Bonefeld, "Free Economy," 16.

**40** Werner Bonefeld, "History and Social Constitution: Primitive Accumulation Is Not Primitive" in *Subverting the Present, Imagining the Future*, ed. Werner Bonefeld (London: Autonomedia, 2008), 82.

*A RECORD OF THE CATASTROPHE*

ciety as a result of the dynamism of exchange. I then showed how Reichelt and Backhaus drew on Marx to provide an explanatory basis for the constitution and reproduction of this social dynamic. Finally, I showed how Bonefeld supplemented this analysis by showing how the state as the political form of capital is responsible for instituting policies that perpetuate this social dynamic. These points can be crudely drawn together as follows: The critical theory of society holds that capitalist society is a negative totality that consists in the domination of external nature for the purpose of valorization; as the political form of this purpose, the capitalist state is responsible for insuring that this type of domination is perpetuated. I believe such a notion of critical theory can be shown to be relevant to contemporary society by illuminating how and why the current government of Canada under the leadership of Prime Minister Stephen Harper has so enthusiastically promoted energy policies of unrivalled ecological destruction.

Much of the critical commentary on the Harper government and the "petro-state" they have turned Canada into consists in condemnation that might be said to resemble traditional theory or contemporary Habermasian and Honnethian critical theory in its moral criticisms of bad types of capitalism, non-representative democracy, or the prime minister's character flaws. These commentaries thus fault "corporate ideology," "neoliberal ideology," "libertarian ideology," and even provide psychological analyses of Harper himself as "paranoid and narcissistic," and even as a "useful idiot."[41] In these and other cases, these criticisms engage in what Adorno referred to as "surface critique," providing an asocial account that focuses on individual decisions or abstract normative notions of democracy rather than the social dynamics that compelled these decisions. I think the present conjuncture can be better explained by drawing on the line of analysis we have just reconstructed.

From this perspective, the domination of nature for the purpose of valorization and the state as the political form of this purpose provide the basis for a more deep-seated explanation that reads the state of extraction as exemplary of the neoliberal expression of this social logic. This can be seen by contextualizing the development of the contemporary regime of extraction accumulation within the context of the neoliberal project and then tracing the consequences of such a dynamic in terms of the pronounced domination of nature and the increased immiseration and maiming of individuals.

As Jim Standford and Sam Gindin point out, the neoliberalization of the Canadian economy began in response to economic stagnation in the

---

41 For example, see Andrew Nikiforuk, "Oh Canada," *Foreign Policy*, Jordan Michael Smith, "Reinventing Canada: Stephen Harper's Conservative Revolution," *World Affairs*, March/April 2012; Murray Dobbin, "Has Harper Finally Gone Unhinged? Putin, Petrodollars and Canada's Useful Idiot," *Counterpunch*, April 22, 2014.

1970s.[42] As Gindin shows, the neoliberal project was part of a global offensive to raise profits at the expense of the Western working class by securing property rights, market freedoms, and profits through various forms of economic restructuring. This was particularly true in Canada where the workforce was sharing an unprecedented share of the GDP. The state, as the political purpose of capital, played an instrumental role in instituting this project by implementing policies that assured this restructuring. As Bonefeld indicates, these decisions can be seen as examples of the state's role in facilitating "the order of economic freedom" by "sustaining the capitalist relations of production and exchange," and seeking the further progress of the system of free labour. Finally, this process of neoliberalization contextualizes the present.

Let's consider the two policy decisions that Stanford attributes to the neoliberalization of Canada: the dramatic shift in monetary policy in the early 1980s, which was engineered to make mass unemployment a "deliberate, permanent feature of the economy," and the Free Trade Agreement with the USA. The consequences of these policies, especially in the case of the FTA, laid the institutional and political framework for a huge shift in the focus of Canada's economy. As Stanford also notes, "several factors" coincided with these policies that further weakened Canada's traditional exports, at the same time that demand for resource commodities skyrocketed, shifting Canada's economy to renewed dependence on the extraction and export of raw natural resources (or "staples"), "led by a massive expansion of bitumen production and export from northern Alberta."

From this perspective, a critical theoretical reading of the state of extraction comes into light. Such a theory does not fault Harper or read this development as a deficit in democracy, but rather views this type of state-backed production for exchange as representative of the domination of nature for the purpose of valorization *qua* neoliberal capitalism. Consequently, the numerous state policies, which have been shaped "around maximizing the extraction of wealth from the country's natural resources"[43] can be seen as further expressions of the state's role in sustaining these particular capitalist relations of production and exchange. For not only is this type of neoliberal production, and the state policies that foster this production, an instance of securing property rights and symptomatic of globalization and free trade, it is also relatively mechanized, requiring a small

---

42 Jim Standford, "Canada's Transformation Under Neoliberalism," *Canadian Dimension*, https://canadiandimension.com/articles/view/canadas, and Sam Gindin, "Beyond the Impasse of Canadian Labour: Union Renewal, Political Renewal," *Canadian Dimension*, May 21, 2014, https://canadiandimension.com/articles/view/beyond-the-impasse-of-canadian-labour-union-renewal-political-renewal.

43 Marianne Lenabat, "What Happened to Canada?" *n+1*, April 10, 2014, https://nplusonemag.com/online-only/online-only/what-happened-to-canada.

workforce and thus contributing to permanent unemployment, the erosion of living standards, and wage depletion.

As a result, as Stephen Leahy shows, although Canada's overall GDP increased from $600 billion to $1.7 trillion over the course of the last 20 years, income inequality has actuality increased:

> [While] the Alberta tar sands are the world's largest industrial project with investments in the hundreds of billions of dollars, only 20,000 people worked there in 2011. For all its rapid growth Canada's oil and gas sector created only about 16,500 new jobs between 2000 to 2011, the same period in which 520,000 manufacturing jobs were lost.[44]

This has led to a situation in which one in seven children lives in poverty and income inequality has increased faster than in the US, with the rich getting richer, and the poor and middle class losing ground, over the past 15 to 20 years. In other words, this is an exemplary instance of the neoliberal project. Leahy cites Daniel Drache, a political scientist at York University: "Most of Canada's increase in wealth went to the big shareholders in the resource industries. It mainly went to the elites." This is to say nothing of the unparalleled degradation, and domination of nature, that this type of valorization consists in, nor of their environmental impact.

What's more, as these statistics indicate, this economic dependence on extraction seems to have set up a dynamic in which the petrodollar has further weakened other export industries, making the economy more reliant on it and thus compelling the state to institute more policies that further expand this type of accumulation, meaning that these inequalities and degradations are only set to increase. We can here see the relevance of Adorno's characterization of human history as "progressive natural domination," continuing "the unconscious one of nature, of devouring and being devoured." We see how the "law which determines how the fatality of mankind unfolds itself is the law of exchange" through the internal relation between the state and the economy. And we see a point where this process of dominating second nature spews out tatters of subjugated nature to the point where it might annihilate natural history.

In providing a single existential judgement against this new barbarism by unfolding a strand of critical theory that views these developments as an instantiation of the conceptuality that holds sway in reality and views the state as a political purpose of this reality, premised on the continued dom-

---

44 Stephen Leahy, "Blame Canada Part Three: The Bigger Canada's Energy Sectors Gets the Poorer People Become," *Desmog Canada*, March 21, 2013, http://www.desmog.ca/2013/03/20/blame-canada-part-3-bigger-canada-s-energy-sector-gets-poorer-people-become.

ination of external and internal nature, I hope that I have not only demonstrated the relevance this strand of critical theory holds for contemporary society, but have provided a lens through which to understand the genesis of these developments, in order to negate them. ⬢

# Parties / Partying / the Party

## OLIVE BLACKBURN

1. Party Invitations

1.1

Interactive Social Contract / Rally No. 3

Meet the new gods. Experimental beer-backed currency. Hypno software. Guaranteed sincere love and excellent sex for all attendees. All the latest propaganda techniques and cult tactics will be harnessed to achieve turbo zen at the third and unforgettable charismatic show down. I'm your plus one.

1.2

comrades,

we are coming to town to smoke you out of your holes. check it: wednesday, feb. 8th. go tell your fucking friends. believe the hype. we would love to have you.

cheers,

the PR dept

1.3

ALL WELCOME. Refreshments—stiff, copious—provided.

1.4

Invites you to be the party that we're at.

1.5

Anyone who's trying to come to my welcome back party, it's all summer long on the corner of 22nd & Sanchez.

2. Parties

2.1

The party party

The party of non-partisan non-party politics

The party of slush-fund liars

The party of lost ground

The party for the continued withering of party politics

The party for total affiliation

The party for the circumvention of the party

The party for the evaporation of aims

The party for the infinite division of the party

2.2

A group of characters (A, B, C, D, E, F, and W) are at C's place for dinner.

2.3

let's be too much, every second of a never ending night. let's make each second too loud, too fast, too hot, too close, too bright, too dark, too blurry. we want more, then twice that amount. and then we falter for a second, everyone disperses, and it's gone.

2.4

Conceptual Parties.

Have a party for an hour. For the second hour, reenact the party that just happened. For the third hour, reenact the first hour playing someone else.

Have a party for an hour which is documented by video. Watch the documentation of the first hour during the second hour.

2.5

function of social groups: killing time; jockeying for position vis-à-vis status, hierarchy; confessional

2.6

The people by the door are a bit uncomfortable. Please take a moment to make yourself more comfortable. There are some chairs here in the front.

3. After-Parties

the sounds of a failing legitimation. of streets overturning, of cars used only as shields. distant scuffles. the whistling of leaves. a soft breeze. the best days in the city are days where everyone has forgotten about going to work. too much to do. At the window, scanning, scouring, inspecting, discussing. to the desk, discussing, discussing, writing, arguing, writing. to the street, walking, lifting, holding, pushing, waiting, waiting, leaving. going downstairs, drinking, drinking, holding, leaving.

# From Epigrams (1961)

## ERNESTO CARDENAL

I give you these verses, Claudia, because they're yours.
I've written them simply so that you'll understand.
They're only for you, but if you don't care,
one day they might spread through all Latin America...
And if you also scorn the love that dictated them,
others will dream of this love that was not for them.
And you might see, Claudia, that these poems,
(written to win you over) inspire
in other enamored couples as they read them
the kisses that the poet did not inspire in you.

*

Of these movies, Claudia, of these parties,
of these horse races,
nothing will remain for posterity
just the verses of Ernesto Cardenal for Claudia
                    (if that)
and Claudia's name that I put in those verses
and those of my rivals, if I decide to save them
from oblivion, and include them also in my verses
so as to ridicule them.

# Notes to Complicate Cardenal's Epigrams

## ALEJANDRO DE ACOSTA

*Q. — ¿Why this sudden flowering of the epigram?*

*A. — Poets found that this brief, light poetry was a very appropriate form for certain kinds of things.*

*Q. — ¿Do you mean that it was the expression of a socio-political reality?*

*A. — Yes. In a country with a dictatorship it was quite appropriate to write an epigram. But others were just personal: there have also been many romantic epigrams.*

...except that the reader, and then the translator, and then another reader, might notice that there seems to be no *just personal* epigram at all. Start here: Claudia is interpellated twice: first, with a note of condescension, as one who needs the simple version (the epigram *is* the simple verse); second, as one to whom the address is already sliding. They are hers, but also belong to all Latin America, they will spread, *circulate—*

and this *circulation* is not only continental but already, in anticipation, historical. That is why he puts his name there, in the second of this excerpt-series I've made for you, reader, *because it is yours*—but let's not take that as some ordinary signature. Three points then to begin my complication of these matters: *first*, that, before they appeared as

You girls who will one day read these verses, excited,
and dream of a poet:
know that I wrote them for one like you
and that it was in vain.

*

This will be my revenge:
That one day you will be handed a book by a famous poet
and you'll read these lines the author wrote for you
and you won't know it.

*

They told me you loved another
so I went to my room
and wrote the article against the Government
for which I am now in jail.

*

You who are proud of my verses
not because I wrote them
but because you inspired them
even though they were against you:

                    You could have inspired better poetry.
                    You could have inspired better poetry.

*

I've handed out subversive flyers,
shouting **LONG LIVE FREEDOM** in the street
defying the armed guards.
I participated in the April Rebellion:
but I turn pale as I pass your house
and one glance from you makes me tremble.

a book, the series of epigrams circulated in clandestinity as a sheaf of mimeographed papers; *second*, that the excerpt Neruda published in a Chilean journal was attributed to an *Anónimo nicaragüense*; *third*, that when the first edition of the book finally appeared (Mexico 1961), it was dense with translations of Martial and Catullus. EC was not only author, but translator—

> [It would seem that EC wrote *epigramas* in Nicaragua over the years 1952–1956. Having already published a few books in 1946 and 1947, as well as a thesis on recent Nicaraguan poetry, EC spent two years in New York. There he read enough Pound to get the idea of a direct engagement with the ancients. The translations were mainly push and motivation for the brief style, though; all subsequent editions, half the length, struck them.]

this call to posterity (the girls in the future, *you who one day* reads *these lines*) is undermined, self-undermining. In any case that is my claim, that the epigrams indeed *as a series* undermine their own status as future classics, and so become another kind of classic, which I learned when I saw that how they stage their problem staged a problem for me—and that is the complication.

This reaching out for posterity, the anticipation of it, its almost simulation, is a hollow gesture maybe, erotic frenzy of a young man taken by a supposed power of poetry—

*I am now in jail:* not that eros stops at the gates, but from this point on, the efficacy of the epigrams is double: first, the one we know about, how they strike with satire, especially at the end,
*in cauda venenum,*

> [what makes the epigram political? is it? it is not, not necessarily. *For the Romans and Greeks this just meant a short poem*, he says, but he will go on to say that as brief and biting they are appropriate for a dictatorship—maybe for any situation where a reality has to be expressed bluntly, the writer's strong emotion showing and armed. So perhaps only in the sense that they overflow the *just personal* realm with their stinging tails—thus poetry of circumstance becomes engaged/combat poetry]

# IMITATION OF PROPERTIUS

I do not sing the defense of Stalingrad
or the Egyptian campaign
or the landing on Sicily
or the crossing of the Rhine by General Eisenhower:

I only sing the conquest of a girl.

Not with jewels from the Morlock Jewelry Store
or Dreyfus perfumes
or with orchids inside a plastic box
or with a Cadillac—
only with my poems did I win her over.

And she prefers me, though I am poor, to all of Somoza's millions.

\*

You have worked twenty years
to amass twenty million pesos.
But we would give twenty million pesos
not to work the way you have.

\*

You don't even deserve an epigram.

\*

Suddenly a siren sounds out in the night,
a long, long alarm, the gloomy howl of the siren
of a firetruck or the white ambulance of death,
like the cry of the cegua[1] in the night,
that draws nearer and nearer across the streets
and houses and rises, rises, and falls
and grows, grows, falls and withdraws
growing and falling away. It's neither fire nor death:
                                          It's Somoza passing by.

1   cegua: monstrous witch-like creature of folklore

[the obverse of the poems: the flyers and the cry

**¡VIVA LA LIBERTAD!**—]


short and biting, satirical,
bilious even; the second is a surprise, and here EC may pass to posterity:
the instability of the *you*—someone who inspired—

*you could have inspired*—

at first it is just a lateral
shift: spurned love becomes the anti-Government article and then jail—or
the felt contrast between the armed guards and

*your house*

*your*

*gaze*

—or, ultimately, that the power of the
poems themselves is a conquest. A metaphorical conquest? No, never, not
quite—the power of a poor man as against the Dictator's millions is also
what makes this awful, familiar metaphor possible. And vindicates it, that
he conquers her—

So that now, heady with the conquest, he can address the Dictator
directly, affirming poverty against his wealth—I have to follow the series
here, as it was laid out, as I have excerpted its most pressing poems—
denying him a name in this epigram, even writing that one, a contradictory
one-liner aiming to subtract him from posterity altogether.

[In 1983, so in the future of the *Epigrams*, far enough into the future
that Somoza's dictatorship was over, though his name had not yet
been forgotten, the Trinidadian-Canadian poet Dionne Brand wrote
*Epigrams to Ernesto Cardenal in Defence of Claudia*. I leave us this
note to remark, remind...]

It is difficult to speak to the distant desired. It is impossible to talk
to the dictator. Neither is listening. There is a place, so I learn from EC,
where we stockpile all the language addressed to ones not listening, and it
is a messy place.

Somoza is at first the oligarch. But is he even a person? He does
not answer, will not be spoken to. He is perhaps just a presence, now a
terrible omnipresence, fear in the night, known and unknown.

The epigrams are at their most unstable when we are brought to
look at a simple dinner only by contrasting it with the dictator's meal—

We heard some shots last night,
We heard them by the Cemetery.
No one knows who got killed, or who killed them.
No one knows anything.
We heard some shots last night.
That is all.

*

If you are in New York
there is no one else in New York
and if you're not in New York
there's no one in New York.

*

But at night you see your rice and refried beans,
with fresh curd cheese and a warm tortilla,
or a fried plantain,
                you eat them without bodyguards.
And your pitcher of tiste² is not first tasted by an assistant.
And afterwards if you like you play a country song on your guitar,
and you don't sleep surrounded by floodlights, barbed wire, and guard towers.

*

Oh pitiless you,
        crueler than Tachito.³

*

My sweet kitten, my sweet kitten!
How my sweet kitten trembles
from my caresses on her face and neck
and your murders and tortures!

2  tiste: corn & cocoa drink

3  Tachito: Somoza!

[impossible everydayness of the dictator]

who gets the venom here? And then this *you*, considered tenderly if
not horizontally, is shattered in confusion. Crueler than *Tachito*? The
Dictator by his nickname—and since there is no other dictator, it must be
the, a, "girl" again. Now the venom is truly unleashed,

[impossible (possible) cruelty of the beloved!]

for this is far, far more perverse
than the trivial sublimation by which one might end up in jail, or the claim
of conquest, its vindication in praise of poetry and as expression of class
hatred. The dreaded comparison?

I need to say more here, clearly—it is not just perverse. One says
horrible things in anger. You speak from *that* place. People *are* that cruel,
privately. Is there room for such venom/

If the epigram allows the private,
subjective satire to stab at the public—the not yet intimate, the formerly
intimate, the anonymous, omnipresent power of the government-jail-
Dictator series—then this cruel retort must be allowed. *You don't even
deserve an epigram*; and *you* don't deserve, in another sense of *deserve*,
to be compared to Somoza. But that is Somoza's omnipresence, that he
gets into our arguments, our spats, our bickering even—and if the epigram
is true, true to form as well as truly venomous, this phase cannot be
censored by EC any more than the political poems can be censored when
they circulate in anonymity.

[i.e. *that* place is impersonal and as it were an anonym *in us*
in the poet at least, if a poet knows how to listen, there]

We are in an illiberal space where private and public, amorous and
political, have been irreparably mixed. I praise this epigrammatic
engagement even as I take my distance from its occasion—I mean EC's
youthful sexpol of girls and conquests. Though I appreciate that he mixed
it in with his political politics, or maybe the other way around.

It could also be that he discovered them to be indistinct in the course of
poetic saying. Was it the Dictator's violence that revealed it—
this *trembling*, indistinctly erotic and fearful?

At this point in the series EC has me. He has my attention. He speaks,

# SOMOZA UNVEILS THE STATUE OF SOMOZA
## IN SOMOZA STADIUM

It's not that I think that the people raised this statue to me
because I know better than you that I ordered it myself.
Nor do I think that with it I will live on in posterity
because I know that the people will tear it down one day.
Nor that while living I wanted to raise to myself
the monument you will not raise to me when I die:
I had this statue raised because I know you hate it.

*

Every afternoon she would walk with her mother on the Landstrasse
and at the corner of the Schmiedtor, every afternoon,
there was Hitler, waiting to see her go by.
The taxis and the buses were full of kisses
and couples would rent boats on the Danube.
But he didn't know how to dance. He never dared to speak.
Later she would go by without her mother, with a cadet.
And then she stopped going by.
Hence, later on, the Gestapo, the annexation of Austria,
the World War.

*

My love, have you not read the **NEWS**:
SENTINEL OF PEACE, GENIUS OF WORK
PALADIN OF DEMOCRACY IN AMÉRICA
DEFENDER OF CATHOLICISM IN AMÉRICA
THE PROTECTOR OF THE PEOPLE

                              THE BENEFACTOR...?
They rob the people of its language.
And they counterfeit the people's words.
(Exactly like the people's money.)
That is why we poets polish our poems so.
And that is why my love poems are important.

not for the last time, like a newspaper headline. At the same time he can directly parody Somoza's imagined voice, always this move of the oppressed, also an anonymous impulse: to grant more concern and thought to the oppressors than they perhaps have in their cruelty. Maybe he only sees it because he can admit his own cruelty, anyone's cruelty. The poem speaks from spite: Somoza's for the people, EC's for Somoza. And though here we find immediate resonances of the recurring question of memory and posterity in the epigrams, EC will take an entirely unexpected step and deposit us in another place and time, explaining—

> [explaining! but
> epigrams do not
> explain!]

another dictatorship as the result of a spurned love—certainly here the poet does not exactly blame the girl (though the causal link is brutal enough)—but he does suggest what may be called a psychohistorical thesis—

*Hence*

that expands the amorous-political knot. It is easy enough here to diagnose geopolitical delirium, an entirely wanton, irresponsible transposition. That, it seems to me, is where *Epigrams* leaves us and where I leave this complication I have only sought to underline for you, the reader. I would add a question, a note perhaps—

the poet EC says in several of these epigrams that the poet will purify the language, as against the dictator, who is spoken of

## IN CAPITALS            IN HEADLINES

which are already, visibly, in the **ROMAN** memory of the epigrams, the writing carved into the side of the stone monument, the inscription at the base of the statue of Somoza unveiled by Somoza in Somoza Stadium. And also the theft of the words of the people. Well, first,

> [I already had these questions,
> I rediscovered them in trans-
> lating, I sharpened them on

# EPITAPH FOR JOAQUÍN PASOS

He walked these streets, without a job or position,
and not a single peso.
Only poets, whores, and junkies knew his verses.
He never traveled abroad.
He was in prison.
Now he's dead.
He has no tombstone.
                        But
remember him when you have concrete bridges,
great turbines, tractors, silver granaries,
good governments.
Because in his poems he purified the language of his people
in which trade agreements will be written one day,
and the Constitution, love letters and decrees.


                        *


Our poems cannot yet be published.
They circulate from hand to hand, handwritten,
or copied by mimeograph. But one day
the name of the dictator against whom they were written
will be forgotten
and they will go on being read.

                                                    his epigrams—I hope they do
                                                    not sting me]
is the purification of the language, as Joaquín Pasos did in his vanished
verses—is this purification not in effect betrayed when a trade agreement,
a Constitution, a *decree* is written in it? Why is the poet, vanished (in his
vanished poems) in any sense vindicated, not in fact betrayed, dead again
under the *silver granaries*?

                                                    Second, how can
the poet EC say his love poems are important for the same reason? Do
they not survive, like the Latin ones, because of their perversity as well?
Is this perversity (from garden variety adolescent-*cum*-macho talk of
conquest to the dreaded comparison, the irresponsible geohistorical
delirium) retroactively justified if it can be shown that his poems were
still *against* the Dictator?—

          (when they were also against the "girls", often enough). The
name of the dictator *can't* be forgotten, because, like that of the poet,
it is written into the epigrams. We even know his nickname! Very well,
then, I agree that we need poems, even love poems, even these perverse
epigrams, with their cruelty not just reported but enacted (to Claudia
and all the others). But I will merely say that I don't understand why we
need to purify the language at all, whether we can do it at all, or whether
it ultimately matters if someone can come and write a constitution or
a trade agreement with the words we purified in our poems. All I want,
I think, is the epigram's bite, its capacity to circulate, which is also its
capacity to be translated. There is something else, though, which is that
the addressee does not listen, does not share the language. One can amuse
oneself writing an epigram, as Jonson did to the Small-Pox,
                    *thou hast shown thy malice, but hast failed.*
That, today, is my pessimism, not about translation or epigrams, but about
the political space, the shared language.

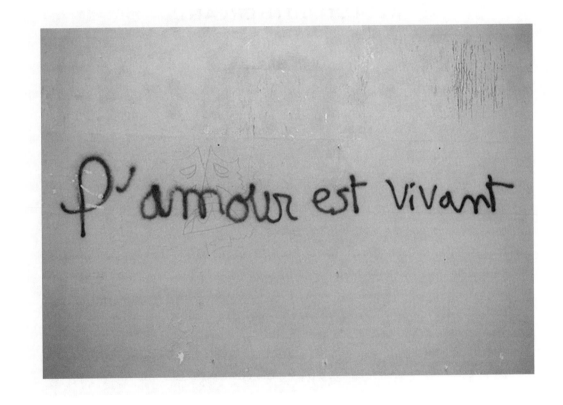

# Simplicity

## KESTON SUTHERLAND

*For Andrea*

*As if you swallowed love with singing love*

In his first acknowledged publication, the *Differenzschrift* of 1801, Hegel describes, in what for him is an unusually quick and simplistic narrative outline, the advance of Reason toward "objective totality." The "objective totality" toward which Reason advances is not "objective" in the common sense that it is like an object already there, in a position to be stumbled upon by the subject, who may not even be looking for it; "objective totality" is not found: it cannot be founded, but must be reached; and the subject who does actually reach is extended in that act, which is the ardent work of Reason that Hegel in the *Phenomenology* calls "the strain of the concept." The action of this strain is travel and stretching at once: It is both the movement of the subject, the advance of Reason toward "objective totality" and the "expansion" of the subject. This expansion is not just growth, but also inclusion: the subject expands through the work of Reason that is inseparably both ardent and "comprehensive," in the sense that every objective "substance" that "becomes subject" remains active in the logic of self-consciousness and the advance of Reason: every object on which the right work is done is comprehended in life. Expansion itself, together with a simultaneous contraction that will be described shortly, "completes" or "accomplishes" the "objective totality" toward which the subject has advanced. The quick outline of the narrative of Reason in the *Differenzschrift* does not explain any of this, but just efficiently plots the essential action of the logic. The overview is rounded off in what may be the most simplistic formulation of absolute knowledge in all Hegel's writing, virtually the bathos of shorthand. "[I]n this way," he sums up, "the system advances until the objective totality is completed. Reason then unites this objective totality with the opposite subjective totality to form the infinite world-intuition, whose expansion has at the same time contracted into the richest and simplest identity."

Nothing in Hegel's writing could be simpler than this. It is disarmingly not unlike the sort of identity-tagging that is lambasted in the *Phenomenology* as opprobriously "schematic," just joining up the dots or putting back together the scattered bones of a laboratory skeleton. "The system advances until the objective totality is completed." The efficiency of this synopsis makes it hard to resist Adorno's judgment that the *ardent work* required to advance Hegel's system to its totality is also, in a crucial respect, "serene indifference," since "nowhere in [Hegel's] work is the primacy of the whole doubted." The primacy of the whole is not only not doubted, but it is also capable of being posited in extravagantly simplistic logical terms. Reason unites everything objective, all the objects in the world, with everything subjective, the least wish, drive, desire, or memory, or the most hyperbolic, so that infinity is still at last where life is too: "The task of philosophy," Hegel writes earlier in the *Differenzschrift*, is "to posit the finite in the infinite, as life."

What is thus arrived at and at last comprehended in this simplistic overview of the narrative of Reason is "the richest and simplest identity." It is not the identity of a person, but that of "the infinite world-intuition"; but perhaps as a person it is difficult to hear about this identity and not wish it could be your own, or at least that it could be possible for people. Hegel does not directly rule out people from achieving the identity that he reserves for "the infinite world-intuition," however formidably he may multiply the conceptual difficulties of reconciling the destiny of Reason, or of the subject, with the life of just any person. It is true that "the richest and simplest identity" may not be possible for just any person to live; it may not be available for persons at all; people commonly do not infinitely expand and at the same time infinitely contract like "the infinite world-intuition," and Hegel does not say there is another way to achieve "the richest and simplest identity." In the *Phenomenology*, Hegel argues that it is the fate of substance to become the subject, as subject and object are progressively united in the comprehension of absolute knowledge. This may be a more thoroughly speculative description of how "the richest and simplest identity" is achieved, a narrative with greater conceptual power to posit the universal; but its power as speculative thinking consists in some significant and crucial measure in its ineradicable distance from a mere story of a life. The *Phenomenology* is not biography; what "the subject" achieves in the fulfillment of its destiny is not just what any person achieves by living. But since at the same time what any person achieves by actually or really living cannot be other than self-actualization and self-realization, so what any person achieves by being alive is always progress toward "objective totality" (for Hegel, real living is the inseparably both ardent and comprehensive effort to keep infinity within reach). What just any person does by really living must be the activity of advance, the absolute unrest and straining of the concept, that is, it must be the activity of the subject: Just any person is not and is the subject, just any finite life is not and is in the infinite, the *Phenomenology* is not and is biography, and not just anything or just anyone can achieve "the richest and simplest identity" and just anything or just anyone can achieve that identity, right now.

Later in his life Hegel took oblique revenge on this simplistic early formulation of absolute knowledge as "the richest and simplest identity." In the *Philosophy of Right*, simplicity is belittled in its natural form as "crude," suitable perhaps for Rousseau but not for the subject. Here Hegel again defines the task of Reason, whose "end" it now is "to banish natural simplicity, whether the passivity which is the absence of the self, or the crude type of knowing and willing, i.e. immediacy and singularity, in which mind is absorbed." Whereas earlier it had been the fate of mind, in the shape of "the infinite world-intuition," to be comprehended in "the richest and simplest identity," here the simplicity that matters is natural, and natural simplicity is not comprehensive but merely engrossing. What is the relation, if any, between natural simplicity, which is crude, and the perfect simplicity of identity that is at last achieved by the infinite expansion and contraction of the subject? How is it possible to know when simplicity is natural? Perhaps simplicity is natural whenever Reason banishes it. The same action of banishing what is natural in order to achieve unity is central to Hegel's account of marriage, which must be both love and a contract at the same time, and in both respects thoroughly ethical. In marriage, men and women must "renounce their natural and individual personality to this unity of one with the other." Hegel then directly adds, reproducing again the essential logical motif of his thinking: "From this point of view, their union is a self-restriction, but in fact it is their liberation, because in it they attain their substantive self-consciousness." Simplicity, when it is the last predicate of "identity," or the most comprehensive achievement of the subject, defines the destiny of Reason, "the finite in the infinite": "the richest and simplest identity." Later, natural simplicity meant engrossment in crude distractions, a category that can safely be abandoned to culture, in which "immediacy" as a whole could be dumped. (This judgment on immediacy by the author of the *Philosophy of Right*, whom Marx in his letters called "Old Hegel," was disastrously impressive to Lukács, who made stubborn, flexible use of it in his essays on the theory of literature, and who was driven on by the intrinsic stubbornness of the concept itself to strike stubborn attitudes about artworks whose sub-

**How is it possible to know when simplicity is natural? Perhaps simplicity is natural whenever Reason banishes it. The same action of banishing what is natural in order to achieve unity is central to Hegel's account of marriage, which must be both love and a contract at the same time, and in both respects thoroughly ethical.**

stantial particularity could then more easily be liquidated in abstractions, and it was thereby disastrous for Marxist aesthetic theory, which wasted a lot of energy wrangling to dispute it and has perhaps never yet altogether eradicated its transparent shadow: In reality, intensity is impossible without immediacy and revolutionary subjectivity makes immediacy itself ardent.) Hegel had always been a ruthless critic of bad or clumsy thinking, and his whole philosophy requires and also relentlessly reiterates the absolute distinction between "the dry-as-dust Understanding," an activity of mind and of the subject that has no contact with the absolute and is a mere "clinging to formalities," and Reason or speculative thinking, which is the movement of the absolute itself. Primitively conceptualized versions of the same absolute distinction appear in Hegel's unpublished early writings, for example in "Eleusis," the poem written in August 1796 and addressed to Hölderlin, in which "scholars" are barred from contact with divinity, in the person of the god Ceres, for what is virtually their sin of valuing "curiosity" [*Neugier*] over the true "love of wisdom" (the phrase is broken across a line-ending: *Liebe / Zur Weisheit*: "their curiosity greater than their love / of wisdom"). This stubborn attachment to the routines of empirical consciousness is the work of the Understanding, which explains why it is that, when they "dig for words" (*graben* [...] *nach Worten*: *Grab* is the German for grave), scholars come up with nothing but "dust and ashes" to which life will not return.[1] The first page of the *Phenomenology* warns its would-be interpreters that there is "the way in which to expound philosophical truth" that will be found in its pages, and no other way. It is not surprising to hear him years later berate "the crude type of knowing and willing," because he always did that; but to find that "the crude type of knowing and willing" is now "natural simplicity," rather than the labors of intellectual gravediggers, at least hints at a metastasis in the identity of absolute knowledge, which has gone from being, at first, the perfection of richness and simplicity, to, at last, the end and activity of a Reason whose progress depends on the expulsion of natural simplicity. And yet, moments away in the same text: "Love, the ethical moment in marriage, is by its very nature a feeling for actual living individuals, not for an abstraction." Is love then not by its very nature largely a feeling for what must be expelled, since the existence of an actual living individual who is not at least very often "natural" and "simple" in Hegel's sense can scarcely be imagined? Hegel surely cannot mean that individuals can only be loved when in an emphatic sense they are "actual" and "living," unless he means that love is not stability of attachment but on the contrary what exceeds and disrupts it in moments of radiant intensity and unrest. But perhaps this is really a contradiction, and the natural simplicity that must be banished in the advance of Reason nonetheless remains present and able to be loved, since it is what "actual living individuals" cannot actually live without? What just any person achieves by living is to be an actual living individual for whom love is intended by its very

---

1   "Eleusis," *Werke I: Frühe Schriften*, Frankfurt am Main: Suhrkamp, 1986, 231–32. Slavoj Žižek, in *The Ticklish Subject* (London: Verso, 1999), 97, attempts (in his usual brisk and telegraphic style) a perverse reading of this distinction in Hegel, according to which Reason is after all nothing but "Understanding" itself "deprived of the illusion that there is something beyond it." But for Hegel it is Reason and not Understanding that dispenses with the prop of a spurious Beyond. Understanding cannot by itself escape from the logic that posits the existence of an absolute beyond its reach. See Hegel, *Faith and Knowledge*, trans. Walter Cerf and H.S. Harris (Albany: SUNY Press, 1977), 56: In the philosophies of Understanding, "the eternal remained in a realm beyond, a beyond too vacuous for cognition so that this infinite void of knowledge could only be filled with the subjectivity of longing and divining." Reason alone abolishes the beyond and extinguishes "the subjectivity of longing." Cf. John Wieners, "Supplication," on "the / hurts of wanting the impossible / through this suspended vacuum." From the perspective of Hegel's logic this poem is the lucid ventriloquism of the Understanding.

nature, even as nature is the very condition in which the simplicity of life will be crude and barren of reason. Any person is preferable to an abstraction, for love, no matter what the abstraction or how powerful or indispensable it may be for philosophy, or however the advance of reason or even speculative thinking as a whole may depend on it. For love, any person is preferable to the subject. But love consummated and preserved in the renunciation of "natural and individual personality to the unity of one with the other" is the love of the subject itself: what "is by its very nature a feeling for actual living individuals, not for an abstraction" is itself, as "unity," the greatest abstraction of all, the ultimate and essential abstraction that is disclosed in all concrete universals and everything anywhere in the world. Love is "by its very nature a feeling" that is an activity of the very subject whose unity with the world is achieved by banishing "natural simplicity," but at the same time, if anything begins in natural simplicity or in "knowing and willing" that is "crude" in the sense of "immediate" and "singular," and indeed in "passivity which is the absence of the self," it is love: the description of the "natural simplicity" that Hegel says must be banished is a description of the scene in which love, in the only reality we actually live, always erupts.

Just as speculative thinking cannot be altogether banished from Marx's historical materialist critique, so natural simplicity cannot be altogether banished from the work of speculative Reason in Hegel's philosophy, except in both cases by denial of the reality of love. Hegel even knows this, because he defines love as "mind's feeling of its own unity," and unity for Hegel must extend right back to the start of Reason's advance, before even natural simplicity is yet possible. Natural simplicity in its totality is comprehended in the unity of mind that is felt as love, by the very action of its perpetual banishment. Baudelaire wrote that genius is childhood recalled at will, a formulation that looks crude and simplistic, and that seems to propose a virtually mechanical account of inspiration, beside the powerful speculative exploration of the contradictory relations between childhood, will, and genius in *The Prelude*; but the formulation captures a particular truth of poetry by the very nature of that determined, extravagant simplicity. Somehow obscurely essential to the whole substance of poetry is an inextinguishable confidence in the power of just any person to get to the end, where life and the logic of its advance to unity will at last be comprehended, since people are what love is by its very nature meant for, and since, like love, perhaps even exactly like it, poetry always erupts in the scene that Hegel calls "natural simplicity," where, in the conscious confusion of passivity which is the absence of the self, in the immediate grip of crude knowing and willing, and in singularity of expression, in which mind is both absorbed and emptied, "the richest and simplest identity" may seem in actuality to be just any person, at least for right now, when just any other person is there too, recalled at will. ⬢

# The Pigeon and Me

## SERGIO HYLAND

I saw something interesting last night. It was after midnight and I was outside shoveling snow. In prison, any job you can get that allows you to work outside of "normal" hours and "normal" circumstance is always a good thing. So, as a maintenance worker, I'm usually among those who get the first shot at jobs of that nature (think the "roof job" in the movie *The Shawshank Redemption*).

I enjoy doing snow removal late at night. I find serenity, and some level of inner peace. I find an opportunity to do some deep thinking, without having to worry about the normal hysteria that takes place during the prison's regular hours of operation. After midnight, I can relax while still working hard.

It was quiet, and very cold. It didn't matter much to me, as my mind soon began to focus on what my eye's peripheral had just caught: something in the snow. It was alive and struggling to move. Too small to be a skunk, too large to be a mouse. I approached with curiosity, and immediately recognized its walk, a very distinct wobble. I'd seen it plenty of times before. It was a wounded pigeon. I couldn't tell exactly what the nature of its injury was, but it was serious enough to keep it from flying away as I drew closer.

I felt terrible. It was freezing outside. I wanted to help, but the closer I got the more panicked it became. As it scurried towards the middle of a large field—where I suppose it thought it would be safe—I couldn't help but to think that me and this pigeon may have more in common than it would appear.

I looked around, nervously, making sure that I was out of the view of my supervisor—who wouldn't like it too much if he caught me trying to help a bird when I was supposed to be shoveling snow. I wanted to help it. I wanted to pick it up out of the snow and at least place it somewhere warmer. It may have still succumbed to the elements, but I'd feel better knowing that I'd tried. I just wanted to help, because I would want somebody to help me if ever I should find myself in such a precarious situation.

But I couldn't help. Between the watchful eyes of my supervisor, and the hurried feet of the fowl, I was stuck. So I watched as it ran away from the only person out there who was willing to—or at least really trying to—help it.

More often than not, I feel just like that pigeon. I relate to it in so many ways. Far away from home, alone, in a dark and cold environment, where people don't usually offer help without strings being attached, I can relate to its helplessness, and its sense of hopelessness. How would *you* feel if you had wings that were meant to fly, but couldn't?

I don't blame the bird for not trusting me. After all, I *am* human. And humans can be wolves, or they can be foxes. See, the wolf salivates at the very sight of the injured pigeon. And the fox? It smiles at the pigeon, dances with it; it may even pull the bird out of a jam. But at the end of the day, both the wolf and the fox aim to make an easy meal out of the injured prey.

So no, I don't blame that pigeon for running away from me—even though I was only trying to help. I run from help all the time. And for precisely the same reasons. Because when you're down, and wounded, and alone, the world seems a lot colder, and a lot darker; you start to feel more helpless, more hopeless. Friend mimics foe.

It's all in my head.

There must be *somebody* out there who I can trust.

But who?

Run, pigeon...

Run.

Sergio Hyland #FX1537
State Correctional Institution (SCI) Greene
175 Progress Drive
Waynesburg, PA 15370

# The Ones Who Walk Away from Omelas

## URSULA K. LE GUIN

With a clamor of bells that set the swallows soaring, the Festival of Summer came to the city Omelas, bright-towered by the sea. The rigging of the boats in harbor sparkled with flags. In the streets between houses with red roofs and painted walls, between old moss-grown gardens and under avenues of trees, past great parks and public buildings, processions moved. Some were decorous: old people in long stiff robes of mauve and gray, grave master workmen, quiet, merry women carrying their babies and chatting as they walked. In other streets the music beat faster, a shimmering of gong and tambourine, and the people went dancing, the procession was a dance. Children dodged in and out, their high calls rising like the swallows' crossing flights over the music and the singing. All the processions wound towards the north side of the city, where on the great water-meadow called the Green Fields boys and girls, naked in the bright air, with mud-stained feet and ankles and long, lithe arms, exercised their restive horses before the race. The horses wore no gear at all but a halter without bit. Their manes were braided with streamers of silver, gold, and green. They flared their nostrils and pranced and boasted to one another; they were vastly excited, the horse being the only animal who has adopted our ceremonies as his own. Far off to the north and west the mountains stood up half encircling Omelas on her bay. The air of morning was so clear that the snow still crowning the Eighteen Peaks burned with white-gold fire across the miles of sunlit air, under the dark blue of the sky. There was just enough wind to make the banners that marked the racecourse snap and flutter now and then. In the silence of the broad green meadows one could hear the music winding through the city streets, farther and nearer

and ever approaching, a cheerful faint sweetness of the air that from time
to time trembled and gathered together and broke out into the great joyous
clanging of the bells.

Joyous! How is one to tell about joy? How describe the citizens of Omelas?

They were not simple folk, you see, though they were happy. But we do not
say the words of cheer much anymore. All smiles have become archaic. Giv-
en a description such as this one tends to make certain assumptions. Given
a description such as this one tends to look next for the King, mounted on a
splendid stallion and surrounded by his noble knights, or perhaps in a golden

litter borne by great-muscled slaves. But there was no king. They did not use swords, or keep slaves. They were not barbarians. I do not know the rules and laws of their society, but I suspect that they were singularly few.

As they did without monarchy and slavery, so they also got on without the stock exchange, the advertisement, the secret police, and the bomb. Yet I repeat that these were not simple folk, not dulcet shepherds, noble savages, bland utopians. They were not less complex than us. The trouble is that we have a bad habit, encouraged by pedants and sophisticates, of considering happiness as something rather stupid. Only pain is intellectual, only evil interesting. This is the treason of the artist: a refusal to admit the banality of evil and the terrible boredom of pain. If you can't lick 'em, join 'em. If it hurts, repeat it. But to praise despair is to condemn delight, to embrace violence is to lose hold of everything else. We have almost lost hold; we can no longer describe a happy man, nor make any celebration of joy. How can I tell you about the people of Omelas? They were not naive and happy children—though their children were, in fact, happy. They were mature, intelligent, passionate adults whose lives were not wretched.

O miracle! but I wish I could describe it better. I wish I could convince you. Omelas sounds in my words like a city in a fairy tale, long ago and far away, once upon a time.

Perhaps it would be best if you imagined it as your own fancy bids, assuming it will rise to the occasion, for certainly I cannot suit you all. For instance, how about technology? I think that there would be no cars or helicopters in and above the streets; this follows from the fact that the people of Omelas are happy people. Happiness is based on a just discrimination of what is necessary, what is neither necessary nor destructive, and what is destructive. In the middle category, however—that of the unnecessary but undestructive, that of comfort, luxury, exuberance, etc.—they could perfectly well have central heating, subway trains, washing machines, and all kinds of marvelous devices not yet invented here, floating light-sources, fuelless power, a cure for the common cold.

Or they could have none of that; it doesn't matter. As you like it. I incline to think that people from towns up and down the coast have been coming in to Omelas during the last days before the Festival on very fast little trains and double-decked trams, and that the train station of Omelas is actually the handsomest building in town, though plainer than the magnificent Farmers' Market. But even granted trains, I fear that Omelas so far strikes some of you as goody-goody. Smiles, bells, parades, horses, bleh. If so, please add an orgy. If an orgy would help, don't hesitate. Let us not, however, have temples from which issue beautiful nude priests and priestesses already half in ecstasy and ready to copulate with any man or woman, lover or stranger, who desires union with the deep godhead of the blood, although that was my first idea. But really it would be better not to have any temples in Omelas—at least, not manned temples. Religion yes, clergy no. Surely the beautiful nudes can just wander about, offering themselves like divine soufflés to the hunger of the needy and the rapture of the flesh. Let them join the processions. Let tambourines be struck above the copulations, and the glory of desire be proclaimed upon the gongs, and (a not unimportant point) let the offspring of these delightful rituals be beloved and looked after by all. One thing I know there is none of in Omelas is guilt. But what else should there be? I thought at first there were not drugs, but that is puritanical. For those who like it, the faint insistent sweetness of *drooz* may perfume the ways of the city, *drooz* which first brings a great lightness and brilliance to the mind and limbs, and then after some hours a dreamy languor, and wonderful visions at last of the very arcana and inmost secrets of the Universe, as well as exciting the pleasure of sex beyond belief; and it is not habit-forming. For more modest tastes I think there ought to be beer. What else, what else belongs in the joyous city? The sense of victory, surely, the celebration of courage. But as we did without clergy, let us do without soldiers. The joy built upon successful slaughter is not the right kind of joy; it will not do; it is fearful and it is trivial. A boundless and generous contentment, a magnanimous triumph felt not against some outer enemy but in communion with the finest and fairest in the souls of all men everywhere and the splendor of the world's summer: this is what swells the hearts of the people of Omelas, and the victory they celebrate is that of life. I really don't think many of them need to take *drooz*.

Most of the procession have reached the Green Fields by now. A marvelous smell of cooking goes forth from the red and blue tents of the provisioners. The faces of small children are amiably sticky; in the benign gray beard of a man a couple of crumbs of rich pastry are entangled. The youths and girls have mounted their horses and are beginning to group around the starting line of the course. An old woman, small, fat, and laughing, is passing out flowers from a basket, and tall young men wear her flowers in their shining hair. A child of nine or ten sits at the edge of the crowd, alone, playing on a wooden flute. People pause to listen, and they smile, but they do not speak to him, for he never ceases playing and never sees them, his dark eyes wholly rapt in the sweet, thin magic of the tune.

He finishes, and slowly lowers his hands holding the wooden flute.

As if that little private silence were the signal, all at once a trumpet sounds from the pavilion near the starting line: imperious, melancholy, piercing. The horses rear on their slender legs, and some of them neigh in answer. Sober-faced, the young riders stroke the horses' necks and soothe them, whispering, "Quiet, quiet, there my beauty, my hope..." They begin to form in rank along the starting line. The crowds along the racecourse are like a field of grass and flowers in the wind. The Festival of Summer has begun.

Do you believe? Do you accept the festival, the city, the joy? No? Then let me describe one more thing.

In a basement under one of the beautiful public buildings of Omelas, or perhaps in the cellar of one of its spacious private homes, there is a room. It has one locked door, and no window. A little light seeps in dustily between cracks in the boards, secondhand from a cobwebbed window somewhere across the cellar. In one corner of the little room a couple of mops, with stiff, clotted, foul-smelling heads stand near a rusty bucket. The floor is dirt, a little damp to the touch, as cellar dirt usually is. The room is about three paces long and two wide: a mere broom closet or disused tool room. In the room a child is sitting. It could be a boy or a girl. It looks about six, but actually is nearly ten. It is feeble-minded. Perhaps it was born defective, or perhaps it has become imbecile through fear, malnutrition, and neglect. It picks its nose and occasionally fumbles vaguely with its toes or genitals, as it sits hunched in the corner farthest from the bucket and the two mops. It is afraid of the mops. It finds them horrible. It shuts its eyes, but it knows the mops are still standing there; and the door is locked; and nobody will come.

The door is always locked; and nobody ever comes, except that sometimes—the child has no understanding of time or interval—sometimes the door rattles terribly and opens, and a person, or several people, are there. One of them may come in and kick the child to make it stand up. The others never come close, but peer in at it with frightened, disgusted eyes. The food bowl and the water jug are hastily filled, the door is locked, the eyes disappear. The people at the door never say anything, but the child, who has not always lived in the tool room, and can remember sunlight and its mother's voice, sometimes speaks. "I will be good," it says. "Please let me out. I will be good!" They never answer. The child used to scream for help at night, and cry a good deal, but now it only makes a kind of whining, "eh-haa, eh-haa," and it speaks less and less often. It is so thin there are no calves to its legs; its belly protrudes; it lives on a half-bowl of corn meal and grease a day. It is naked. Its buttocks and thighs are a mass of festered sores, as it sits in its own excrement continually.

They all know it is there, all the people of Omelas. Some of them have come to see it, others are content merely to know it is there. They all know that it has to be there. Some of them understand why, and some do not, but they all understand that their happiness, the beauty of their city, the tenderness of their friendships, the health of their children, the wisdom of their scholars, the skill of their makers, even the abundance of their harvest and the kindly weathers of their skies, depend wholly on this child's abominable misery.

This is usually explained to children when they are between eight and

twelve, whenever they seem capable of understanding; and most of those who come to see the child are young people, though often enough an adult comes, or comes back, to see the child. No matter how well the matter has been explained to them, these young spectators are always shocked and sickened at the sight. They feel disgust, which they had thought themselves superior to. They feel anger, outrage, impotence, despite all the explanations. They would like to do something for the child. But there is nothing they can do. If the child were brought up into the sunlight out of that vile place, if it were cleaned and fed and comforted, that would be a good thing indeed; but if it were done, in that day and hour all the prosperity and beauty and delight of Omelas would wither and be destroyed. Those are the terms. To exchange all the goodness and grace of every life in Omelas for that single, small improvement: to throw away the happiness of thousands for the chance of the happiness of one: that would be to let guilt within the walls indeed.

The terms are strict and absolute; there may not even be a kind word spoken to the child.

Often the young people go home in tears, or in a tearless rage, when they have seen the child and faced this terrible paradox. They may brood over it for weeks or years. But as time goes on they begin to realize that even if the child could be released, it would not get much good of its freedom: a little vague pleasure of warmth and food, no doubt, but little more. It is too degraded and imbecile to know any real joy. It has been afraid too long ever to be free of fear. Its habits are too uncouth for it to respond to humane treatment. Indeed, after so long it would probably be wretched without walls about it to protect it, and darkness for its eyes, and its own excrement to sit in. Their tears at the bitter injustice dry when they begin to perceive the terrible justice of reality, and to accept it. Yet it is their tears and anger, the trying of their generosity and the acceptance of their helplessness, which are perhaps the true source of the splendor of their lives.

Theirs is no vapid, irresponsible happiness. They know that they, like the child, are not free. They know compassion. It is the existence of the child, and their knowledge of its existence, that makes possible the nobility of their architecture, the poignancy of their music, the profundity of their science. It is because of the child that they are so gentle with children. They know that if the wretched one were not there sniveling in the dark, the other one, the flute-player, could make no joyful music as the young riders line up in their beauty for the race in the sunlight of the first morning of summer.

Now do you believe in them? Are they not more credible? But there is one more thing to tell, and this is quite incredible. At times one of the adolescent girls or boys who go to see the child does not go home to weep or rage, does not, in fact, go home at all. Sometimes also a man or woman much older falls silent for a day or two, and then leaves home. These people go out into the street, and walk down the street alone. They keep walking, and walk straight out of the city of Omelas, through the beautiful gates. They keep walking across the farmlands of Omelas. Each one goes alone, youth or girl, man or woman. Night falls; the traveler must pass down village streets, between the houses with yellow-lit windows, and on out into the darkness of the fields. Each alone, they go west or north, towards the mountains. They go on. They leave Omelas, they walk ahead into the darkness, and they do not come back. The place they go towards is a place even less imaginable to most of us than the city of happiness. I cannot describe it at all. It is possible that it does not exist. But they seem to know where they are going, the ones who walk away from Omelas. ⬡

𝔗𝔥𝔢 𝔊𝔢𝔯𝔪𝔞𝔫 𝔠𝔢𝔫𝔰𝔬𝔯𝔰 —— —— ——
—— —— —— —— —— —— ——
—— —— —— —— —— —— ——
—— —— —— —— —— —— ——
—— —— —— —— —— —— ——
—— —— —— —— —— —— ——
—— —— —— —— —— —— ——
—— —— —— 𝔦𝔡𝔦𝔬𝔱𝔰 —— ——
—— —— —— —— —— —— ——
—— —— —— —— —— —— ——
—— —— —— —— —— —— ——
—— —— —— ——

—Heinrich Heine, *Reisebilder II*, 1827

# Exiting the One-Dimensional

## NINA POWER

*Note: A version of this piece was originally commissioned for an Australian feminist magazine, which turned it down due to the discussion of Marilyn Monroe, who was deemed to contravene both their no "pop culture" and no "brand" policy. Despite pointing out that it is Monroe (as discussed by Jacqueline Rose) who questions her role as a "commodity"—indeed, this is the point of the piece—the editor wouldn't budge. I find it revealing that a certain strain of feminism, ostensibly anti-capitalist and anti-consumerist, would incorporate a kind of purism into this politics, as if they would be tainted by a discussion, however critical, of those deemed to be "brands" or "popular." My feeling is that life is much more complicated than that—as if we could put our fingers in our ears and block out all the "undesirable" culture in the world (and with it all those supposed to "go along" with such culture). I'm not for a moment suggesting that a politics based on pointing out the subversive elements of popular culture will do, either—indeed, feminists like Angela McRobbie in* The Aftermath of Feminism *(2009) suggest that this strategy, one adopted by many in the 1980s and 1990s, was an abject failure at the level of advancing genuine political change. Nevertheless, as part of a broader politics, one that both subverts and overturns, I don't see how we can avoid an engagement with "brands," especially when those "brands" turn out to be better placed to understand commodification than those po-facedly pretending their middle-class, "tasteful" brands are exempt from the same logic.*

*—N.P.*

In 1964, Herbert Marcuse wrote *One-Dimensional Man*, which, among other things, examined the ways in which capitalist society generates false freedoms and presents consumerism and a flattened-out culture as highly desirable. In 2009, I published *One-Dimensional Woman*, a play on Marcuse's title for sure, but a short text which also tried to look at similar questions regarding consumerism and culture in our own era, with a particular emphasis on how these related to the representations and realities of women in capitalist societies. I wanted to go beyond some of the tired, but widely accepted, claims regarding the negative impact of images of women—around embodiment, around women's roles, around how women are "supposed" to act—and ask the question *why*? Why would a culture that prides itself (hypocritically) on individual liberties, the freedom to choose, simultaneously present such narrow images of beauty, success, appearance? Why was the range of roles for women in television, cinema, magazines so often so impoverished, so, well, one-dimensional?

As a teenager growing up in the 1990s, a language of "empowerment" came to the fore: Women could be or do anything they wanted in principle. A worthy sentiment, to be sure, but one that was inevitably co-opted by advertising along the lines of "because you're worth it," a flattened-out image of women as gaining self-confidence purely from their appearance. Aspiring to be a "worthy" woman was equated with being wholly compatible with consumerism, a narrow range of physical types, and an absolute compatibility with capitalism and the political status quo. It is easy, of course, to be cynical about the media, to claim that *of course* these are the kind of images it will choose to project—to create false needs, to generate unrealistic aspirations, to push people to spend money they don't have on things that won't work—but I was curious about the step beyond this: How does capitalist society benefit from presenting women in this way? What does it get out of them (beyond their cash)? I was interested in the post-war mass entry of women into the workforce—sometimes referred to as the "feminisation of labour" in the literature—and how this emancipatory historical fact had not translated into greater equality in every area. I was sure there was some connection between the cultural portrayal of women and the way in which employment both welcomed women but also kept them at arm's length when it came to pay, maternity, and the higher echelons of power.

When we examine the media portrayal of women, we are struck not only by the general absence of a great many characters—older women, women deemed less attractive by the logic of consumerism iconography, complex women, clever women—but also by how little they speak, and how minimal their range of interactions are permitted to be. If a man is not involved in the discussion or an interaction, the portrayal simply doesn't exist (the Bechdel test has long been used as an insightful yardstick in this regard, asking if a work of fiction features at least two women who talk to each other about something other than a man—the majority of films and other cultural products fail). From advertising to big-budget films, women are presented as essentially passive creatures, consumers at one end, and props for male action at the other. Women are not supposed to "act," or to be agents, they are supposed to be looked at, to be subjects and subjected to the gaze of the other. Although they are permitted to be creators of children, to be carers and comforters, they are rarely ever portrayed as generators of new ideas, as producers, as makers of history. And almost never are they portrayed as all of these things at once, unless we count the odd depiction of the female CEO who has children and a high-powered job: Then we are allowed to ask "how does she do it?" or "can we really have it all?" The answers being respectively "no idea" and "nope, probably not."

What struck me repeatedly when thinking about these one-dimensional portrayals—the girlfriend-as-prize in cinema, the advert-woman smiling at the thought of her shampoo, the happy-but-badly-paid worker—was how little relation to reality they possessed. Women I knew were completely different—of course, most men are not Spider-Man either, but men, when they are not regarded as neutral, as humanity as such, are permitted to be complex, to talk, to act, where women are barely saying anything. Recent research (2013) by the Center for the Study of Women in Television and Film reports that:

> Female characters remained dramatically under-represented as protagonists, major characters, and speaking (major and minor) characters in the top-grossing films of 2013. Females accounted for 15% of protagonists, 29% of major characters, and 30% of all speaking characters... Female characters were younger than their male counterparts and were more likely than males to have an identifiable marital status. Further, female characters were less likely than males to have clearly identifiable goals or be portrayed as leaders of any kind.

One solution is obvious—more diversity in the production of media images, more female producers, more older women on screen, more women of different backgrounds in a much greater variety of roles and positions of control and direction. But even while these things get better all the time, this trend does not overturn the dominant set of images, though it might go some way to undermining them. And the money will always go to those who play it safe and repeat old stories, no matter how untrue they are.

So what of feminism today? It appears to be convulsing in a series, not exactly of new waves, but of permanent micro-revivals. "It is time to return to what feminism has to tell us. It is time to make the case for what women have uniquely to say about the perils of our modern world." So begins Jacqueline Rose's new book, *Women in Dark Times*. Rose chooses three quite different women, Rosa Luxemburg, the artist Charlotte Salomon, and Marilyn Monroe, who she calls "the stars," to define what she calls a "scandalous feminism, one which embraces without inhibition the most painful, outrageous aspects of the human heart." These three women are all, Rose says, "truth tellers," and not victims but subjects of their own destinies, despite their terrible deaths in each case (Luxemburg murdered by the government after a failed revolutionary uprising in 1919, Salomon—then five months pregnant—murdered in Auschwitz in 1943, Monroe dying in mysterious circumstances in 1962). While Rose chooses these three women, she also wants to make a broader point, perhaps one that explains the poverty of the images we are daily bombarded by: "A women is terrifying because you never know what she is going to come up with." The mismatch between the reality of women's lives, whether they be political heroes, artists, mothers, workers, or all of these things at once must be partly explained by this fear. It is the fear of something already known—women have never been one-dimensional, but have constantly been portrayed as such by those who have something to lose.

In her final interview, quoted by Rose, Marilyn Monroe said: "I don't look at myself as a commodity, but I'm sure a lot of people have." It is the gap between how she saw herself and how others did that provides a template for an escape from today's one-dimensionality. ⬢

---

Postscript: I discussed *Women in Dark Times* with Rose in December 2014 on *Novara FM*, a radio show run by Aaron Bastani and James Butler on London's Resonance FM (http://novaramedia.com/2014/12/ women-in-dark-times). We covered a range of topics from war, revenge, and justice to desire, laughter, and protest. While we agreed on much—particularly the need to undermine and question the dominant mainstream feminist rhetoric of positivity and perkiness, our major disagreement came when Rose suggested that the question of violence was always undecidable, in the sense that we are all capable of violence. It's not exactly that I disagree completely with this claim, only that we cannot discuss the question of violence outside of its material, institutional forms. My claim is that violence is, for the most part, a form of classed, gendered, and raced *training* in which certain people are taught how to be violent against the majority who are not "naturally" violent. Violence *comes from* state power, from the police, from patriarchal norms, and from imperialism, not from our supposed inherent brutality. While Rose felt that this represented a "soft," "humanist" position, as against her psychoanalytic approach which emphasized the "complexity" of the psyche, I assured her that my emphasis on "militant empathy" did not in the least mean that I didn't *hate*. On the contrary, it is hate *without* the need to hurt those *without* power, but to overturn those *with* the monopoly on violence that seems to me to represent the true revolutionary position. I would like a feminism that understood hate, justice, and revenge but also understood the reality of most violence as it currently exists, in all its myriad forms.

The idea of the class struggle can be misleading. This is not a trial of strength to decide the question: Who wins, who loses? Nor is it a wrestling match as a result of which things will go well for the victor but badly for the vanquished. Thinking like that means romanticizing and therefore hushing up the facts. For whether the 1% wins the struggle or loses, it will still be doomed to decline in consequence of the inner contradictions that will prove fatal as it evolves. The question is only whether it collapses spontaneously or is brought down by the 99%. The survival or end of three thousand years of cultural development will be decided by the answer. History knows nothing of an evil never-endingness in the image of the two fighters slugging it out forever. The true politician reckons only in terms. And if the abolition of the power and influence of the 1% is not achieved by the time an almost predictable moment of economic and technological development has been reached (rents, melting glaciers, hydraulic fracking, mass migrations of refugees, drone warfare, robot labor, and automation all point to it), then all is lost. Before the spark hits the dynamite the burning fuse must be cut through.

For the politician, intervention, risk, and tempo are technical matters—not matters of chivalry. When the ship goes down, so too do the first-class passengers.

# Contributors

**EMILY ABENDROTH** is the author of *Exclosures* (Ahsahta, 2014) and a member of DecarceratePA.

**OLIVE BLACKBURN** is a dancer, writer, and Marxist feminist from Northern California. She is the author of *Communism is up there and we are down here but it is happening now* (Timeless Infinite Light, 2014).

**TISA BRYANT** is the author of *Unexplained Presence* (Leon Works, 2007), where "The Problem of Dido" first appeared. She teaches at California Institute for the Arts.

**CACONRAD** is the author of *A Beautiful Marsupial Afternoon: New (Soma)tics* (Wave, 2012) and *Ecodeviance: (Soma)tics for the Future Wilderness* (Wave, 2014).

**ALEJANDRO DE ACOSTA** is the author of *The Impossible, Patience* (LBC, 2014) and the translator of Jorge Carera Andrade's *Micrograms* (Wave, 2011).

**RICHARD DYER** is a professor in the department of film studies at King's College, London. "In Defense of Disco" was first published in *Gay Left* in 1979. He is the author of *White: Essays on Race and Culture* (Routledge, 1997), *The Culture of Queers* (Routledge, 2001), *In the Space of a Song: The Uses of Song in Film* (Routledge, 2011), and many other works.

**TANYA ERZEN** is a Soros Justice Media Fellow who directs a college program in the Washington Corrections Center for Women and is finishing a book about faith-based programs in American prisons and the conservative movement for prison reform. She is the author of *Straight to Jesus: Sexual and Christian Conversions in the Ex-Gay Movement* (University of California Press, 2006) and *Fanpire: The Twilight Saga and the Women Who Love It* (Beacon Press, 2013). She has written for *Guernica*, the *Nation*, the *Boston Globe*, and the *Chronicle of Higher Education*.

**SILVIA FEDERICI** is an activist, scholar, and professor emerita of political philosophy and international studies at Hofstra University. She is the author of *Caliban and the Witch* (Autonomedia, 2004) and *Revolution at Point Zero* (PM Press, 2012) among other works and has deep roots in the radical autonomist feminist Marxist tradition. "Precarious Labor: A Feminist Viewpoint" was first delivered as a lecture at New York's Bluestockings Radical Bookstore in 2006.

**JOEL FELIX** is the author of *Limbs of the Apple Tree Never Die* (Verge, 2013) where "Fieldbook: Pharsalia" first appeared.

**FERNANDO FORTÍN** is a poet from Honduras.

**DAVID HADBAWNIK**'s ongoing translations of Vergil are available from Little Red Leaves. He is the editor and publisher of *Habenicht Press* and the journal *kadar koli*.

**ROBERTO HARRISON** is the author of *Bridge to the World* (cannot exist, 2011) and *bicycle* (Noemi Press, 2015). Between 1997 and 2008, he co-edited *Crayon* magazine.

**DANIEL HARTLEY** is lecturer in English and American literature and culture at the University of Giessen (Germany). He specializes in Marxist literary and cultural theory. His book, *The Politics of Style: Marxist Poetics in and beyond Raymond Williams, Terry Eagleton, and Fredric Jameson*, will be published by Brill in 2016.

**SERGIO HYLAND** is imprisoned at SCI Greene, a supermax facility near Waynesburg, Pennsylvania.

**MITCHELL INCLÃN** is an anarchist writer currently living in the Puget Sound and San Francisco Bay areas.

**SAMI R. KHATIB** is a Berlin-based critical theory scholar. He has taught courses about media and cultural theory at Freie Universität Berlin and is the author of a book on the messianic idea in Walter Benjamin's philosophy titled *Teleologie ohne Endzweck: Walter Benjamins Ent-stellung des Messianischen* (Tectum Verlag, 2013). The English translation is forthcoming.

**URSULA K. LE GUIN** is the author of many novels, poems, children's books, and short stories including *The Farthest Shore* (Atheneum Books, 1972), *The Dispossessed* (Harper and Row, 1974), *Lavinia* (Harcourt, 2008), and many others. "The Ones Who Walk Away from Omelas" first appeared in a 1973 science-fiction anthology titled *New Dimensions 3*.

**MIRANDA MELLIS**'s most recent books are *The Spokes* (Solid Objects, 2012) and *None of This Is Real* (Sidebrow, 2012). She teaches at the Evergreen State College.

**CHARLES TONDERAI MUDEDE** is a Zimbabwean-born film critic, filmmaker, and writer for *The Stranger*, a weekly newspaper based in Seattle. Mudede collaborated with director Robinson Devor on two films, *Police Beat* and *Zoo*, both of which premiered at Sundance—*Zoo* was also screened at Cannes. Mudede has contributed to the *New York Times*, *LA Weekly*, *Village Voice*, *Black Souls Journal*, *C Theory*, *Cinema Scope*, and is on the editorial board for the *Arcade Journal* and *Black Scholar*.

**CHRIS O'KANE** is currently an adjunct professor at Portland State University. He is also a contributing editor of *Historical Materialism*.

**PATRIK ØÖD-NOIR** is from San Francisco.

**NINA POWER** is a senior lecturer for the philosophy department at Roehampton University, the author of *One-Dimensional Woman* (Zero Books, 2009), a translator of Alain Badiou, and a contributor to the *Guardian*.

**STUART SMITHERS** is chair of the religion department at University of Puget Sound. He is also the president of the Rubicon Foundation and part of the Smoke Farm collective. "The Logic of the Martyr" was originally presented at the 7th annual Critical Theory Conference in Rome, 2014.

**EIRIK STEINHOFF**'s essay "Making Nothing Happen: Poetry and Sabotage" appeared in 2015 in *postmedieval*.

**KESTON SUTHERLAND** is the author of *Stupefaction: A Radical Anatomy of Phantoms* (Seagull, 2011) and of *Odes to TL61P* (Enitharmion, 2013). He teaches at the University of Sussex.

**STEPHEN VOYCE** teaches English and critical media studies at the University of Iowa. He is the author of *Poetic Community: Avant-Garde Activism and Cold-War Culture* (University of Toronto Press, 2013), the editor of *A Book of Variations: Love—Zygal—Art Facts* (Coach House Books, 2013), and the director of the Fluxus Digital Collection.

**CATHY WAGNER**'s most recent book is *Nervous Device* (City Lights, 2012).

**ALLI WARREN** is the author of *Here Come the Warm Jets* (City Lights, 2013).

**PETER WIEBEN** is an American artist who recently moved to from Cairo to Belgium. His book about the Egyptian revolution is called *It's Time to Move* (2013). His artwork and reportage from migrant camps in Calais, France, recently appeared in the *New Republic*.

# Encyclopedia of the Catastrophe

**ABSENCE**: Enlightenment thought and capitalism converge in the production of modes of living that are highlighted by the absence of life and presence. This ontological crisis is investigated in Hegelian and Marxian themes of emptiness, void, alienation, second-nature, zombies, fetish character, ghosts, and apparitions. The illusion of appearances especially includes the neo-individual's illusory sense of self—at once absorbed and directed by the spectacle and the screen. As Guy Debord wrote: "The spectacle in general, as the concrete inversion of life, is the autonomous movement of the non-living."

**ADNAN**: A poet, essayist, novelist, and painter, Etel Adnan is the author of *The Arab Apocalypse*, *Seasons*, *Sitt Marie Rose*, and many other remarkable works. Adnan is an inspiring visionary poet who sees what we have forgotten: "Death is the interruption of a monstrosity."

**ADORNO**: Affectionately known as "Teddy," Theodor Adorno was a 20th-century genius who wrote widely as a member of the Frankfurt School of philosophy and social criticism. Born Theodor Ludwig Wiesengrund, he began publishing his early works as Theodor Wiesengrund-Adorno (Adorno being part of his mother's maiden name). In California, he attempted to legally change Wiesengrund to "W." This curious gesture was not allowed by the authorities and he became "Theodor Adorno." Adorno is most famous for *Dialectic of Enlightenment* (co-written with Max Horkheimer), *Negative Dialectics*, and *Minima Moralia*. He also made a few famously bad decisions, such as calling the police to break up a student protest in Frankfurt and taking a tram up the Matterhorn against his doctor's advice. This bad decision was his last, as he died afterwards.

**AGAMBEN**: Philosopher, writer, sub-rosa presence. In his essay "Tiananmen," Giorgio Agamben maintains that the state cannot tolerate in any way those "singularities" who form a community without affirming an identity. He warned that in the coming struggle between the state and humanity (the non-state), "wherever these singularities peacefully demonstrate their being in common there will be a Tiananmen, and, sooner or later, the tanks will appear." This advice, while still relevant in the 21st century (see "Ayotzinapa"), might have been confusing to pre-Columbian residents of the Americas (see "Arawak").

**AMAZON**: A forest in Voltaire's *Candide*, a mythical race of women (who were said to remove the right breast, the better for shooting a bow), and a corporate cannibal. The corporation known as Amazon eats other companies in ways large and small, eats the time of its workers, and eats government through tax avoidance, all to create a cash-generating machine. Amazon (the corporation) is also compared to a tyrant: It rules through terror and, left unencumbered, will destroy swaths of the US economy. Amazon (the corporation) should be approached with great caution.

**ANTHROPOCENE**: The ironic denouement of a centuries-long fable in which humanity believes itself to have great influence over the planet—and is highly distressed when that delusion becomes a reality.

**APACHE**: Like Cheyenne, Black Hawk, Lakota, and Comanche, Apache is the name of an attack helicopter. A mysterious convention of US Army tradition uses names from indigenous people of North America (also known as "Indians") it once hunted and slaughtered to designate its more lethal aircraft.

**APOCALYPSE**: Revelation, unveiling, to see the lived illusion of "life" as *bare life*. The falsity of the normative Western imagination of the apocalyptic consists in projecting onto the world the absence (which see) of presence, the absence of remorse or conscience, and mourning for the loss of civilization and the catastrophe of the status quo. It is not the world that is lost, but *we* who have lost the world and go on losing it. It is not the world that is going to end soon, but we who are *finished*, amputated, cut off in a hallucinatory way from *vital contact with the real*. The catastrophe is not economic, ecological, or political—*the catastrophe is above all a crisis of the lack of presence*. According to John of Patmos (author of the Book of Revelation), the *ringing* of the bell (see "aporetic dissonance") is meant to signal the beginning of the apocalypse—also the beginning of *presence* and real life as life-in-common.

**APORETIC DISSONANCE**: An affective condition. The believer's *discovery* within herself or himself of a dissonant ring of perplexity, puzzlement, confusion, and loss concerning the integrity of capitalism's self-presentation, rhetoric, and ideology. This ring is most often absorbed by the system and quietened—but in rare cases of collective and combined dissonance, the ring's vibration might result in the spontaneous rupture of "the moment" or augenblick (which see).

**ARAWAK, DECIMATION OF**: A beginning disguised as an ending. In 1492, the Arawak might have benefited from a warning like the one from Agamben (which see).

**ARCADES**: Romantic, bygone forests of commerce and culture; a prelude to barricades.

**ASSANGE**: Julian Assange is an Australian citizen who currently lives in London as a guest of the Ecuador-ean embassy, just a few yards from the Grand Temple of the Commodity Form: Harrods department store. As the result of award-winning excellence in online publishing and journalism, Assange has been under threat of arrest and a guest of the Ecuadoreans since 2012. He is also the co-founder of WikiLeaks. For releasing restricted documents, videos, and other material (some apparently supplied by Chelsea Manning) about US actions in Iraq, Assange was called a "terrorist" by the sitting US vice president. Some presidential candidates and public "intellectuals" have called for his assassination.

**ASSIMILATION**: A means of survival or suicide, depending on whom you ask.

**AUGENBLICK**: Literally, German for "eye glance" or, more colloquially, "blink of an eye"—*moment*. According to Lukács, there is a dialectical interaction between subject and object in the historical process, but in the crucial moment (augenblick) of crisis, this interaction results in a form of revolutionary consciousness and praxis that provides the direction for the events. In that instant, the fate of the revolution—and therefore of humanity—"depends on the subjective moment." This does not mean that revolutionaries should wait passively for the arrival of this augenblick.

**AUSTERITY**: An ancient superstition according to which a starving person could put on weight by fasting. In more recent times, a neoliberal governing and extraction program in which capital continues to refine and adapt methods of "accumulation by dispossession" (the modern metamorphoses of Marx's idea of "primitive accumulation") through state and other institutional means. Epitomized by the European Union's monetary policies regarding Greece, austerity consists of creating a continuous crisis in order to avert an actual crisis. These policies are akin to well-known counter-insurgency practices of "destabilizing in order to stabilize" which, for the authorities, involves deliberately producing chaos so as to make order more desirable than revolution. The present neoliberal crisis of austerity is no longer a classic crisis or the decisive moment (see "augenblick"). On the contrary, it is an endless end, a lasting apocalypse (which see).

**AUTOMATION**: Marx seems to have gotten this right. He suggested that as capitalist industries mature, they increasingly tend toward automation: Utilizing machines, substituting human workers, and creating higher and more efficient modes of productivity. An excellent 2013 study of the impact of technology on future employment by Frey and Osborne (Oxford University) predicted that 47 percent of all US jobs were at high risk of disappearance within a decade due to automation technologies.

Several contradictions and challenges emerge from this situation, the most central being: What will happen to all of the permanently unemployed and unnecessary workers? The interests of the capitalists (more profit) and the workers (more free time and shared benefit) are at odds. Will the global growth of redundancy and the creation of unemployed "surplus" populations lead to the spontaneous moment of rebellion or revolt (see "augenblick")?

**AYOTZINAPA**: On September 26, 2014, in the Mexican state of Guerrero, 43 students from the Ayotzinapa Rural Teachers' College disappeared after commandeering buses to attend a protest. Families and friends continue to demand that authorities find and return the students. The absence of these students reminds the world that freedom will never be tolerated by power. Life in the 21st century continues to follow a tendency toward violence, nakedness, and survival. While the reduction to "bare life" is experienced by all classes in different ways, the absence of life among the rich goes mostly unrecognized.

*With apologies to Matt Stoller, Glenn Wallis, Michael Löwy, G.I. Gurdjieff, the Invisible Committee, St. John of Patmos, and Wikipedia for the brazen and perverted dispossession of ideas, terms, and phrases.*

# In poor places, corruption is a means to an end.

# In rich places, corruption is an end in itself.

# About PM Press

PM Press was founded at the end of 2007 by a small collection of folks with decades of publishing, media, and organizing experience. PM Press co-conspirators have published and distributed hundreds of books, pamphlets, CDs, and DVDs. Members of PM have founded enduring book fairs, spearheaded victorious tenant organizing campaigns, and worked closely with bookstores, academic conferences, and even rock bands to deliver political and challenging ideas to all walks of life. We're old enough to know what we're doing and young enough to know what's at stake. We seek to create radical and stimulating fiction and non-fiction books, pamphlets, T-shirts, visual and audio materials to entertain, educate, and inspire you. We aim to distribute these through every available channel with every available technology—whether that means you are seeing anarchist classics at our bookfair stalls; reading our latest vegan cookbook at the café; downloading geeky fiction e-books; or digging new music and timely videos from our website. PM Press is always on the lookout for talented and skilled volunteers, artists, activists, and writers to work with. If you have a great idea for a project or can contribute in some way, please get in touch.

PM Press
PO Box 23912
Oakland, CA 94623
www.pmpress.org

# Friends of PM Press

These are indisputably momentous times—the financial system is melting down globally and the Empire is stumbling. Now more than ever there is a vital need for radical ideas. In the years since its founding—and on a mere shoestring— PM Press has risen to the formidable challenge of publishing and distributing knowledge and entertainment for the struggles ahead. With over 300 releases to date, we have published an impressive and stimulating array of literature, art, music, politics, and culture. Using every available medium, we've succeeded in connecting those hungry for ideas and information to those putting them into practice. Friends of PM allows you to directly help impact, amplify, and revitalize the discourse and actions of radical writers, filmmakers, and artists. It provides us with a stable foundation from which we can build upon our early successes and provides a much-needed subsidy for the materials that can't necessarily pay their own way. You can help make that happen—and receive every new title automatically delivered to your door once a month—by joining as a Friend of PM Press.

Please visit **www.pmpress.org** to become a Friend of PM Press
and to learn about different levels of support.